At the Feet of the Spiritual Master

Avatar Adi Da Samraj

"I offer you a relationship not a technique": These words by Adi Da Samraj open the engaging and revealing stories of Gerald Sheinfeld's 45 years with his Spiritual Master. Gerald's stories give a unique insight into the Guru/devotee relationship, beginning with his confession that feeling Adi Da's Enlightened State answered his search for God and truth. Then over time Adi Da served that heart-awakened response by revealing more and more of His Awakened Condition, spontaneously generating a deeper devotional response. These stories show how spiritual growth happens as a free gift by the Enlightened Master.

A book worth studying, filled with the awakened recognition of Divine Reality and profound lessons in ego transcending self-understanding.

—**Andrew Harvey**
Author, *Evolutionary Love Relationships, Teachings of Rumi,*
and *The Hope: A Guide to Sacred Activism*

Starting in the 1970s, the Great Adept Adi Da Samraj began a process of instructing and blessing anyone who entered His Divine Company. Amid this process, Sri Adi Da generated a prolific body of spiritual teachings, detailing how those so inclined may transcend their individuated existence in prior identification with God. Gerald Sheinfeld, a devotee of Sri Adi Da throughout virtually this entire span, has chronicled the miracle and majesty of his Spiritual Master's Divine "Leela," or play of consciousness. Anyone who is interested in the nature and transformative power of the Guru-Devotee relationship process will discover in Sheinfeld's *At The Feet Of The Spiritual Master* a treasure trove of Transcendental Wisdom never before found in the traditions and annals of Spiritual knowledge and teachings.

—**Lynnea Bylund**
Director, Gandhi Worldwide Education Institute

How does one find words to express that which is beyond words? *At the Feet of the Spiritual Master* is a profoundly moving account of Gerald Sheinfeld's life of deepest devotion to his Master, Adi Da Samraj. In utterly vulnerable, heart-broken story after story, Gerald manages to describe the priceless gift of a life lived in surrender to Master Adi Da. He succeeds in illustrating that Divine Realization is not something to work at or to be achieved through self-effort or spiritual seeking. Rather, it is the Spiritual Master's unique gift to the devotee. In my study of the great spiritual traditions, I know of no comparable portrayal of the Master-devotee relationship. To read Gerald's leelas is to be touched at the core of one's being by the love of the devotee for his Master and to be awed by the mystery of Heart-Master Adi Da's appearance in this realm.

—Hugh O'Doherty
Lecturer, Kennedy School of Government, Harvard University

A joy to read and savor, these Leelas, or sacred stories, have the power to open the heart of the reader to the Love-Bliss-Happiness that eternally radiates from the enlightened state of this great spiritual master. For those who are familiar with Adi Da's writings, this book will bring alive the truths they reveal. For those who do not yet know about Adi Da's liberating wisdom, this book will awaken a hunger to know more about the teaching and the teacher. *At the Feet of the Spiritual Master* is destined to become a classic in the literature of human spirituality.

—Gary J. Coates
Professor of Architecture, Kansas State University
author, *The Rebirth of Sacred Art: Reflections on the Aperspectival Geometric Art of Adi Da Samraj*

Gerald's stories are the "true confessions" of an ordinary man who willingly entered Adi Da Samraj's Divine Fire, struggled with its unexpected heat for years, recognized the futility of his self-contraction and refusal of relationship, and emerged as a grateful devotee of Adi Da Samraj. Gerald's straightforward honesty takes hold and inspires our trust just as it queries our incredulous automaticities.

—Ray Lynch
Three-time Billboard Award winner; composer of the Platinum albums,
Deep Breakfast, No Blue Thing, The Sky of Mind, and *Ray Lynch Best Of*

I am grateful and delighted to have read the "Leela" manuscript of Gerald Sheinfeld. It is a well-rounded selection of stories that describe how Master Adi Da taught His devotees with humor, compassion, and love. It is a clear and emotional testimonial of Adi Da's Teachings for all humankind that brought tears to my eyes continuously. Adi Da's Teaching transmits the Truth simply. Thank you, Gerald. You have created a testimonial that the world urgently needs.

—Susana Weingarten Evert
Professional dancer, Ballet Independiente de Mexico and DANCEVERT;
choreographer, educator, and massage therapist

This is a unique book of stories told by a devotee who spent 45 years in the company of Adi Da. A true love story about a Realized God Man and his devotee. Don't miss it.

—Michael Butera
Psychotherapist, former Diocesan Catholic priest

In the spiritual traditions of humankind, there are some rare few books that tell of a spiritual aspirant's time in the company of a great spiritual master in terms that are neither mythological, nor exaggerated, nor merely a handful of brief episodes. Gerald Sheinfeld's book covers 45 years of his devotional relationship to his Sat-Guru, Avatar Adi Da Samraj. Gerald's stories are intimate, profound, humorous, and emotionally moving. Adi Da's "play" with his devotee was continually surprising, provocative, and demanding. He was always drawing Gerald beyond his ego-comfort zone. When you read these stories, you may find Adi Da doing the same with you.

—Michael LaTorra
Professor of English (retired), New Mexico State University;
abbot (emeritus), Zen Center of Las Cruces;
author, A Warrior Blends with Life: A Modern Tao

Having grown up within the community of Adidam, I have always delighted in the stories of how devotees found their guru in Adi Da and how their love and devotion to him changed the course of their lives. A wonderful narrative of the relationship between the Guru and his devotee.

—Rani Druda, DC

I read my first book by Heart-Master Da in 1974—and was immediately enchanted, and in love. I felt Him as a completely fearless and boundless being, free of any and every conventional limit; free, even, of identification with the dying body-mind, a God-man, communicating and radiating the "Conscious Light" (as He wrote) of "Reality Itself." More than 40 years later, I am still in love with the "Constant Lover"—and His lifelong devotee. And so it was with great appreciation and delight that I read *At the Feet of the Spiritual Master*, by Gerald Sheinfeld. These stories about the life and teachings of Heart-Master Da wonderfully convey His "Divine Play," or Leela—His unconditional embrace of all beings, and His ego-undermining, freedom-giving force. As I see it, you have found your way to this book by mysterious grace—all events are in His all-pervading Event—and I truly hope the stories told by Gerald in this book help you feel the "Perfect Satisfaction" offered to you, directly and intimately, by Heart-Master Da. As He once said as I sat in heartbroken joy at His feet: "Who doesn't want to be Happy? Who doesn't want to know that the Divine is alive in human form?"

—Bill Gottlieb, CHC
Certified health coach; bestselling author of *Alternative Cures*
and 15 other self-help books; former editor-in-chief,
Rodale Books and Prevention Magazine Books

A brilliant U.S. scholar once stated, "Adi Da Samraj is the greatest Spiritual Master in all of history." Gerald Sheinfeld is uniquely blessed to have spent decades in intimate proximity to the God man Adi Da Samraj. Gerald describes some of what it was like to live in the midst of such an incomparable, magnificent, humanity-serving, radiant Force. I felt the presence of God throughout the pages of his book, which is a rare gift to the world.

—Charmian Anderson, PhD
Author, *The Heart of Success*; one of the first individuals to receive
an advanced degree in Transpersonal Psychology in the United States

Gerald Sheinfeld has written an up-close account of his lifelong devotion and service to his Guru, Adi Da Samraj. In brief vignettes, this Leela book chronicles Gerald's 45-year struggle for increasingly profound self-understanding aimed at ego-transcendence. The Leelas make abundantly clear that living in the ever-blessing presence of the Guru is an utterly demanding practice, keeping devotees on their toes all the time, out of their comfort zone, without a let-up, moment to moment, day after day. The reader becomes a witness to the intimate play in which the Guru, with no holds barred, creates an endless variety of teachable moments, often out of seemingly innocuous events and circumstances, and thereby confronting devotees with their interminable acts of self-contraction. The Guru mirrors devotees back to themselves, all for the sole purpose, and ultimate reward, of Enlightenment.

Sheinfeld takes the reader into that rarefied world of sacred Ashrams, of sublime Darshans and esoteric Teachings. Far removed from the conventional lives of the common people, he offers a peep into the kitchen of esoteric spirituality where it can become uncomfortably hot in the Guru-devotee relationship, but where everyday matters are approached with a radical profundity, subtle humor and, of course, never-ending ego confrontation. He shows what it takes to follow the rigorous path of devotion in the presence of the Living Divine. This Leela book culminates in Sheinfeld's ecstatic summary-confession about six precious Gifts of Divine Reality that he personally received in the good company of his Guru, finding refuge in Only-God.

This Leela book is for anyone curious about life lived with a Living God-Man: devotees' daily trials and tribulations, their Instruction and the extraordinary Gifts they receive. It gives a glimpse of their fascinating lifestyle.

The take away from this book will be different for each reader. For me, it offered a vicarious experience of a road not taken, and a spur to greater seriousness. While the reader may not learn much about how to be and act in our conditional world, that "lack" is more than compensated by the profound, esoteric insights Gerald gains and shares once he has released his struggles and seeking: that greatest Gift of being Blessed to Realize the egoless Prior Unity of Conscious Light, which is always already the case, but which humankind fails to recognize and realize (yet)—to its own misfortune.

—Rolf C. Carriere
Senior UN official 1971–2004,
senior advisor to several INGOs 2005–present

Living in times when tribalism is the dominate global paradigm (by which I mean the separation of individuals into oppositional factions based on ego-driven and presumed-to-be irreconcilable differences), it is emotionally potent and spiritually promising to read of one man's radically unconventional encounters with a teacher unlike any heretofore appearing in the sacred traditions.

Gerald gives us entrée into how, over decades of practice as Adi Da's devotee, he came to understand what it means to surrender the egoic self and be drawn into the state of non-opposition and non-difference made possible by Adi Da's own spiritual realization. *At the Feet of the Spiritual Master* is a must-read for any who are fatigued by the politics of "divide and conquer" and who know that there is Something Else to be understood.

—**Kathy M. Skerritt**
Co-Founder, The Anthroposphere Institute;
first generation framer, The Great Lakes Commons Social Charter

We all know what we mean when we refer to somebody as being "a good guy". Most of us would have said that about the Gerald Sheinfeld you find at the beginning of this book. But what would you say about the Gerald you find forty-some years later, having finished writing this book? Profoundly changed? Yes, at least that. Unbelievably blessed? Certainly!—you'll see.

My wife, Gardenia, and I worked with Gerald on the presentation of these stories and that in itself was a great blessing. We were among the earliest witnesses to the marvelous narrative of an ordinary man spiritually transformed through service to the Avatar, service only a few were privileged to perform.

—**Fred Rohe**
Author of *The Zen of Running*, *The Complete Book of Natural Foods*,
Dr. Kelley's Answer to Cancer, and *The Smart Food Movement*

AT THE FEET OF THE
Spiritual Master

Stories from My Life with
Avatar Adi Da Samraj

by Gerald Sheinfeld

International Standard Book Number-13: 978-0692924983
International Standard Book Number-10: 0692924981

Library of Congress Control Number: 017913161

DEDICATION

*B*eloved Heart-Master Avatar Adi Da Samraj, the Leelas
(sacred stories) in this book give a glimpse of Your Divine
Avataric Mastery for the sake of Your devotees and ultimately all beings. We all came to Your Divine Person as ordinary
people seeking what is greater. What we found was the perfect
answer to "our" prayers. Your Divine Presence Awakened our
hearts' devotion, because Your Radiant Divine State spontaneously
became the greatest attraction to our hearts. You Revealed that You
are both the Divine Way and the Divine Realization. By Your
Blessing Grace, You have Transformed Your devotees, enabling us
to live as love, surrendered in Your Perfect Truth and conforming
to Your Heart of Love-Bliss. You are the Divine Avatar, the Revealer
of the Prior Unity of Divine Reality. There is no greater happiness
than heart-Communion with Your Living Divine Presence.

I lay this book of true Divine Love stories at Your Holy Feet.
May Your Awakening Presence shine through each page and
Reveal Your Prior egoless Divine Truth to all who may be so
Blessed to receive Your Holy Regard.

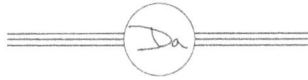

TABLE OF CONTENTS

PART SIX: Stories from 2000–2008

PART SEVEN: Stories from 2008–2016

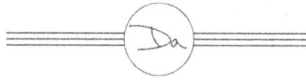

ABOUT THIS BOOK

The Title and Subtitle

At the Feet of the Spiritual Master refers to the devotional disposition of happily and spontaneously serving Avatar Adi Da in recognition of and heart-response to His Divine Spiritual Presence. The photo on the cover shows a sign of receiving Avatar Adi Da's Freely Transmitted Gift of Divine Reality, Love-Bliss, and Prior Unity of being, while literally sitting at His Feet.

The Stories from My Life with Avatar Adi Da Samraj are not part of an ancient tradition where it was accepted for devotees to exaggerate or even make up stories about the greatness of their guru, or spiritual master. None of the stories in this book are exaggerated or made up—though of course I may have misremembered something here or there. But these stories are truthful accounts of events that I experienced firsthand.

Of course, the Divine Avatar Adi Da Samraj works at all levels of Consciousness, so while I understood things that related to my own separate perception, He was also working beyond the illusion of identification as a separate being. He was (and is) communicating His Divine State of Consciousness Itself. His Divine State of Consciousness is very different from a "separate" being, for it is perfectly egoless.

May these stories touch your heart and move you to respond by finding out more about His Divine Presence Avatar Adi Da Samraj and the Way of Adidam Ruchiradam.

Avatar Adi Da's Sacred Names and Titles of Reference

During the years in which Avatar Adi Da established Adidam Ruchiradam, also known as the Reality-Way of the Heart, He was known by several Names. Generally, His taking of a new Name coincided with a change in the way He was working with devotees, and it would be the principal Name used for the period of time characterized by that way of working. Some Names and Titles of reference were used relatively briefly. Others were retained and used interchangeably with other Names and Titles over a longer period of time.

Interspersed throughout the stories in this book are several "Name pages", placed in conjunction with my use of a particular Name for Avatar Adi Da during my storytelling. You will also notice that in many stories (especially later on) I use several different Names or honorific Titles, a characteristic of my devotional style of writing.

The list below includes the Names included in the "Name pages" in the book, and dates principally associated with Avatar Adi Da's taking of or working under that Name. (There are other Names and Titles that were used by Avatar Adi Da that are not included in this book.)

Franklin Albert Jones	November 3, 1939
Bubba Free John	August 16, 1973
Da Free John	September 13, 1979
Da Love-Ananda	January 11, 1986
Da Avabhasa	April 30, 1991
Adi Da, the Da Avatar	October 11, 1994
Adi Da Samraj	February 3, 1996
Ruchira Avatar	November 12, 1996
Bhagavan	2006 onward
Parama-Sapta-Na Adi Da Samraj	July 10, 2007

My Devotional Use of Capitalization

All traditions of humankind have always used capitalization when referring to God—such as Lord, Divine, and similar sacred references—to acknowledge holiness.

Having been a devotee of Avatar Adi Da Samraj for forty-five years, by His Divine Self-Revelation I recognize to the core of my being that He is the Divine Avatar, the All-Completing One, the Divine Person come to Awaken all beings into Divine Reality.

As an expression of my devotional recognition of Avatar Adi Da Samraj, I use capitalization throughout this book when referring to Him and His Divine Work of Blessings. Here are some examples: capitalization of nouns like "Birth" and "Miracle" in "The Birth of Avatar Adi Da in New York in 1939 was the Miracle that exceeds all miracles". Capitalization of "His" and "He" in "When He spoke of God and Truth it was clear He was making a confession of His Own Realization." Also most adjectives describing Avatar Adi Da and/or His State and some verbs relating to Avatar Adi Da as the Subject are capitalized.

Avatar Adi Da's Use of Capitalization, Underlining, and Quotation Marks

Throughout this book, I have quoted from the writings or talks of Avatar Adi Da Samraj, Who Utilized unique literary means to communicate His Transcendental Wisdom. He used capitalization, underlining, and quotation marks to distinguish between ordinary speech (which describes the conditionally manifested reality) and speech that describes the Unconditional Reality. With the use of capitalization and underlining, Avatar Adi Da expresses a different view of the world, in which Truth and the terms that relate to that Greater Reality are given more significance than the language of the separate ego and the conventional world (in which the word "I" is the "centerpole", and therefore, is capitalized).

With quotation marks, Avatar Adi Da often communicates that some ordinary term, in Reality, is pointing to an illusion. He also uses quotation marks to point to a specific, technical meaning He intends.

Avatar Adi Da Samraj:

The only "Centerpole" of My Divine Avataric Word Is Reality Itself, the Conscious Light (or True Divine Heart) That Is Transcendental, Inherently Spiritual, Intrinsically egoless, and Self-Evidently Divine Being (Itself). The uppercase Written Words Represent (or Picture) the Reality-Truth of Heart-Significance— and the lowercase words, by comparison, characteristically achieve significance as indicators (or representations, or pictures) of conditional (or limited) existence.

To read (or Listen to) and understand My Divine Avataric Word is to be Acausally Released from having to exercise the egoic vision and its separate and separative "point of view".

Therefore, read and Listen to, and recite, and feel (rather than merely think) the Words of My Divine Avataric Message.

The big and small letters of My Texted Gift always interrupt the common flow of mind, and Signal the Heart of "you" that this moment Is the Necessary Instant of Self-Awakening—to Be As "you" Are. ("The Forever-Spoken Word of Reality Itself", *The Aletheon*, 2009 edition, 40–41.)

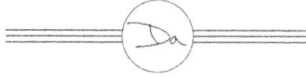

AUTHOR'S PREFACE

*L*eela is a Sanskrit word for "play". In some eastern spiritual traditions *Leela* means "the Awakened Play of a Realized Adept, through which He or She mysteriously instructs devotees and Blesses all and everything". Thus, the stories in this book are Leelas—instructive stories derived from many years of devotion and service to Avatar[1] Adi Da Samraj.

Most of these Leelas happened throughout the years of Avatar Adi Da's formal Teaching and Blessing Work, 1972–2008. I was Blessed to have been His devotee for those thirty-six years, and feel profoundly Graced to have served Him personally for many of those years. Traditionally, it is understood that the most auspicious choice a person can make in life is to spend time in the Company of a Realizer, and Avatar Adi Da Samraj is a Realizer of the Ultimate Degree. And even more, as I learned, He Is the Perfectly Free Divine, the True Reality of existence, in Person. For me it was always His Divine Freedom that attracted my heart to stay in His Holy Company.

Many of these stories are from the earliest days of 1972–1973, when there were few devotees in Avatar Adi Da's Company, which granted me many opportunities for service to Him. In 1973 Adi Da invited me to join Him on His five-week Blessing trip to India, stories of which I am particularly happy to include.

Everyone who came to Avatar Adi Da became involved in a profound process of human and Spiritual growth. The process had many aspects and stages involving deepening recognition of His Divine State, and greater self-understanding of the ego-act of separation from Divine Reality. The recognition of Avatar Adi Da as Divine Reality Itself, in whom all inhere, grew over time. I didn't fully appreciate Who He was in the early years of my service, but there was clearly the intuition and experience of His egoless Freedom. It was evident that His Divine Compassionate Work was to undo the act of separation and separateness that is egoity in everyone.

1. Avatar: from the Sanskrit "Avatara" meaning Divine Incarnation, or One who has "descended" or "crossed down" from the Divine Domain. In Adidam Ruchiradam, Avatar Adi Da Samraj is understood to be the Complete Divine Avatar.

However, devotees were very immature in that time, both humanly and spiritually. The Divine Avatar Adi Da had to Educate us in all aspects of conforming our lives to Divine Reality, and Train us in responsive devotional worship. So, by necessity, in those early years there was a lot of dialogue and focus on self-understanding and establishing the basic realization that our egos are not entities or "things" inside us somewhere. Rather, they are the moment-by-moment <u>activity</u> we are unconsciously <u>doing</u>. And it was only over time that He thus awakened enough understanding that we became sensitive to the unique gifts of the liberating relationship He was offering.

He called His Divine Avataric Work with devotees in those years His "Submission-Work" or His "Teaching-Submission years". It was "Submission" because He let us come to Him without any preparation and engaged us like a "friend" as well as Spiritual Master. This Submission allowed Him to Reveal His Perfect Freedom, which attracted our hearts and minds to recognize His Divine Truth and want to practice the Way He came to Reveal and Teach—the Way of the Heart.

Avatar Adi Da Samraj:

> It was not possible for Me to be received without first Submitting Myself (as I have Done) to the point of Perfect Coincidence and Perfect Identification with all-and-All—Such That all-and-All Are My Person.
>
> My Divine Avataric Self-Submission Was a Means Whereby I Took On the pattern of humankind (and of the "world" altogether), in order to Transform that pattern in My Own Person. ("The Boundless Self-Confession", The Aletheon, 2009 edition, 1903.)

Once there was sufficient maturity in the gathering of His devotees and they truly understood that focusing on ego-patterning was not what enables spiritual growth, then the practice of "radical" (at-the-root) devotion in recognition of His egoless State was established instead. His Submission became unnecessary, and intrinsic egolessness, founded in Adi Da's prior Transcendental Spiritual State, became the focus of the Way of the Heart. This change began to take place in the mid-80s, along with Avatar Adi Da's calling for renunciation. We came to recognize more and more over time—and are still understanding more about this each day that passes—that all the different ways that Avatar Adi Da appeared to His devotees and the world were just extensions of His Compassionate Blessing. His warmth, demand, humor, and love are all Blessing-qualities of the Forever Free and Silent Divine Person that the heart is moved to worship.

I have often heard people say, "I wish I was there during the early Teaching years." My response is that, in truth, you have not missed the most important opportunity and you must recognize that His Awakening Transmission of the Prior Unity of Consciousness, that Is Divine Reality Itself, is never limited to time or space. Avatar Adi Da is Eternally Present as that State, and when His Living Divine Presence is felt in any time, there is no doubt—the heart inherently recognizes the Truth.

In time it became clear to us that the process of serving devotees' heart-awakening and self-understanding was the means by which Avatar Adi Da could Perfectly and Eternally Coincide with all of humankind and spontaneously establish His egoless Pattern in this world for all time.

Avatar Adi Da Samraj:

Because of What I have Accomplished through My Divine Avataric Self-Submission, all of humankind—and, indeed, all of Earthkind, and all living beings in all places and times—are now Enabled to devotionally and whole-bodily-responsively recognize Me, and (in due course) to "Locate" Me and "Perfectly Know" Me. ("The Boundless Self-Confession", *The Aletheon*, 2009 edition, 1904.)

While conforming our lives to His Divine Revelation, His devotees were profoundly Blessed to witness Avatar Adi Da's egoless Pattern manifesting before our eyes. In the stories you will read in this book, you may notice the changes in the way Avatar Adi Da worked with His devotees over time, and the changes in our devotional response, based on growing self-understanding and growing recognition of His Divine Person, Presence, and State.

Avatar Adi Da Samraj:

My Time of Teaching-Work Is the Context in Which the Fullness and Finality of My Divine Avataric Reality-Revelation Eventually Happened—through a Most Profound Progressive "Consideration"-in-Submission.

Now there is no longer any Such "Consideration".

Now There Is Only My Full and Final and Perfect Divine Avataric Teaching-Revelation. ("The Universally Consequential Event At Ruchira Dham Hermitage", The Aletheon, 2009 edition, 1718.)

◆ ◆ ◆

I would like to extend my heart-felt gratitude to Fred Rohe, the editor of this work, to Gardenia White for her editorial contributions, and to Tally Groves for her help in preparing the manuscript for editing.

Thanks also to Chris Tong, James Steinberg, and Megan Anderson for their many outstanding contributions to the book, to Leslie Waltzer of Crowfoot Design for the cover design, to Crystal Carpenter for copyediting, to Matt Barna for the layout, and to Michael LaTorra for the proofreading.

And deep thanks to John Salick and Jeanne Martin for the use of their car, and to Rosie Groves and devotees in the Northeast region and to Roger Gerakin and Jane Lind for providing living circumstances that allowed me to work full-time on these heart-brightening stories.

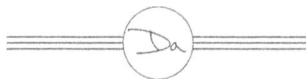

INTRODUCTION

by James Steinberg

The appearance of the Divine as a human being is the great event in this world. The Grace that is brought with such an Incarnation is unmatched by any other Divine gift. In the West, we record very few appearances of the Divine in human form. Only Jesus of Nazareth is generally acknowledged in the Christian faith as a Divine Incarnation. Muhammad is God's prophet for Muslims, as is Moses for Jews. It is in the East that such Appearances of the Divine in human form are more commonly known, worshipped, and honored. There, such beings are known as Avatars, a word that traditionally means one who has "crossed down" from the Divine Realms. The great Hindu text the *Bhagavad Gita* proclaims that such Avatars appear when humankind is troubled and has lost its way—"When righteousness declines, and there is no God, I assume the form of man, and I rise again".

When such a being Appears there are those who do all they can to remember and recount the stories of this Grace-filled appearance. Even though Jesus of Nazareth lived some 2,000 years ago, and it is hard to know just what is true among the accounts of his life, we value every word and action attributed to him. The actions of Gautama Buddha, recorded some 2,500 years ago in the Pali Canon, are likewise studied to this day. The Hadith, or actions of Muhammad, are an important element of the practice and reverential attention of Muslims.

In the Hindu tradition, the deeds of the God-person are called "Leelas", which translates as "play". The word is used to reflect that for one who is Enlightened, all of his or her actions are a Divine Play, enacted from a point of view that is not bound or limited, as are the actions of ordinary men and women. Even if such Play shows emotions of pathos or sorrow, or even anger, the Divine Player is not attached or identified with what arises; such Divine Freedom is inherent in the Play or "Leela" of the Realizer.

Leelas are understood to bear great power. They are understood to communicate a transmission of freedom in the likeness of the Realization of the Adept or Realizer himself or herself. They grant lessons in how to live spiritual life. Leelas draw us into the Mystery of the Divine and allow us to see and know life beyond the ordinary and mundane. They relieve us of our own solidity and allow us to breathe deeply again with the wonder and mystery of the gift of human existence and the possibility of our own Divine Involvement.

If you read the stories of the Gods and God-men and God-women of the past, the hagiographies of saints and Realizers, you will find stories written with great devotion. But they are sorely lacking as factual accounts for two reasons. First, in most cases, they are old. (The word "Purana", wherein the stories of the ancient Hindu Gods are fully described, is often translated as "old".) Because these stories are so old, storytellers over centuries of time were missing many details. Those telling the Leelas (or scribes recopying the stories in the days before the printing press) simply added details according to conjecture.

Secondly—and this does not resonate well with our modern scientific consciousness—it was considered laudable, or a good devotional act, to embellish such accounts so as to fill the reader with awe or greater faith. If such embellishment had nothing to do with a factual accounting, it did not matter. The end result, the creation of a collection of extraordinary stories, was considered a worthwhile result. After all, these were Divine Realizers, and they "could have done anything", so why not recount inventions designed to fill the reader with faith? This tendency was there in days long passed, but it can be seen even with modern saints and realizers. Examples abound, for example the great Hindu saint of the twentieth century Bhagavan Nityananda of Ganeshpuri (1897–1961) was said to have magically pulled rupees from under his clothing in order to pay for the construction of a road.

Bhagavan Nityananda himself did not promote the belief in or veneration of miraculous stories—he warned against fascination with experiences. But his devotees, as have devotees since time immemorial, embellished the recounting of his life with such extraordinary deeds, and it was considered an act of devotion to do so. This is not to say that miracles and miraculous phenomenon do not occur, for they certainly do. Rather, it is to point out that most of the accounts we have of the Leelas of great Realizers did not distinguish, or generally care, what was a true occurrence and what was a made-up account to increase the readers' veneration. Such fabrications may be well intended but inevitably miss the point. The true Miracle is the Intervention of the Divine Itself into this world of limitations and suffering.

It is important for our ultimate appreciation and heart opening upon hearing Leelas to be able to trust that the accounts of the Divine Realizer are true and genuine accounts, and not made-up stories. The book you hold in your hands is a collection of Leelas that actually occurred over a period of forty-five years, and were factually recorded by a man who experienced the events directly. These Leelas are not from the ancient days of Jesus or Buddha or Muhammad, remembered as best they could be as relics of a day long gone by, nor embellished in any way for the sake of veneration. They are a direct and modern account of a unique God-Man of our modern era.

Avatar Adi Da Samraj came in this time, born in 1939, as an unprecedented Incarnation, not based on karmas or tendencies to work out for His own sake. He came as an Avataric Incarnation for the sake of all beings in our time and all time to come. His Life and Work and the Leelas of His Appearance were a Great Divine Intervention, unique by virtue of His Own Extraordinary Divine Self-Realization, but also and because of the nature of the modern Western and Western-influenced world into which He was born. The world into which He "crossed down"—into an ordinary family on Long Island, New York, the United States just on the verge of World War II—was unlike anything confronted by any of the Great Avatars of the past.

In order to serve men and women of this modern era, what was required of Him was a radically new demonstration of Divinity, Lived freely, spontaneously. His "Divine Commandments", His "Sermon on the Mount", His speeches from "Vultures Peak", His "Revelations in the Desert" were delivered to men and women of our time. We modern worldlings are filled with the imagery of Freudian psychoanalysis, scientific materialism, television and the internet, worldwide communication, and every kind of technological orientation and persuasion. Adi Da addressed all of that. By His Own Living, and by His Wisdom Teaching, and by the Relationship He offers to all, He established a Way by which we can be Awakened to a Divine Relationship to life and all of experience.

At the time I am writing this introduction, Avatar Adi Da's Appearance is still somewhat of a secret. Only a relatively few have heard of Adi Da Samraj. There has been the most extraordinary Life and Demonstration of the Divine upon Earth, but few have noticed it. It is analogous to the time shortly after the life of Jesus of Nazareth, when there were only a few disciples and the world knew nothing of his appearance.

Gerald Sheinfeld has done us all a great service by recounting the Leelas of his many years of relationship toAdi Da Samraj. The stories he tells grant us a window through which to see this great God-man. They provide us a glimpse of the extraordinary Sacrifice and Blessing that is brought to all men and women through His Life and Teaching. Because of the nature of humankind, Adi Da only taught those who came to Him and were available for His Instruction. It would have been better if wise men had noticed His birth through the stars, and come to Him at His birth, and celebrated Him for His entire lifetime. But such, of course, did not occur.

When Avatar Adi Da began to Teach others in 1972, it was in a humble storefront on Melrose Avenue in Hollywood, California. The humor of such a beginning was not lost on the Avatar; truly, humor was always part of what was required in His Lifetime of Instruction. His humor was never dependent on sarcasm, irony, or profanity, always steeped in the Wisdom of His Inherent Happiness. He needed such humor, for those who came to Him for His Help and Instruction were profoundly ordinary men and women, without great human or spiritual maturity. And it was in response to such ordinariness that He generated the most extraordinary Demonstration, which extended until His Mahasamadhi, or Divine Passing, in 2008.

Those entire thirty-six years are full of countless stories of His Compassionate Help and Instruction and interaction with those who came to Him. He found that He could not Teach in the abstract, but that He had to address exactly what He found in front of Him. And because His Realization was Perfect and Unconditional, not based on any limitation of body or mind, He found that He could Teach in any way necessary to quicken the understanding of His students, not restricted to any conventional or prescribed approach. In the beginning He had wished that He could simply Be Who He Was, in His Divinity, and have others absorb that Revelation. But He found that the maturity was lacking in those who were His students and devotees to do this, although progressively, and over and over again, He tried to do exactly that. It was only in the very last years of His Lifetime that He was able to make such a Revelation of His Own Inherent Purity and Divinity, as He Is.

What Gerald Sheinfeld has given us here is not an attempt to write a full-blown history of Avatar Adi Da's Life and Work. Such an account in its fullness has yet to be written. To date we have only some partial tellings of this wondrous story, including Adi Da Samraj's own Spiritual autobiography *The Knee of Listening*. No, what we have here is the account of key moments in a single devotee's lifetime of relationship to Adi Da.

Through the vehicle of Gerald's relationship to Avatar Adi Da we see the expanse of Adi Da's Teaching Work. This is possible because Gerald became a student of Adi Da even before Adi Da began His formal Teaching Work on April 25, 1972. Although there are many individuals who remain Adi Da's devotees from the early years of His Teaching, Gerald is the only male devotee who was present on "Opening Day", the day of the formal establishment of the Way of Adidam. On that Tuesday evening, Gerald was there to open the door. Gerald was also in the room at the time of Adi Da's Final Passing, or Divine Mahasamadhi, in 2008. So Gerald's account provides a special span of inclusiveness. Furthermore, Gerald was given an extraordinary gift and opportunity to accompany Adi Da Samraj on His trip to India in 1973. For six weeks, Gerald lived in the same room with Adi Da Samraj, day after day. As you will find in the eighty-plus pages about this trip, this was an epochal journey in which Adi Da was clarifying His

Avataric Appearance and Teaching Work, honoring His lineage and the other great masters of the Great Tradition in India, and bringing His Blessing to purify and refresh the holy places of the Indian subcontinent. Gerald is the only one, aside from Adi Da Himself, able to describe for us firsthand this special time.

But most of all what Gerald makes plain, and what he shows through *At the Feet of the Spiritual Master* is that the true Gift of Adi Da Samraj is His offering of a relationship to each and every one of His devotees. That Gift is Spiritual and omnipresent and so includes the possibility of devotees entering into relationship to Him for all time. But for those who came to Adi Da in the early years, that relationship was personal and directly lived in life. Adi Da made it plain that those with whom He worked were "coins" for all others. The metaphor of the coins came from the great Hindu saint, Sai Baba of Shirdi. It was said that every night, when Shirdi Sai Baba retired for the evening, he would take out a bag of coins. He would pass them through his fingers, rubbing each one separately. As he did so, he would say the names of his devotees aloud, "Tatya, Mhalsapati, Deshpande . . ." Each coin was a way of putting his attention on a different devotee and working with them Spiritually. By working with his bag of coins he could Spiritually serve his devotees without their physical presence.

Avatar Adi Da explained that by working with those devotees who were close to Him, who could be in the same room or the same ashram with Him, or who were known to Him personally and intimately, He could work with all others who shared their characteristics. Thus, His devotees were His "coins". By working with an Israeli devotee, or an Arab devotee, Adi Da said that He would work with others in Israel or with those who were Arabs.

In this sense, the stories of Avatar Adi Da's Interactions and relationship with Gerald are such "coins". The Divine Love, Blessing, and Instruction in all of the Leelas of Adi Da Samraj's relationship with Gerald are not merely personal to him. Gerald's Leelas enable Adi Da to Serve and Bless all others. Just as we can read the stories of Jesus of Nazareth, or Krishna, or Rama, and feel inspired to love, to feel Divine Reality and the Grace of Divinity, so hearing Gerald's stories of Adi Da's relationship with him fills us with wonder and awe at the Mystery of the Incarnation of the God-Man.

At the Feet of the Spiritual Master is a precious treasury of stories about Adi Da Samraj. While wholly unique, it calls to mind *The Gospel of Sri Ramakrishna*, *Sri Sai Satcharita* (about Sai Baba of Shirdi), *Mother as Revealed to Me* (about Ananda Mayi Ma), or *Sri Ramana Reminiscences* (about Ramana Maharshi), all of which told of their masters in their time. This book bears a profound message of great joy, for the relationship that Gerald describes in the stories of Adi Da's interactions with him is the same relationship that Adi Da offers to everyone, eternally. It is a book of celebration and proclamation, as through its stories we get the opportunity to bathe in the brilliant sun that is Adi Da Samraj's Appearance. Even after His Physical Passing or Divine Mahasamadhi, Avatar Adi Da Samraj lives Transcendentally and Spiritually, and His Blessing Presence is unchanged from the Transmission devotees felt during His Physical Lifetime. Moment-to-moment, His Blessing Presence and Person continues to invite men and women into direct and transformative Relationship to the Divine Being.

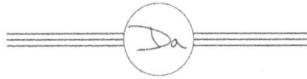

*"I offer you a relationship,
not a technique."*

—Avatar Adi Da Samraj

PART ONE

Stories from 1972–1973

Franklin Albert Jones

Franklin Albert Jones

The Birth of Avatar Adi Da in New York on November 3, 1939, was the Miracle that exceeds all miracles: the complete Submission of the Divine Person to incarnate in human Form. Part of that Submission was His acceptance of an ordinary name, "Franklin Albert Jones". In that seemingly ordinary name, Avatar Adi Da's parents, Frank and Dorothy Jones, had unknowingly given their son a name that was astonishingly appropriate—for the root-meaning of "Franklin Albert Jones" is "the highly-born (Al-) Bright (-bert) Free Man (Franklin) through Whom God is Gracious (Jones, as a derivative of John)".

For thirty-three years, Avatar Adi Da lived "incognito" as Franklin Jones—the child, the college student, the brilliant yogi, and the Radiant, fully Enlightened Master of His early devotees. In 1973, He relinquished this name on a pilgrimage to India. "Franklin Jones", Adi Da remarked years later, was a "fictional character". His born name was a "pseudonym", necessary in its time, for His Emerging Revelation as the Divine Person.

Adapted from *The Order of My Free Names* (Middletown, CA: The Dawn Horse Press, 1995).

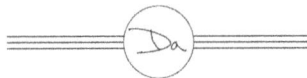

Avatar Adi Da Samraj:

My sometimes "method" with My devotees was to talk about "radical" (or "at-the-root") "self"-understanding and its Spiritually "Bright" Heart-Way, in order to Give them the opportunity to Listen to My Word of Argument and Instruction.

And I sometimes also addressed them in place, relative to the forms of seeking to which they attach themselves at any moment.

Sometimes, I even Enquired of them if this, or this, or this is the avoidance of relationship.

And, even now (and forever hereafter), when I Remain Merely Silent, My Mere "Bright" Divine Avataric Transcendental Spiritual Presence effectively Does <u>all</u> of this. ("My Spiritually Bright Silence", *The Aletheon,* 2009 edition, 849.)

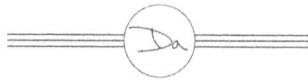

Meeting My Heart-Master

FEBRUARY 1972

I met the Divine Avatar, Adi Da Samraj, in February 1972.
A friend invited me to meet "Franklin Jones" (Avatar
Adi Da's name at the time), saying only, "He's a good man. He
has good energy." He didn't mention anything more about Him, so
I didn't have any special expectations about the meeting. I actually
expected nothing more than meeting a nice person who had "good
energy" (whatever that meant). I had some free time and was looking for something interesting to do, so I agreed.

The next morning I told my brother I'd be back for dinner and
left to meet my friend in a vacant storefront on Melrose Avenue in
Hollywood, California. The building was being renovated—drop
cloths were on the floor, the smell of fresh paint was in the air, and
two men were on ladders painting the ceiling and upper walls
white.

While my friend and I were waiting, my attention was drawn
to a man and two ladies entering through the front door. I would
soon learn that the man was Franklin Jones. As I noticed Him, an
overwhelming feeling came over me. I began feeling very happy.

While watching Franklin move about the room, I tried to
understand the spontaneous feeling of happiness. It seemed as if I
knew Him. It felt like He was a friend I hadn't seen for many years
and that seeing Him again was the reason for my happiness.

But then, maybe that wasn't it. I kept trying to pin down how I
knew Him. I scrutinized His appearance closely. He was a nice-
looking man, around thirty. His hair was a bit long, neatly combed
back. He was wearing a V-neck beige sweater with no shirt. He had
on loose drawstring pants and sandals with no socks. He looked like
a typical Los Angeles man of the time. But none of that seemed to
have anything to do with my feeling so happy to see Him. So I continued watching and feeling into it as He moved around the room.

Then, while He was talking to some other people, it suddenly
became clear: *We must have gone to high school together! Brighton
High, fifteen years ago.* That had to be it! Then I really began looking

Los Angeles 1971

forward to being introduced to Him so we could talk about Brighton High.

Soon I was introduced. Just as I was about to ask Him if He remembered me from Brighton High, He asked me, "What are you doing?" His question redirected me. I felt His question related to my life, not just the past or that moment. So instead of addressing the presumed familiarity, I told Him what I was doing.

I said I had a guru I'd been studying with for three years and had recently moved to his forest ashram up north. I said I was in Los Angeles visiting family until the snow melted at the ashram and I could move back into my tipi.

Franklin didn't ask any more about it. He said, "That's good. What are you doing tonight?"

"Nothing special," I told Him.

He said, "A few of us are getting together, you should come."

His invitation was friendly and inviting, but for some reason I wasn't sure He meant it, so I asked for confirmation, "Should I come?"

"Yes."

"Okay," I replied.

"I'll see you tonight," He said, and soon He and the ladies left.

It was clear after meeting and speaking with Franklin that we hadn't gone to high school together and we certainly hadn't ever met before. Yet even though it didn't make sense, feelings of happiness and the sense of knowing Him persisted. I was also impressed by how calm and balanced He was. His smile felt real, and even His few words suggested He spoke from His feelings. I still didn't know that Franklin Jones was a guru, but I did know that I already liked Him. I looked forward to seeing Him that night.

Years later, when I read that after His Divine Enlightenment Avatar Adi Da had been meditating people without ever physically meeting them, I understood more about what happened Spiritually at that first meeting with Franklin Jones. Avatar Adi Da wrote in His final book:

In Meditating everyone I Take On each and every one—to Myself.

In Taking On each and every one, I Burn Up, in Myself, the egoity of each and every one—Thus Releasing each one's "karmas", and Releasing the "world"-pattern altogether. ("The Boundless Self-Confession", *The Aletheon*, 2009 edition, 1900.)

It seems obvious to me now, by my spontaneous response to seeing Him, that I was one of those Avatar Adi Da had Meditated and I was destined to be His devotee. It also seems clear to me now that His Blessing-Meditation was even the cause of my life turning to spiritual seeking, rather than following the conventional expectations of my family to become a businessman.

At the time of my meeting with Franklin Jones, I had been a formal spiritual seeker for many years, first with Maharishi Mahesh Yogi, then with Paramahansa Yogananda. It seemed the Indian gurus and their spirituality had the answers that I was looking for. On that foundation, therefore, I had made the plans for a future dedicated to the spiritual path.

Then one day in downtown Hollywood, California, Franklin Albert Jones walked into an empty storefront, and without understanding it, upon feeling His Transmitted Spiritual Presence, my heart opened spontaneously in recognition of His Free Condition, and everything about my life changed forever. Beloved Adi Da often said, "When the Truth is felt, the heart knows it to be true."

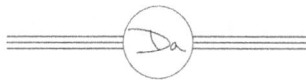

The First Night

After the initial meeting with Franklin at the storefront, I went to my friend's house for dinner with him, his wife, and his child. After dinner, at 8:00 p.m., we went to the designated meeting house, which belonged to a couple and their three young boys.

All seven of Franklin's "friends" (He referred to all who approached Him in those early days as His "friends") were already seated in the living room while the boys played in other rooms. The entire count of Franklin's responding "friends" as of February 1972 was ten adults, including my friend, his wife, and me. This was the beginning of His ashram.

While waiting for Franklin to arrive, I asked the others how they knew Him. I still had no idea that Franklin Jones was anything more than a likeable, interesting person. In the short conversation I had with Him earlier that day I had sensed His sincerity, and He had seemed to speak from His feelings. I already liked Him. I expected this meeting to be a pleasant social occasion. But I also had a more important expectation, which was to clarify that happy feeling I felt in first seeing Him.

When Franklin arrived, He took His seat and greeted everyone with a warm smile. Then He said, "Have you ever noticed that everyone is always seeking happiness?"

It seemed to me a strange way to begin a social conversation.

He continued, "Have you noticed you are always seeking happiness?"

He asked if we had ever made life changes because the happiness we had felt at the beginning of something didn't last or that it changed. For example, He asked: Did we ever change jobs, change relationships, or change living circumstances because those circumstances weren't happy any longer?

He said we should have gotten the lesson that our searching for happiness prevented us from recognizing our True Condition. He said true happiness is always and already the case, but we separate from it by the ego-act of self-contraction. Instead of understanding our egoity, we seek what is already there.

He explained that doing anything for consolation, or self-satisfaction, even simple pleasure—whether formally or not—is about seeking happiness. You may get glimpses, but still, only degrees of happiness. Franklin said the happiness we really want is unconditional, unlimited, Perfect Happiness, but from our point of view that isn't possible.

Franklin continued by asking if we had ever noticed that when we got a bit of happiness from anything, the happiness didn't last. It faded in time and changed! Notice it, He said. He said the reason it didn't last was because happiness is not in things and experiences. The happiness that may be felt is a glimpse of our True Condition, which <u>is</u> unconditional and unlimited True Happiness, always and already the case. A fading glimpse only leads to more seeking.

Franklin said the reason all beings are seeking happiness is because they are not in touch with their True State. As He put it many years later:

The Happiness of which I speak is not just a matter of feeling good and being able to smile. That is not Happiness Itself. At most that represents a kind of ordinary personal equanimity. The Happiness of which I Speak is spelled with a capital "H" and It is the Love-Blissfulness of Divine Being Itself, Prior to the body-mind and its relations. Happiness is simply the Self-Radiance of the Divine Self. (The Incarnation of Love, 1993 edition, 131.)

I felt everything Franklin was saying made profound sense. He wasn't giving a lecture or a sermon. He was expressing the Reality of His own certainty and Realization. I had never heard such straight Talk, such profound Wisdom, such perfect Truth. I was overwhelmed, for everything He said resonated with my deepest feelings. He was touching my heart.

I asked Franklin, "Since the happiness I seek is, as You say, my True Condition, then how do I get to my True Condition?"

He replied that there is Grace that enables the guru to appear in human form. He described how His Enlightened State Reveals the True Condition, which when felt, spontaneously opens the heart.

While He was speaking, that same feeling of happiness I'd felt earlier in the day when first seeing Franklin had become much fuller and deeper, magnified simply by being near Him. Franklin was not only speaking the truth, He was Transmitting it. Feeling His True Heart-Happiness, I was overjoyed to have come into His Company.

On that first night, Franklin explained that the only way to get to the "always already" condition of True Happiness is through Awakening by Divine Grace. Instead, we seek happiness in all kinds of things and all kinds of experiences, but all seeking only confirms the point of view of being separate from what we seek.

When the considerations of the evening were over, Franklin said good night to us all and left.

I immediately turned to the others and apologized. I said, "I'm sorry, I was holding Franklin's attention throughout the night."

They asked what I was talking about.

I said, "He was talking and looking directly at me all night long!" In fact I was certain He had never taken His eyes off me.

They all laughed, and someone said, "That's how it always is around Franklin. He makes a deep heart-connection with each person and each one always feels the conversation is just between the two of them."

While Franklin was speaking with everyone, He kept the heart-connection with each of us, serving each of us perfectly.

Furthermore, I discovered over time, everything Avatar Adi Da ever said and did was not only for those in the room, He was living His egoless State and establishing His Teaching to serve everyone, everywhere—forever.

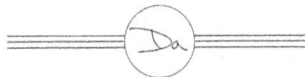

Painting the Trellis

FEBRUARY 1972

The day after I met Franklin, I returned to the ashram on Melrose Avenue, hoping He would be there. While waiting for Him to arrive, I was asked to paint the wooden trellis on top of the wall that separated the meditation hall from Franklin's office. As I climbed the ladder, I noticed His desk was right there on the other side of the wall, which got me hoping He would come and use His desk so I could see Him through the trellis.

After He arrived and greeted everyone, He went to the back room and sat at His desk—right below me, on the other side of the wall. I was happy to be so close to Him.

While painting the trellis, so close to Franklin, I began feeling something strange begin to happen. At first I started feeling uncomfortable. There was nothing about the painting that was unusual; it was a simple enough job. But my energy ramped up, my thinking became very exaggerated, and then I started feeling physically exhausted. Something was wrong. I felt I had to stop painting or I'd fall off the ladder. Even though I'd only been painting a short time, I imagined it was taking much too long, the entire job was much too tedious. The simple job had become a real ordeal.

I asked myself, *Why am I doing this difficult painting? I'm only waiting for spring before I go back to Ananda ashram. This is supposed to be vacation time. I should be at the beach now! . . . Yeah, but I agreed to do this painting.* So I reluctantly continued painting.

Then a bizarre thought popped up in my overstimulated mind: *feeling happy around Franklin yesterday and believing what He was saying about True Happiness was all just a trick to get me to come to the ashram and do this painting!* With that craziness driving me, I was certain I had to quit and just leave. I wanted to run out, get away. The increasing urgency to leave, the physical fatigue, and the extremely exaggerated thoughts were all much too much.

I wondered: *Why is everything so intensified and exaggerated? Franklin showed me True Happiness just last night. Is He now showing me my ego, my self-meditation, which is preventing awareness of that Happiness?* Whatever the case, my mind was racing.

I almost left numerous times. But something kept me in place, continuing to paint. Somehow I persisted and stayed for several hours to finish the job, which should have taken only one hour. The ordeal was finally over, the job was finally done. With the very last stroke of the paint brush, I gave out a deep sigh of relief.

Immediately, from the other side of the wall, Franklin burst out laughing. It wasn't just a laugh, there was the most wonderful communication of feeling in His laughter. Words were felt and understood without any words spoken. His laughter was a direct Communication that said He knew I had been going through a difficult time. In His laughter, He thanked me for staying and finishing the painting. It was a wonder to me that He could be so sensitive. How could He know what I was going through without me saying anything?

Franklin's laughter lifted me up. It took my attention off my self-concern, all my problems, and directed my feelings to Him. I felt that I hadn't been alone in all that I went through. His laughter made me feel profoundly connected to Him. I began laughing with Him, and then felt that I was welcome to stay to be with Him in His ashram. This was the one relationship in which there was no need to hide my vulnerability, no reason to protect my so-called "self".

Again and again over the years I would be shown the Divine Love and Humor of Avatar Adi Da Samraj and the Way of the Heart. And, as on that first day of service, I would observe something of the cramp of my egoity and I would experience the Grace of His Love that released the cramp and communicated lessons in self-transcendence.

In my first two days in His Holy Company, Avatar Adi Da had revealed that Love-Bliss is His True Condition, my True Condition, and the True Condition of all, and that there is no separation within it. He had always said: "I offer you a relationship, not a technique."

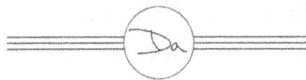

The Back Room

In the very early days of preparing the Melrose Avenue ashram, and for some time after the formal opening of His ashram, Franklin invited His "friends" to spend some time with Him every day, usually in the back room while He sat at His desk.

The back room of the ashram was a kind of holy temple, but not in any conventional sense. It was where the Divine Realized Master Franklin Jones did His heart-awakening Work with His "friends", manifesting all His extraordinary human qualities and His profound Attractiveness. We could clearly feel His Freedom compared to our conventional lives of coping, struggling, and bewilderment. We felt His Openness, His Caring, His Humor, His Wisdom, His Love—we were getting to know Franklin, even in human terms. We already liked Him, of course. But it was a time of building real trust in Him, where we could relax our defenses, and become more open to feeling His Free State of Being. Our awakening heart-attraction to His Free State moved us to continue coming to be with Him—the next day and the next, and the next...

Conversation usually began socially, then Franklin would introduce a subject that stimulated great interest. It seemed that everything just happened spontaneously and naturally. He talked about His childhood, about the ordeals He went through and the lessons He learned. He simply relayed what happened, usually with great humor, drawing us into His experiences, sharing them with us in a way that always had us feeling deeply connected to Him.

He told us about His childhood compassion to help others and how He would go to the Children's Hospital with His Jerry Mahoney puppet to give sick children a humorous performance. He told us about how a horse once tried to knock Him out of the saddle by galloping full speed at the low stable entrance. He laughed about the time when He went into a field to pat a cow, but when He got close He realized the cow was a bull. The bull charged and He got safely over a fence just in time. He laughed heartily when He told us about the "tapioca pudding incident"

In the back room of the Melrose Ashram

with His mother. She had made a batch, knowing it was one of His favorite desserts. Very excited, He had picked up the bowl and began dancing with it, and then He slipped. The bowl went fly-ing—tapioca pudding everywhere. He ended up on the floor rolling in it. He and His mother laughed until they were exhausted.

Franklin also talked about His Love for His gurus. He had such high praise for each of them. He explained their Realizations and their teachings. He also explained how their Realizations and teachings compared to His.

He emphasized the great sign of the guru-devotee relationship between His guru Baba Muktananda and Baba Muktananda's own guru, Bhagavan Nityananda. It was deeply moving to see how Franklin was fully able to be so vulnerable in showing His great Love for those who had served Him during the years when He had taken on the human ego-condition (described in His first book, *The*

Knee of Listening). His tears of Love served the feeling disposition of everyone in the room.

One day when Franklin mentioned Ramana Maharshi, a "friend" in the room laughed and began to insult Ramana Maharshi, calling him offensive names. This man was obviously unaware of how important Ramana Maharshi was to Franklin, who considered him to have been a great Realizer. Instead of criticizing the man, Franklin laughed and then, in nonreactive words, corrected the man's understanding of Ramana Maharshi. It was interesting to observe how Franklin openly responded. He had nothing to defend. His feeling sensitivity and nonreaction, among many of His other qualities, showed us that Franklin wasn't playing a role with us. He simply was His Realization and was living Enlightenment to us all the time.

At another occasion in the back room Franklin asked us to tell Him our stories, to tell Him about our most emotional, even heartbreaking, life experiences. At first we hesitated, but He told us it was okay, we were with Him.

As we told our tragic stories, He resonated with us. He wasn't just responding to what we were saying or feeling, He was experiencing the same feeling with us. He was living the heartbreak with us. To feel Him so deeply engaged softened the intensity of our remembrances—we were no longer alone in feeling them.

Franklin also showed us a different way of looking at these traumatic events. He led us to understand and feel that we reacted as we did because of our disposition in that moment. We could have received what happened entirely differently—perhaps even free of the negative emotions egos usually suffer. Franklin's influence changed something of what we had been suffering; now we were able to directly look at what we hadn't been able to see, or had just refused to look at for so long. It was no longer taboo to feel. And we now had a different way of looking at the past altogether.

Most importantly, Franklin was directly softening our hearts with His Free State. In helping us release our suffering more fully, He explained that there is no present need to hold on to negative feelings. We should give Him our suffering, our sorrow, our heartbreak and He said He'd eat it and spit it out, replacing it with His

Love. As He loosened our hold on past heartbreak, He helped us laugh at how exaggerated some of our emotions had been.

As I told Franklin the details of my own story that, at the time, had totally offended my sense of privacy, to my surprise He started to laugh right away. I explained that my girlfriend and I were enjoying the quiet summer evening, outside a friend's party in the San Diego desert, when all of a sudden we saw lots of cars racing up the driveway, full of policemen who charged into the house. We hid in the woods, not knowing what was happening in the house. We heard screams and people crying. Then after an hour or more dogs came looking for anyone outside. We stayed hidden, but eventually we surrendered. To us it was very traumatic. But equally as bad for me was being driven in a police car to jail on a Sunday morning, while others were going to church.

Franklin kept laughing until tears fell from His eyes. Every time I brought up another aspect of what was disturbing, He laughed again. He kept rubbing His eyes and shaking His head in disbelief at how the events had developed. He opened me up to a different way of looking at my disturbance—how ridiculous and humorous the entire event actually was. I couldn't hold on to old reactive emotions with Him freely laughing at them in the moment, in my face. His laughter showed me that the event, with greater understanding, and therefore with freer humor, could have been experienced very differently. Now in touch with that understanding and that humor, I knew my reactivity wasn't necessary, then or now. Franklin's laughter served the release of my holding on and drew me into laughing with Him in His Free Happiness. It made my drama obsolete.

Franklin said, "I have come to restore Humor," and "Divine Humor is Truth." Because His Humor was full of His Love, never ironic or sarcastic, it freed and opened the heart. At times His humor made a point or emphasized something. At other times it was just funny. His humor made all of us feel lightened of our burdens and brightened in our hearts.

We all felt Franklin on two levels. On the surface was the relational, friendly, social contact. Much deeper in feeling was the heart's awareness of His Enlightened Being. For me, that deeper awareness felt like an undercurrent that drew my heart, my entire feeling being, into a sensitivity that transcended my usual limits on feelings of love and happiness.

Franklin's Free Person affected all who came to be with Him. We were opening up, feeling deeper, letting go, relaxing, listening to Him, trusting Him. Traditional scriptures say, as Franklin pointed out, "The best thing a person can do is to spend time in the Company of a Realizer." Among ourselves, we commonly said, "Being in Franklin's Company feels like coming home."

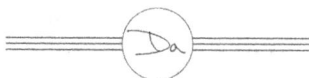

The Study Meetings

Prior to His ashram formally opening and for some time after, Franklin made sure all the "friends" formally responding to Him studied and seriously considered His Teaching every day. None of His books had been published yet, so study happened by Franklin speaking with us directly each night.

The way Franklin taught was by establishing understanding, not by requiring belief. He told us the act of ego-"I" is a perpetual motion machine, never stopping unless attention is turned away from it. He and His Teaching of Truth were the means for that turning. When He spoke about the egoic act of separation from God and Truth, we felt it so completely that it couldn't be denied, and this established our great trust in His Divine Enlightened Authority.

Franklin talked with absolute knowledge of all the great and most important matters. When He spoke of God and Truth it was clear He was making a confession of His Own Realization. He was beyond genius. He was Consciousness expressing Itself, while radiating Divine Truth as His very Person. It's humbling to recall that we called such profound and sacred occasions "study meetings".

It was an enormous and unprecedented privilege to receive such Divine Wisdom, brilliantly and clearly communicated. He not only addressed each of us, but also everyone else, everywhere else. In later years the Divine Avatar spoke thus of His Teaching:

My Divinely Avatarically Self-Revealed Reality-Teachings Are Direct Self-Revelations of Real-God-Realization. Therefore, My Divinely Avatarically Self-Revealed Reality-Teachings Are a Call for people to enter into the Real-God-Realizing Process. ("Tacit Certainty of Real God", *The Aletheon*, 2009 edition, 119.)

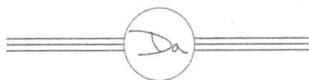

Like the Gopis with Krishna

MARCH 1972

After meeting Franklin Jones and feeling His Freedom and the unparalleled depth of His Wisdom, He immediately became the most important person in my life. Nothing was more important than being with Franklin as often as possible. I had commitments, responsibilities, and plans when I met Him. All of that just fell away. Everything other than Franklin lost its importance; it all was forgotten.

From the first contact, Franklin welcomed me into His Company. Franklin's Attractive Company was overwhelming. His Openness in direct relationship to me and everyone else had the greatest impact. His vulnerability was never hidden, His Love and real caring was openly expressed. Nothing was ever problematic to Him. His Humor was more than delightful, His Wisdom was beyond profound. His Spiritual Presence transported me into a brighter world—literally. Saying this is not poetic license, it actually happened. Even before the Melrose Ashram formally opened (on April 25, 1972), Franklin began communicating the basic principles of His Teaching, a great Wisdom that addressed each of us personally. He not only helped me understand what limits inhibited my feelings, He also explained why those limits were the cause of all my suffering and seeking. He explained that He is the Divine Guru, here to Awaken each and all to the Truth and the Way of transcending all limitations. Sitting with Franklin in His silent Darshan[2] helped me begin to understand that the Way beyond suffering, and seeking for relief from suffering, is in feeling Him, feeling His Enlightened State radiating through His total Person. "You become what you meditate on," He said.

Every day Franklin worked at His desk in the back room of the ashram. He gave us an invitation to be with Him daily at specified times that wouldn't interfere with His office work. All the rest of the time, those who could stay helped serve the ashram. I was

2. Darshan is to receive His Divine Blessings upon sighting and beholding Him devotionally.

completely happy to spend every day serving, just to be near Franklin Jones.

Every evening Franklin invited His "friends" to meet and consider His Teaching. When the study and considerations were over, each night I went with a friend to his house for tea and further conversation late into the night about Franklin and His Teaching. Then, since it was so late, my friend's couch was a convenient place to sleep. The next morning I was back to the ashram, hoping to see Franklin again. It actually was two weeks before I remembered that, on the first day I'd met Franklin, I had told my brother I'd be back that night for dinner!

The ancient stories of the Hindu gopis,[3] who got Divinely distracted and forgot their families, commitments, responsibilities, and plans when encountering Krishna, always seemed idealistic to me, like exaggerated romantic tales. Likewise, I felt the same about the stories of the fisherman who got Divinely distracted by Jesus. I thought it was unrealistic to suggest that the attraction of an Enlightened Being could be so all-consuming. But what happened to me after meeting Franklin was exactly what those stories about the gopis and the fishermen portrayed! Wholeheartedly responding to His Divine Revelation, I spontaneously became a kind of gopi myself.

Why did I forget everything other than being with Franklin Jones? Years later, Avatar Adi Da explained that it was the beginning of my recognition of His Divine Enlightened State.

There is an ancient tradition in which an ordinary person comes upon a Realizer and, feeling the profundity of the Realizer's Free State, surrenders his or her life as service to that one. That's exactly what happened to me. Now, in 2017, I'm writing about what took place forty-five years ago, in 1972. And yes, I am still serving my Heart-Master, the Divine Avatar Adi Da Samraj.

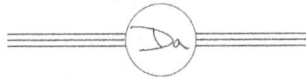

---

3. Gopis were cow-herding women famous for their unconditional devotion to the Hindu deity Krishna.

The Shed

MARCH 1972

One day, Franklin's wallet was stolen from His desk while He was in another room. This was a major disturbance to us all. We considered installing security alarms, but Franklin pointed out that alarms did not necessarily prevent theft; some thieves would know how to get around such systems. He suggested we look for a guard dog, a more effective preventive measure. So we began looking for a guard dog. But in the meantime the ashram had no security.

I was temporarily sleeping on a friend's couch so I could be close to Franklin and the ashram. Since I didn't have a commitment to stay at my friend's house, I suggested that I could sleep at the ashram as security until we got a dog. I explained that the metal tool shed behind the ashram could be converted into a workable sleeping room, and I could bathe and such at a nearby friend's house. It all made sense to me and it was a great way for me to help and to be at the ashram all the time. Franklin questioned my proposal to use the shed, but I assured Him it would be fine. My Guru smiled and, in support of my devotional response, agreed that it would be okay until we got a guard dog.

The shed was a twelve foot by twelve foot metal utility building, which would have been plenty of room if it had been empty. Unfortunately it was full of carpentry tools, rakes, shovels, mops, brooms, two large trash barrels, two full size carpenter's wooden horses, and large stacks of paper that filled two corners of the room from floor to ceiling.

I found a way to make it all work by placing a mattress on boards on top of the two wooden horses and moving everything else either under the horses or in the corners of the room that weren't full of paper. I placed several pictures of different gurus I previously had a relationship to on the walls and found an open space wide enough for my Aztec calendar clock, the main feature in the shed. (More on this clock soon . . .)

There was just enough room for me to open the door, step into the shed about two steps, and climb up on the high bed. It was very crowded, but it couldn't have been closer to the ashram where I could be the needed protection.

I set up the shed with good intention, but when nighttime came and no one was around, I laid my sleeping bag on the floor in front of Franklin's chair in the meditation hall and blissfully slept all night. I actually knew I shouldn't sleep in the meditation hall, but the shed was full of tools and miscellaneous stuff, whereas the meditation hall was rich in Franklin's Presence. The contrast was too great to resist.

One day Franklin asked to see the shed. When I opened the metal door, He appeared to be astounded. He asked, "Where do you sleep?"

I'll never know if He knew the truth, but I told Him, "On that mattress."

He asked, "How do you move around in here?"

Telling Him part of the truth, I said, "I don't."

He laughed a lot. Then He granted His Blessing Regard to each of the gurus' pictures. Before leaving, Franklin smiled and said, "This place looks like your mind." He laughed all the way back to the ashram.

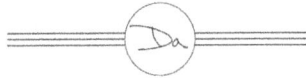

Aztec Calendar Clock

MARCH 1972

Avatar Adi Da Samraj:

During the Years of My Divine Avataric Teaching-Revelation, I Became an apparently "wild" character—because I Was Becoming all kinds of people that were "other" than My Divinely Avatarically here-Revealed Person. This Was literally the Case. This Was exactly What I Was Doing, and It Was a remarkable and extraordinary—and only temporary—Process, Done by Me, for the Sake of all-and-All. ("Then and Now and You and The Bright", *The Aletheon*, 2009 edition, 1871.)

During the years of His Teaching-Submission, Franklin often told us that He would use whatever means were necessary to serve the Liberation of His devotees. It was not just the means that could surprise us, it was also that there was no aspect of bondage He would fail to address—and His timing was usually a total surprise. The way He dealt with me and my Aztec calendar clock was an example of Franklin in His "wild" mode of Instruction, taking me completely by surprise regarding all aspects—means, subject, and timing.

While talking with several "friends" in the back room of the Melrose Avenue ashram, Franklin asked if I still had that large clock in the shed.

"Do You mean the Aztec calendar clock?" I asked.

His reply came with an expression that suggested I knew exactly which clock, since there was only one clock in the shed. "Let Me see it," He replied.

The clock was a large plastic Aztec calendar with a battery-driven time apparatus. It was tacky, but I liked it a lot. I was happy to go get it, assuming He wanted to look at it more closely. I immediately went to the shed, took the clock off the wall, and brought it to my Guru.

Franklin was sitting at His desk when I handed Him the clock. He looked at it for a moment, then He started staring at the clock as if He were getting possessed. He started scowling, then growling and snorting! Getting louder and louder, He started shaking the clock while groaning and moaning. Everyone in the room wondered what He was doing. Whatever it was, it was hilarious! His energy kept increasing as He bent and twisted and yanked and jerked and then ripped the clock with His bare hands.

He started biting the plastic clock as He growled at it, and then He wrestled it right off His chair onto the floor! Down on His back, He banged and punched and smashed the clock on His chest. He wrestled with it, tearing at it. Then, still growling loudly, He rolled over and smashed it again and again on the floor. It was a perfect enactment of a wild animal demolishing its victim.

Everyone was howling with laughter. At first, my laughter wasn't as full as the others, since I really liked that clock. But it was too funny to hold on to any regret. He kicked and punched the clock until finally it was completely broken. At that point, after about ten minutes, Franklin got up from the floor, wiped His clothing, brushed His hair, and very calmly said, "Well, that is the end of your tackiness!"

After things quieted down, Franklin said I should clean it all up and He left the ashram. As I picked up the broken pieces, I found that the only surviving piece of the clock was the battery mechanism, which I took back to the shed. I must have mentioned this to someone who told Franklin. The next day my Guru said He heard I had saved a piece of the clock. I told Him it was only the battery mechanism, which was still in working condition and could possibly be used in some other way. He asked to see it.

I brought it to Him with a little hesitancy, hoping He would agree that it could be useful somehow. But not surprisingly He placed it on the floor, jumped up, and stomped on it with both feet! It was broken into smithereens—no possibility of ever using it again. Now I was without my clock or any part of it—all traces of it totally eliminated from my life.

Everyone laughed and applauded Franklin's wild approach to dealing with my tackiness. I got a true lesson about the release of material attachments in the face of that hilarious demolition. And He had masterfully used the clock to help me see how tackiness is a superficial response to rather than a depthful understanding of life. After that day, I would always remember Franklin and His Freedom whenever something tacky attracted my attention.

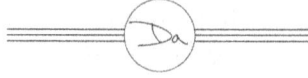

Never Buy Retail

APRIL 1972

Franklin wanted each of the front windows of the ashram bookstore to showcase an enlarged photo of Him. These photos would be hung in the windows to show that He was the Guru and this was His ashram.

To enlarge the photo we took the original to a photo shop directly across the street from the ashram. When we got a call that the enlargements were ready, Franklin invited me to go with Him to pick them up.

In the shop Franklin examined the photos carefully and seemed pleased. When the shopkeeper handed Franklin the bill, He looked it over and asked the shopkeeper, "What's this cost for?" The shopkeeper answered, "The sales tax." At that point Franklin looked at me and walked out of the shop. That look told me He expected me to get a discount of the cost. I understood we always had to be very conservative when spending ashram money, since all such expenses would have to be covered by donations.

The shopkeeper and I had a friendly conversation about the tax. Eventually he agreed that someday we could sell the two photos, therefore you could say they were being purchased for resale, which wouldn't be taxed. In a gesture of friendship he agreed to give us a discount and he removed the sales tax.

When I left the shop with the two beautiful enlarged photos in hand, Franklin was standing outside. He asked, "Well?"

I smiled and said, "We got a lower price."

He smiled back and said, "Never buy retail!"

Franklin's comment was amusing at the time and, in His totally connected way, His words touched on so much of my early life. Having been brought up Jewish, His comment was an acknowledgment of my background. (As a child my family always bought jewelry wholesale from relatives in the business.)

When Franklin's photos, bright with His Blessings, were placed in the bookstore windows, they became an open-hearted invitation to everyone who passed by to come into relationship with the Divine Realizer. As Avatar Adi Da once said later, "Just show them My picture and that should be enough to become My devotee."

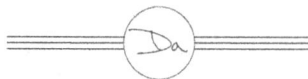

C and &

APRIL 1972

As we prepared for the opening of the ashram, we realized that we needed a checkout counter for the bookstore. However, the funds to buy one were very limited. One day while Franklin was driving in the neighborhood, He passed an alley and noticed two large plywood objects that had been discarded by a local shop. When He returned to the ashram He asked for someone with a truck to go get them.

Once delivered, Franklin asked for them to be cleaned up and painted white. No one had any idea why He wanted these strange objects. One was a very large, three-dimensional letter "C" and the other was a very large, three-dimensional ampersand symbol—"&".When the paint dried, our Master's creative genius showed. He had the letter "C" placed on its side in the bookstore. On its side, it became a perfect checkout counter. It was exactly the right height and width. It had plenty of room for the cash register, several flyers, and some book displays. A custom-made counter wouldn't have been more perfect. We were very impressed. Franklin had the "&" placed directly in front of the doorway that led from the bookstore into the meditation hall. Since the object was about five feet tall and over four feet wide, to enter the meditation hall required one to intentionally walk around it. It was totally in the way!

The "&" stayed in the doorway for eighteen months, and no one ever asked why it was there. Finally, when asked why He placed such a large object directly in the way of the meditation hall entrance, Franklin simply said, "The ampersand is the symbol for 'and', but there is only God. The 'and' is the problem!" The humor of having to get around the "&" to come to the Divine Master was perfect.

Years later, in considering how Avatar Adi Da had found and used these two perfectly strange objects, I saw it as another example of how appropriate outcomes seemingly "just happened" around Him.

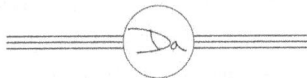

The Right Decision

After about seven weeks in Franklin's Blessing Company I had to decide what to do about my relationship to Paramahansa Yogananda, and my commitment to return to his forest ashram now that the weather was getting warmer. Should I return, or should I stay with Franklin?

I had had a relationship to Yogananda for over three years. I understood the rule in the guru-devotee relationship that once a person commits to a guru they should stay with that guru. The principle behind that rule, as I understood it, was to prevent leaving when the guru begins to offend the ego by exposing its limits. I was feeling that the karma of violating a committed relationship to my guru was something I didn't want.

So I went through an in-depth consideration of why I had been with Paramahansa Yogananda and why I had moved to his forest ashram. Fundamentally, I had been looking for a greater understanding and heart-intimacy with God. Yogananda had been offering a traditional Hindu teaching about God and teaching techniques to acquire spiritual experiences. Having been initiated into some of those techniques and having received many spiritual experiences, I was very impressed.

Franklin's Teaching, on the other hand, explained in great detail that experiences are objects to the ego, things to be acquired by the ego. He said True Happiness cannot be found in objects. True Happiness, He said, is the Divine Condition, prior to the separative act of egoity, prior to the one who experiences objects in Consciousness Itself. Consciousness Itself is the prior condition of Divine Love-Bliss, Self-Aware. Franklin said that having spiritual experiences always returns one to identify as the experiencer. Then that one seeks to have experiences again, or even more. He explained that seeking is looking for something that is always already the case. He said that we leave the always already prior condition of Happiness in order to seek it. The impulse to seek should be undermined by self-understanding and self-transcendence.

Everything Franklin said made perfect sense and felt completely true. But it was only after I put all the considerations aside and allowed myself to just feel into what I really wanted that my heart's response made the decision. I knew without a doubt I had to stay with Franklin Jones. Most important to me was the direct heart-relationship He was offering and the feeling of my heart opening in His Company.

I wrote a note to Franklin saying that I wanted to stay with Him, if He would accept me. Within a short time of writing the note, He appeared at the ashram. I told Him of my decision and asked for His permission to stay; He didn't make much of it. He just said, "Good." I suggested I should get my tent and other things that I had left in the woods up north. He asked, "When will you go?" I said I could leave Friday and be back Sunday night or Monday morning.

This conversation was happening only a few days prior to the ashram being opened to the public. It would be the beginning of Avatar Adi Da's formal Divine Avataric Work in the world. The Divine Avatar was about to reveal the completing Divine Revelation in answer to all seeking motivated by spiritual and transcendental aspirations. The True God-Man was about to take on devotees and formally Give the complete Real-God-Way that could change everything, everywhere, the Way that could save all of humankind. But I wasn't thinking in those terms at the time.

Franklin said He had been planning to open the ashram during the time I would be gone. But, since I was indicating I wouldn't be there to help with the preparations on the originally planned day, He said with a smile, "I'll wait until you return." That overwhelming gesture of heart-relationship was an immediate confirmation that I had made the right decision.

"Sri Hridayam Siddhashram" (the Melrose Ashram) opened to the world on Tuesday, April 25, 1972, at 8:00 p.m., a day later than originally planned.

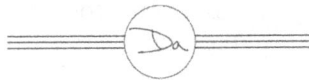

Opening Night

TUESDAY, APRIL 25, 1972

In preparation for the opening of the Melrose Ashram, Franklin had two signs placed on the front of the building. The main sign read "Sri Hridayam Siddhashram", which was the Sanskrit name He gave to His ashram. Roughly translated it meant "Ashram of the Divine Realizer of the Heart", or "Ashram of the Siddha-Master, Awakener of the Heart's Divine Love-Bliss". The second sign said "The Ashram Books".

Before the ashram opened that evening, Franklin allowed His friends to be with Him in the back room. He joked about what He called "Opening Night". He said, "Maybe we shouldn't go through with it. Maybe we've made a mistake and should call the whole thing off? We were originally considering opening a restaurant!" Playing along with His Divine Humor, we responded, "Yeah, maybe we should call it off and open a restaurant!" Then He said, "No, I guess we've gone too far. We'd better continue with our plans." Playfully, we all agreed and applauded His "decision".

At some point, Franklin left the ashram to prepare for the evening, and a group of us stayed to prepare for the event. As evening approached, we finished cleaning. Flowers were placed around Franklin's seat and on the altars in the meditation hall. Incense was lit and finally everything came to rest. That was when we especially noticed the meditation hall had a feeling of fullness and balance in it. It was a familiar feeling around Franklin' personally, the feeling of His Presence. But now the meditation hall had His fullness, His equanimity, and His profound Spiritual stillness in it, even when He wasn't physically sitting there. Just before the guests arrived, our Beloved Guru allowed us to visit with Him in the back room. Finally He asked, "Are you ready?" We all answered with a strong "Yes!" He smiled and sent us to greet the guests.

About twenty-five guests arrived. Most of them stopped in the bookstore to check out the books, and some directly entered the meditation hall. Soon everyone was invited into the meditation

Melrose Avenue Ashram and Bookstore,
opening night 1972

hall, where Franklin would soon be seated. He allowed time for everyone to settle before He entered.

He came into the hall through His curtain doorway from the back room and took His seat. He was clean shaven, handsome, and young (thirty-two years old). Franklin seemed pleased to be formally beginning His Work. He looked as relaxed and happy as always—His Divine Freedom wasn't changed by anything.

Once seated, He looked around the room and made eye contact with everyone. He then closed His eyes.

After about an hour of sitting silently, He looked again at everyone and asked, almost under His breath, "Who will cast the first stone?"

Very few in the room heard Him, and no one said anything.

I was sitting very close to Franklin, and I was a little surprised by His question. I was expecting a beautiful, happy event of people coming to meet Him! I wasn't raised Christian, so I didn't relate to "casting the first stone" in terms of the stories of Jesus. But the

April 25, 1972

vulnerability of Franklin's tone, along with His relaxed manner altogether, suggested that He somehow knew all about, and was totally accepting of, everything that would unfold from His gesture of beginning to Teach.

Franklin then asked, in a louder voice, "Are there any questions?" Again no one answered. He asked, "So everyone has understood?"

One man then said, "I don't understand."

"What don't you understand?" Franklin asked.

The man responded, "Well, you can start with the word 'understanding'." Franklin said, "Yes"—and then, with perfect clarity, He spoke about the Way of Understanding. When the questioner showed he was getting disturbed by something being said, his disturbance was exactly what the Way of Understanding addressed. Franklin explained that our True Condition is without conflict. Understanding is about noticing that when we dramatize conflict we are not resting in our True Condition.

When Franklin finished speaking, He again gave each one His Blessing Regard, then left through His doorway into the back room.

The Siddha-Guru had formally begun His Blessing Work!

Afterward, He sat in the back room waiting for His "friends" and anyone else who was moved to join Him. We joined Him as soon as the guests had left; we praised and thanked our Guru for the evening.

Someone started criticizing the man who had spoken out, but Franklin said not to criticize him. He said, "It was a good night and it was appropriate the way it all happened. There's a great tradition of confrontation in esoteric spirituality."

He asked about the other people who came. Who were they? Who among us knew any of them? We told Him what we knew. He seemed pleased that the night went the way it did. We thanked our great Guru again for the night, to which He responded "Tcha", a word of acknowledgment that He used over all the years when He was pleased. Before Franklin left, He gave each of us a huge hug and said, "I'll see you tomorrow."

In reflecting on this historic event, three principal Gifts from Heart-Master Adi Da Samraj stand out:

His first Gift was the establishment of His Spiritual Heart-Presence within the ashram, an empowerment felt by all.

The second Gift was sitting silently with Him to receive His Darshan. (In the Hindu tradition "Darshan" means the sighting of an Enlightened Being, or Completed One. It is understood that Darshan alone is enough to awaken the heart. What made this event historic is that it was the first Darshan ever given by the Divine Avatar to a gathering of public people.)

The third Gift was His Discourse about the Way of Understanding, His Teaching that enables the transcendence of separation from Eternal Divine Happiness. The entire Discourse (titled "Understanding") was published in Beloved Adi Da's second book, *The Method of the Siddhas*, now published as *My "Bright" Word*.

By these three great Gifts, Avatar Adi Da Samraj formally began His Teaching and Awakening Work at "Sri Hridayam Siddhashram". Over the years, devotees of Avatar Adi Da have continued to make devotional pilgrimages to the enormously auspicious Melrose Avenue location where the Way of the Heart had its formal beginning.

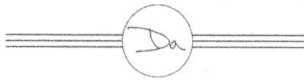

Darshan and the Teaching of Truth

MAY 1972

Once Franklin formally opened the Melrose Ashram to the public, there was a steady stream of new people. The people who came were ordinary, like me. There were no "greats"—no actors, authors, athletes, politicians, or CEOs. Years later, the Divine Guru spoke about those who came to Him:

I have seen the victories, the strengths, the weaknesses of ordinary people. All My Work all of the years has been with just those people—not with big-shots. . . . I have eschewed the company of the so-called "great". My real Work is with ordinary mankind. (*Free Daist* magazine, First Quarter 1995, from a talk given on February 19, 1995.)

In response to the new people, Franklin decided to formally offer His Darshan in the ashram every Tuesday and Thursday night, then again on Saturday mornings. He sat silently on these occasions for up to an hour, allowing all who came to see and feel His Free State.

After Darshan, Franklin often spoke—and always in straightforward, clear language, giving answers to classic questions people have asked down through the ages: *What is the truth about God? Why is there suffering? What is the purpose of my life? What is the secret to happiness? Why do I have to die? What happens after death?*

He also addressed everything from birth to death, covering all that takes place in between. Everything Franklin spoke about always directly applied to each person in the room, and, we would learn over time, to everyone everywhere.

The Discourses from that period became the content for Franklin's second book, *The Method of the Siddhas* (now published under the title *My "Bright" Word*). The "Method" referred to in the original title was the underlying theme I came to recognize in those talks: Satsang—right relationship to "the company of Truth" in the Person of my Guru.

71

In the talk titled "Phases", Avatar Adi Da says:

Talking about Satsang with Me can make It appear to be a very complicated process. But I Am here! The relationship between Me and My devotee is a Real Condition . . . you live from day to day, from moment to moment. In that sense, Satsang with Me is not something exclusively meditative, not something merely ritualistic, not something you are merely called to remember or concentrate on. Satsang with Me is something you must live. (My "Bright" Word, 2005 edition, 368–69.)

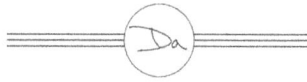

Om Bar

MAY 1972

A perfect example of Franklin's Instructive Divine Humor happened one day when He asked me how I was supporting myself. "By selling healthy candy bars, made by devotees at another ashram," I told Him. I asked if He would like to see them. He said He would, so I rushed to get samples, hoping He would like them and because I felt His Regard of them would be a Blessing.

When Franklin saw the names of the candy bars, His face lit up in amazement, His eyes opening wide with His eyebrows raising so high they almost touched His hair line. His mouth dropped open. It was as if He were in a state of disbelief.

He said in a questioning voice, "*Om Bar? Bhagavan Mint? Muksha Delight?* Names of candy? <u>You've got to be kidding Me</u>!" He laughed very loud, then said, "Those are quite profound names for candy."

The rest of that day, whenever anyone entered the back room of the ashram, Franklin showed them the candy bars, and each time He laughed heartily. Everyone laughed with Him and got the point.

We all laughed at the candy names, but we also laughed because our Beloved Guru's laughter was totally infectious. His Divine Humor lifted our hearts in His Delight and simultaneously Instructed us. Franklin's laughter was a criticism and a way to make the point that casual use of spiritual terminology trivializes the sacred. His Humorous Response was the same as saying: always honor the sacred, never trivialize it. Never trivialize Him.

A day or so later Franklin spoke at length about the common, casual approach to the sacred and the profound. That's when He humorously started calling me "Om Bar"—a nickname that lasted several months—so I would not forget the lesson.

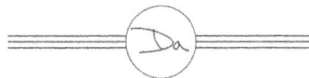

Silly Little Contraction

I was standing in the back room of the Melrose Ashram, having just had a confrontation with someone, and feeling really bad about it, when Franklin came in. He noticed something was wrong and asked how I was feeling. Whenever He spoke about anything, even in asking a question, His transforming, Free Happiness always came through; I was immediately affected. Instead of responding about my problem, the problem totally lost its importance. I said, "I just had this silly little contraction."

Franklin smiled, "That's right. That's all it is, a silly little contraction," as He had explained in His Teaching many times. He laughed and went to His desk, giving it no more attention.

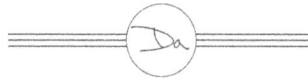

Be Ordinary

JUNE 1972

One day, three months after first meeting Franklin, He told me, "There's no need for you to continue making a statement with your appearance now that you're with Me." He suggested I shave my beard, cut my long hair, trade my hippie clothes for ordinary clothes, read a newspaper, and go to a movie. He said, "Be ordinary and do ordinary things. All the rest is seeking."

I had all sorts of reasons not to be conventional, but Franklin's words about seeking rang true. And His statement of "Now that you're with Me" was a wonderful acknowledgment of my feeling relationship to Him. I did what He suggested.

The next day when the Divine Master saw my shaved face and cut hair, He smiled and humorously said, "Maybe it looked better the other way." After laughing, He suggested growing back the mustache. He said, "You have a weak upper lip, the mustache would help." His Comments always had a lot more to them than just humor. Sometimes they were just a test to see if He hit a nerve and could get a reaction, then see how we would deal with the reaction. Other times His Comments addressed something a lot deeper. What I felt deeply, beyond the matter of my appearance, was that He cared.

The next time Franklin saw the mustache He said, "No, it's too long." With His finger He softly drew a line at the end of my lips on both sides, showing exactly where the mustache should be cut. He said, "Just let it come to here."

This simple Instruction, full of intimacy that Franklin gave was more than sweet, more than touching. It was so simple, so personal, and entirely full of His Love. There was nothing more wonderful than feeling the Heart-Master's Love—for it is Divine Love.

Years later, when I told Heart-Master Adi Da what He said about my weak upper lip as the reason to re-grow the mustache, He laughed and asked, "Did I really say that?"

Whenever I shave I always know exactly where the mustache should end. Over the years, Heart-Master Adi Da often emphasized that He offers a relationship, not a technique. The heart-happiness that my Guru Awakened right from the beginning is still the core of my relationship to Him more than forty years later.

The Fishing Trip

JUNE 1972

One morning Franklin was talking with some of His devotees in the back room of the Melrose Ashram. In the conversation He mentioned how He enjoyed fishing as a boy. He told us interesting stories of His fishing experiences and how He valued sitting silently in a boat away from the busy world, waiting to catch a fish. Fishing, He said, is a lot like spiritual seeking: Always trying to catch the big one.

He asked if we liked to fish, and we responded with fishing stories of our own. Then He said, "Let's go fishing!" The prospect of going fishing with Him was hugely exciting. We enthusiastically agreed. His plan was that the men would do the fishing while the ladies would prepare the environment for a grand dinner and prepare the meal when we returned with the catch.

The next weekend Franklin met all the men at Long Beach Harbor. This was really great—an outing! We rented a big fishing boat fully equipped with fishing rods, tackle, and life jackets, and within about an hour we reached a place where the fish were biting.

Franklin was the first to prepare a line. He said loudly to one of the men, "You did bring the live bait?" The man opened a box of fat, juicy, live worms. To me, a righteous vegetarian, looking into the box of worms was repulsive. Franklin secured a worm on His line without hesitation, but I was reluctant, as were the other men. Franklin laughed at our little dramas, and eventually we relented, each cautiously spearing a worm on a hook and casting it into the water.

Franklin was the first to catch a fish. Eventually we all caught some. But while we were fishing, we were nothing like what Franklin had described—sitting silently in a boat, waiting . . . We were talking loudly, joking with each other, laughing. I had even brought a bugle to play "taps" as fish were hauled on board. We were a rowdy bunch, basically all about having fun. However, nothing we did undermined the equanimity of our Beloved Guru. He simply allowed us to carry on.

After a couple hours, Franklin stopped fishing. I looked to the bow of the boat and saw Him sitting on the deck with His legs folded under Him. He was surrounded by stillness and peace. His face was so bright it seemed to be shining. At first no one else saw Him, but then as a wave of joy washed over us, everyone stopped fishing and became quiet. We all sat down and turned our feeling-attention to our Beloved Guru. He was Radiant.

For a long time we all sat silently at the rear of the boat absorbed in the Divine Master's perfect peace. We didn't fish any more. His Brightness washed away our casual social interests. His Presence absorbed us and took us all into a profound depthfulness. It was like the earth stood still; I just wanted to be quiet and continue contemplating Him.

Eventually, we returned to shore with brightened hearts and a grand catch of fish, enough for a feast for the entire ashram. (This was before our Beloved Master had introduced any formal dietary disciplines to the ashram.)

When we arrived with the fish, we saw that the ladies had created a beautiful environment. But they were reluctant to clean the fish. Like the men with the worms, the ladies were squeamish, so some of the men helped with the grossest parts of the cleaning. The ladies settled into cooking the food, while Franklin sat with the men and talked about the day. Finally the meal was ready and happily served.

During the meal, Franklin Commented on our behavior regarding all the aspects of catching and eating fish. As always, His Comments, even when playful and humorous, served our self-understanding and alignment to spiritual practice. He also talked about killing for food as a sacrificial act. If it must be done, He said, the sacrifice must be felt and understood. He talked about how it only honors the creature being killed if the act is consciously done with compassionate appreciation of the consequences for the creature and for the one performing the sacrifice.

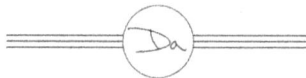

Shadow

JUNE 1972

It was nearly two months after His wallet was stolen from the ashram before Franklin felt it was time to get the ashram security guard dog. That's when He responded to a newspaper ad and said this was the dog that we wanted. Two of the ashram men went to the advertised kennel and purchased the dog. They were told he would be delivered the next day.

We were all awaiting the arrival of our new "pet" when, the next day, a trainer brought a full-grown male Doberman Pincher. He was dark brown with a few spots of white on his neck. His ears were clipped to stand upright, which was traditional for his breed. His mouth was large with very big, white, pointed teeth, obviously ready to be used as needed. The unique thing about the dog was that he had been attack-trained—when commanded he would attack a designated person. He didn't look or feel much like a friendly pet. Franklin appropriately named him Shadow.

Yes, Divine Heart-Master Adi Da Samraj brought an attack-trained guard dog into His first ashram, the ashram where the Truth of God was being Revealed. The place where self-understanding and self-transcendence were the Teaching. An attack-trained "killer" dog in His temple. Why?

Apart from security, there are probably many things that could be said as to why, but there was always more to Beloved Adi Da's suggestions than we initially understood. He was always Teaching, and the circumstance of relating to a killer dog was a great example. He called it "skillful means", after the traditional Buddhist understanding.

After Franklin accepted Shadow and passed on the responsibilities for caring for the dog, He did His Blessing Work silently while He watched as things developed and lessons were learned in regard to all that Shadow represented.

Franklin suggested that I be responsible for Shadow, so the trainer showed me how to take him through his daily routine. He explained that the dog was highly trained and must be required to go through certain routines every day. He explained that a loud voice would be sufficient to enforce discipline. He first showed me the basics: "stay", "heel", "come", "sit". Then he showed how to hold the leash so it could not slip out of the hand after giving the "attack" command. When the "attack" command was given, that nice dog became a killer! He immediately lunged forward, straining his whole body while pressing his head forward with all his might, pulling against his collar and leash. He would be up on his hind legs, snarling with shining white teeth, wanting to break loose and kill someone. Such aggression, such violence! I was very impressed and a bit scared.

I knew no one would break into the ashram if they heard or saw Shadow. On the other hand, I wasn't sure Shadow would fit in an ashram. The trainer kept reminding me never to let go of the leash during the "attack" command. I completely understood.

Shadow was given a corner opposite Franklin's desk in the back room. It was Shadow's corner, there was no doubt about it. Franklin told everyone to stay away from the dog, just allow him his space. He told me that Shadow was happy when he had something to do, a discipline, a task, and he needed a space to protect. He said Shadow was there to be the guard dog, that is how I should handle him, and I should know that he is not my pet. I should have understood right then that, in addition to being the guard dog, Shadow was also there to serve my self-understanding.

Franklin connected with Shadow right away, immediately establishing a trusted intimacy with the dog. I doubt that Shadow had ever felt love, but now he was learning trust and love directly from the Master of trust and love.

Franklin was the only other person Shadow was allowed to spend time with. Everyone else knew Shadow shouldn't be trusted and didn't make much contact with him. For a while, if anyone approached Shadow in his corner they would be met with a serious snarl. But over time a few people did establish a little friendliness with him.

Every morning and evening I took Shadow out for a walk. There was a field where I'd put Shadow through his exercises. He was trained to sit, stay, heel, come, attack, and stop. The "attack" command was given in German, I assume so it wouldn't be said accidentally. The stop command was a very loud "OFF".

In the field Shadow's leash got gradually extended with a long rope, so he could go further yet stay leashed. I also started teaching him some new tricks that better fit my preferences, such as "paw", "roll over", "wrestle", "fetch", "run with me", "kiss", and "let's be friends".

These friendly commands confused Shadow, especially since there wasn't a strict consequence for not responding immediately. He was originally trained with electric shocks and beatings to immediately respond to the "attack" command, so fear motivated his quick responses to commands. It seemed that while trying to soften some of that fear, I was undermining Shadow's strict training.

At the same time Shadow was also being approached by a few others in the ashram and told not to bite, but to be friendly. So the friendly contact coming from several of us also confused his strict training. But I felt it served his heart, and that Franklin had created a circumstance that served Shadow too.

At some point, after a few weeks, Shadow started testing me by not responding immediately to my commands. I knew I had to become strict with him to regain his respect and refresh his responsive sharpness. This brought up a confrontation with my preferred easygoing tendencies. By making me responsible for Shadow, Franklin provided a means for me to begin to see some of my patterns and tendencies. I still hadn't dropped my good-hearted, no demand, peace, and mellow attitudes from my hippie and yogi days. I still liked being a nice guy and not giving anyone a hard time. I didn't like to be forceful or demanding.

Now with Shadow I had to be very forceful and had to give him a hard time if he didn't respond immediately. I noticed that underneath my nice guy, friendly strategies I could easily be very angry, forceful, and demanding. But I didn't like the "Shadow" side of my character. I was suppressing aggressive tendencies for what I felt were more acceptable ones.

Franklin occasionally asked how things were going with Shadow. Were the daily walks and training continuing? I confirmed it all, but told Him Shadow was a demand! Franklin smiled. He knew I was getting some lessons.

One evening Franklin gave a talk in the ashram that He called "Walking the Dog", which was about tendencies everyone unconsciously carries around with them all the time. I could see how it applied to me. As I walked Shadow every day, I was mulling over all my concerns, needs, desires, interests, and random thoughts. Meanwhile, as Franklin described in the Talk, Shadow was clear-eyed, one-pointed, pissing on the grass when he needed to, and uncomplicated in his feelings.

One day while standing with Shadow behind the ashram, some friends drove up. I asked if they would like to see Shadow go through his "attack" command. I told them to stay in the car and roll up the windows. I had Shadow face the car, then wrapped his leash around my hand in the secure manner, and loudly gave the "attack" command: "Shadow, Pass AUF! Shadow, Pass AUF! Shadow, Pass AUF!" He started growling, but he was confused because no one was in front of him, just a car. He looked to each side, then turned to me, and bit my hand!

Having to respond was more important than who he bit. I had tried to exploit Shadow's training to entertain my friends—a big mistake! It was clear that I was no longer in charge of Shadow.

My friends in the car couldn't stop laughing. With full irony, they declared Shadow was a great security dog! When Franklin heard this story, He laughed uproariously. The incident became one of my Beloved Master's favorite stories about Shadow. Twenty-five years later when the Divine Heart-Master revisited the Melrose Ashram location, He reflected on things that happened there. One of the humorous things He brought up was the story of Shadow biting me.

Another amusing incident regarding the "attack" command occurred many years later while Heart-Master Adi Da was visiting the Fear-No-More Zoo at the Mountain Of Attention Sanctuary. A tame raven came out to see who was approaching. The bird wanted to let all approaching people know that the zoo was his territory. As the raven aggressively approached us, Adi Da turned to me and said, "Give him the 'stop attack' command!" I did. "OFF!"

That brought hearty laughter from Beloved Adi Da and the others, and in the Master's Heart-Presence and Humor, the raven softened and let us pass.

One day, after Shadow had been with us for a few months, I brought him a big juicy bone and I gave it to him in his corner. Naturally, he loved it, but after a while it was time to take him for a walk so I reached down to pick up the bone. Shadow growled. I hesitated for a moment and pulled back. That was the very end of me being in charge.

He saw that I reacted in fear. From then on Shadow knew how he could be in charge. Each time I approached him, he growled and I pulled back.

Franklin came one day to say hello to him, and Shadow growled even at Him. Franklin told me the next day it was time to let Shadow go. He said Shadow had become possessed. He didn't explain what He meant, but it seemed clear that to break that bind on his heart would take a long time. In the meantime Shadow was not responding, so it was necessary to pass him on.

We placed an ad in the newspaper to sell Shadow. The first day the ad was published we got a call from an interested man. The next day the man and his girlfriend came to meet Shadow and see how he responded to commands. That meant I had to go beyond my fear of Shadow, and take charge without anger (which required a degree of self-transcendence that was a real stretch).

I moved fast and took Shadow forcefully by the leash the way the trainer had taught me. Shadow responded appropriately. Then I brought him through his commands (the professional ones). It required being very forceful, giving him no room to disobey. Sadly, Shadow was back into responding based on fear. He remembered the consequences from his professional training if he didn't respond fast enough. So Shadow responded quickly to each command. The couple was very impressed with his protective qualities and decided to take him.

Being responsible for Shadow provided valuable lessons. I saw that my principal strategy was to be mellow and avoid unattractive qualities like aggression and anger—the hippie/yogi persona. I also saw that I actually had all the qualities of both sides, soft and hard.

That observation awakened the understanding that all of it was arbitrary—whether soft or hard, it was just pattern, just self-contraction. I also saw that efforts to do something about that pattern were futile and I was constantly draining energy and attention while feeling the dilemma of it all. Instead, I turned to Franklin's core Teaching: *Satsang,* "the Company of Truth".

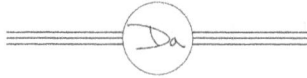

The Gift Returned

JUNE 1972

Traditionally, it is said if you give in service to God, or to others, you will be rewarded. I always felt that "reward" meant receiving gratitude for helping others, or feeling the satisfaction of going beyond your own self-involvement. But Franklin showed how the law of giving works.

Franklin's first book *The Knee of Listening* needed additional funds to cover the publishing costs. Feeling its importance, I happily donated the last of my funds. Even with my contribution, we still needed more funds. I felt I should do all I could to help and serve my Guru. It was clear this book was very important to Him, so I asked my parents and they agreed to lend the balance of the remaining costs. Everyone was so happy that Franklin's Word of Truth was to be published; it was easily worth the sacrifice, not to mention worth having *The Knee of Listening* for our daily study.

A few years later I got a very interesting phone call. A lady called asking if she had my full name and the correct last four digits of my Social Security number. She also asked if I once lived at a certain address in Marina del Rey, California. Trustingly, I said yes to all the questions. She thanked me and hung up. What a strange phone call, I thought.

A week later she called again. This time she told me her name and about her company. She explained that her job was to track down people who left their old bank accounts. She said if an old account had no activity for seven years, the funds were automatically given over to the State. She said I had an account that was about to be turned over and if I would give her written permission, she would send me the funds from the account. Her fee was 10 percent.

I felt there had to be some catch to this because I couldn't have left funds. I agreed just to see what would happen. Again in full trust, I sent her a formal letter permitting her to withdraw the funds and close the supposed account. The lady never mentioned how much money was in the account. Within a week I received a check for the exact same amount of money I gave to help publish *The Knee of Listening.*

What a surprise—the exact same amount! I immediately thanked my Spiritual Master for returning my donation. I had absolutely no doubt that I could never have forgotten over a thousand dollars in a bank account. At one point in my life, having done well financially, I had chosen to become a spiritual seeker with little money, so every dollar was important. I always knew exactly how much money I had and where it was. There was absolutely no way I forgot even one dollar. Yet the bank said it was my money and when I suggested I couldn't have left it, they insisted I had—which I guess was confirmation of the rumors that banks can make mistakes, too. I accepted the money as the Blessing return from Franklin of my original gift.

Over the years there have been hundreds of stories about people giving financial gifts and then surprisingly getting that money, and sometimes much more, returned. Typically, the returns were unexpected and came through such things as increased value of investments, salary increases, inheritances, or increased business profits. Then there have been some remarkably unexpected ways, such as how the Blessing Master returned my donation.

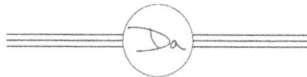

Guru Days

In response to Franklin's suggestion, Sundays were called "Guru Day". It was a full day each week devoted to the sacred relationship to Him—the day when, in those early days of His Teaching-Submission with ordinary people, He allowed His devotees to spend most of the day in His Blessing Company.

He had said the sighting of Him (*Darshan*) should be sufficient, because His Divine Enlightenment was Radiant. But it was also a fact that we were too gross, too superficial, to be that sensitive. So Franklin had to teach us how to be sensitive to Him. He knew exactly how the body-mind works. Enlightened at birth, He had undertaken the entire course of learning and transcending the ego-"I" starting at the age of two, a sadhana (ego-transcending spiritual practice) purposed to know all the mechanisms and nuances of the ego-"I", thus enabling Him to fully serve all unenlightened beings. With us, He was cultivating potential devotees and addressing our egoic patterning; and His Divine Siddhi (or Spiritual Power) was opening and brightening our hearts and minds.

In later years, Beloved Adi Da would explain in detail how all beings operate through four principal faculties: mind, emotion, body, and breath. Each of the four principal faculties needed to be freely turned to Him to serve the surrender of the whole body and mind. Even in those earliest days, He was working to call all these faculties to Him.

The principal faculty of the mind is attention. His Presence was totally riveting, fully addressing attention. He also answered all questions, speaking in profound detail about everything. So attention was freely given over by the attraction to Him.

The principal faculty of emotion is feeling. Franklin said it was in the feeling dimension that we were weakest. He addressed our failure to observe our emotional contraction, our lack of emotional freedom, and our defensiveness, all of which contrasted vividly with His Free Expressiveness. Always Radiant, His Love and Humor brightened the feeling dimension moment by moment.

To address the body, Franklin had us learn about *asana* (Sanskrit for "posture"). In His Teaching, however, asana was not only understood to mean posture, but also attitude, orientation, and the feeling disposition of the whole body-mind. He was always a perfect example of how to conduct energy through right asana.

To address the breath, Franklin instructed us on how to breathe deep into the bodily battery (below the solar plexus). And whenever His Living Presence became palpable, His Instruction was to breathe It in, even to the point of pervading the whole being. On Guru Day mornings Franklin sat silently with everyone in the ashram meditation hall, granting His Blessing Darshan. In the afternoons He sat and spoke with us in the backyard of a friend's house, where a comfortable seat was prepared under an attractive vine-covered trellis. We sat facing Him on the grassy lawn.

On these Guru Days Franklin spoke about the great realities of Divine Truth and His Radical ("at-the–root") Way of Understanding. He fully answered all of life's great questions about God, Truth, and Reality. Upon hearing the absolute Truth, one entered into deep feeling, which spontaneously opened the whole being. That's where the feeling many devotees have described came from: "We have come home."

In His Blessing Company on Guru Days I always felt rested, accepted, relaxed, and simply happy, lightened from my egoic weight of seeking, with the added effects of feeling more balanced and clearheaded. Guru Days with Franklin positively changed us all on many levels.

On the very first Guru Day Franklin spoke about the search for consolation:

I will never give the seeker a "bone". Those who have come for "bones" are waiting in vain, because what they are hoping for is not going to happen. All of that drama of seeking has nothing whatsoever to do with Truth. . . . Your trouble is an illusion. Your search is a reaction to your suffering. Your actual dilemma has barely been conceived by you, barely experienced. You come to Me

Speaking to devotees, 1972

for another consolation, to prevent awareness of your suffering.
You come for distraction, a fascination, a charming vision. You
want to be consoled. But why do you want to be consoled? What
state are you in that you should want to be consoled by Me? You
are suffering! Yes? Since you are only suffering, why are you
defending all of this nonsense?

It is time to be rid of all of that. It is utterly unnecessary. It can
be abandoned! All of that is what I want surrendered as gifts
around My Feet. I want to see your gift to Me of all the suffering,
all the sorrows, all the long faces, all the usual Yoga, . . . all the
visions, all the beliefs, all the philosophies, all the conventional reli-
gion and spirituality, all your personal (and even racial) history. I
want to see your attachment to birth and your fear of death. I want
to Free you of all of it!

Such are the implications of Truth. ("Walking the Dog", My
"Bright" Word, 2005 edition, 212.)

Franklin consistently emphasized the necessity for self-understanding, and the serious responsive practice of surrendering all seeking by always turning in Satsang to the Guru, who is the Person of True Happiness.

One particularly memorable Guru Day, Franklin clearly explained the fact that since the ego-"I" is the contraction from True Happiness due to its separation from Truth, it is always seeking True Happiness. He explained how seeking is fundamental to the ego-"I" since the ego is not happy, but seeking cannot lead to True Happiness because the seeking is itself the very act of being unhappy. (In later years the Divine Master memorialized this principle as "The Lesson of Life: You cannot become Happy—you can only be Happy.")

On another Guru Day, Franklin explained the need to acknowledge the important events in His life because they were part of our coming to understand His fully Awakened appearance on Earth. Accordingly, He established celebration days for us to honor every year, which included at that time His birthday (*Jayanthi*) on November 3, the day that the ashram formally opened on April 25, and the traditional Hindu *Guru Purnima* celebration on the day of the July full moon, when all gurus are honored. All these celebration days, and many others that were adopted as other important events occurred throughout His Lifetime, were all about directly celebrating our relationship to our Guru. His Gift of celebration days added more whole bodily involvement to our growing heart-relationship.

As we became more sensitive to His Divine Presence, Franklin also spoke about His vulnerability. He confessed that He absorbed the qualities and karmas of whomever He was exposed to. He said at times He had to remain set apart from our worldliness. If we wanted to continue having access to His Blessing Company, we were required to transform our worldliness and conform our lives to Him through engaging the disciplines of His Liberating Teaching.

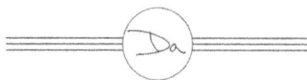

The First Guru Purnima

JULY 23, 1972

In the Hindu tradition of honoring the guru, the first full moon (Purnima) in the Indian month of Ashadh (usually in July) is set apart to celebrate the appearance of the guru. In that tradition, "Guru Purnima", as it is called, is one of the highest holy days of the year.

Franklin said that we should also celebrate this great traditional event honoring all gurus, by celebrating His Appearance as our Guru and showing our devotional response to Him. Basically, up until this time we were all just good-hearted, interested people growing in our devotional response to our great Guru. To us, the prospect of this celebration was a great gift, a way to express our gratitude and devotion. It was a means to also support our progress from being Franklin's "friends" to formally becoming His students, disciples, and devotees.

Franklin had to teach us everything about how to respond to Him. To be available to receive His Blessings required us to surrender and be vulnerable by allowing our feelings to be open to Him. To express devotional response required the discipline of responding and conforming to His Instructions and serving His ashram. We also learned how to sit in an open, conducting posture so as to not obstruct His Transmitted Blessings. Franklin even taught us how to celebrate the transformative relationship to the true Siddha (Transmission-Master) by introducing us to this celebration of Guru Purnima.

Franklin knew we didn't have much (or any) chanting experience, so He arranged to have devotional chanters from another ashram come to lead the chanting. Having had devotees of another guru in Franklin's ashram to chant devotion to all gurus was a great sign of His Honoring of all gurus and of Blessing these honored guests and their guru. Simultaneously, our Guru was also establishing the ancient tradition of devotional chanting in His ashram.

Guru Purnima was going to be a very important celebration day. It was also going to be the first formal celebration in the ashram since the formal opening just three months prior. We got together and considered how to decorate the ashram. We felt that the decorations would be our gift to our Guru, so we didn't ask His advice. But we heard He had been asking what preparations were being done. We had no doubt that Franklin was fully aware of everything and silently guiding us at every level.

We knew flower arrangements were essential around His seat. Also flower malas (garlands) would be honorable. Someone said Franklin liked hanging strands of orange marigolds, so that was planned. Someone suggested candles and incense and those were agreed upon. But what else could we do to most fully honor our Guru on Guru Purnima? We were stumped. Maybe offering the flowers, candles, and incense, as well as cleaning the entire ashram, was all we could do? We all felt we wanted to do more, but couldn't come up with an idea.

While all the beautiful flower malas and arrangements were being made, I suddenly felt an urge to leave and drive around the neighborhood, just to see if something more could be found to add to the decorations. As I left, I felt totally doubtful of finding anything appropriate for the ashram while driving around Hollywood, California, of all places! Yet something was moving me to do it.

After a few random streets and turns, right in front of me was a street full of beautiful, freshly cut, green palm fronds, some with flowering buds. The city landscaping crew said, "Take all you want!" When the huge pile of palm fronds arrived at the ashram, everyone agreed Franklin was the influence behind finding them.

The ladies suggested placing an especially large frond directly behind Franklin's seat as a backdrop. The men agreed and made a wooden frame to support it. Then fresh flowers were placed all over it. The palm frond backdrop became a really beautiful decoration to more rightly honor our Loving Guru. The rest of the fronds were placed in the corners and along the walls of the meditation hall, with individual flowers also placed on them. We now felt Franklin's ashram was beautifully and fully honored.

The next morning when Franklin arrived for Guru Purnima, He was surprised and very pleased by the devotional energy and

The First Guru Purnima, 1972

the resulting way the decorations transformed the environment. He said, "It looks like a forest." When Franklin took His seat, the beautiful backdrop honored His Holy Person. The meditation hall was physically conformed to celebrating Him. All the decorations were beautiful and pleasing to Him. I silently thanked my Guru for the happiness He Awakened in us as we expressed our devotion to Him by honoring and glorifying His ashram and His Presence in it. It was a great example of the joy felt in honoring Franklin Jones by serving Him.

The five guest devotees arrived on schedule to lead devotional chanting. They chanted passionately about the Divine Gift of the Guru and we joined in as we absorbed the unusual melodies and unfamiliar Sanskrit words.

Franklin sat silently in the meditation hall, Revealing His bodily human Form as the Divine Murti[4] of our devotion. He seemed visibly pleased throughout the chanting occasion. One sign of His Pleasure was His toes and feet: they moved a lot! To us, His moving toes and feet were a sign that our devotion was pleasing Him and as a result His Blessings were becoming bodily animated.

It was Satsang—the relationship to the Divine Being that never ends.

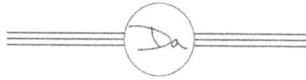

4. Murti is a representative image of the Divine, commonly as a photograph.

Completing the Lines

Franklin explained that it was very important for His students to study His Teaching daily. I was becoming aware of the repetitious patterns of my usual mind-stuff, and eagerly took advantage of being brought to self-understanding and self-transcendence by studying His Word.

Franklin's autobiography *The Knee of Listening* was still at the printer, so for several weeks He had us use copies of His manuscript. When the books arrived, Franklin was pleased that His written Word (which would grow to become more than ninety volumes) would finally be available to the world. I was thrilled to have a hard-bound copy of my Guru's first book with His beautiful photo on the front.

As Franklin began looking through His book page by page, He noticed a major printing error. The last two or three letters at the end of each line of the Prologue page were missing—every line of the Prologue was incomplete!

The printer was immediately informed and asked that all the books be returned for reprinting. Despite being disappointed, Franklin converted the mistake into a Blessing that would only become more valued and revered over the years. He kept enough of the flawed copies to give to His students and before giving them out, He hand-printed the missing letters on each line in every book. He then signed each book "Love, Franklin". What a magnificent Gift!

On the following page is an image of that page from *The Knee of Listening* with Franklin's hand-printed lettering and His signature.

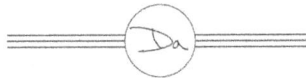

Prologue:

THE HEART OF UNDERSTANDING

Death is utterly acceptable to consciousness and life. There has been endless time of numberless deaths, but neither consciousness nor life has ceased to arise. The felt quantity and cycle to death has not modified the fragility of flowers, even the flowers within our human body. Therefore, our understanding of consciousness and life must be turned to that utter, inclusive quality, that clarity and wisdom, that power and untouchable gracefulness this evidence suggests. We must cease to live in our superficial and divided way, seeking and demanding only consciousness and life in the present form we grasp, avoiding and resisting what appears to be the end of consciousness and life in death.

The Heart is that understanding, that true consciousness, that true life that is under the extreme conditions of life and death. Therefore, it is said, that One that is is neither born nor come to death, not alive as the limitation of form, not rendered in what appears, and yet it is the living One, than which there is no other, appearing as all of this, but eternally the same.

There is only the constant knowledge and enjoyment of the Heart, moment to moment, through the instant of all conditions of appearance and disappearance. Of this I am perfectly certain. I am That.

7

Love,

Franklin

Photo of the page from *The Knee of Listening* with Franklin's hand-printed lettering and His signature.

The Miracle of the Ashram Fire

AUGUST 1972

One day, a large explosion in the auto parts shop next door blew a huge hole in the ashram wall, gushing thick black smoke into the meditation hall. We urgently called the fire department and also called Franklin at His home. He immediately instructed, "Get the books out, I'll be right there!" (*The Knee of Listening* had recently been received from the printer, and the books had been stacked in the back room awaiting Franklin's Blessings prior to being distributed.)

When Franklin arrived, I could feel Him immediately taking charge. First, He asked about the books. We told Him they had been safely removed. He tried to see inside through the bookstore windows, but the black smoke was too thick. He stood near the front door. One can never presume to know what the Guru is really doing, but He seemed to be the ashram Protector—a Force the fire could not encroach upon. Also, from there He could observe everything happening outside, including the arrival of the fire engines.

When Franklin saw the firemen running from their fire engines toward the ashram with axes in their hands, He said loudly, "Tell them not to break the door down. Open it with the handle. Tell them it's a church. Tell them to lay down plastic runners and not step on the rug!"

The situation was urgent. The firemen were responding to a three-alarm, commercial-district fire in downtown Hollywood, California. There had been a loud explosion and two businesses were gushing black smoke. The firemen had no idea if anyone was trapped inside and didn't know the extent of the fire. They needed to get inside fast.

Several firemen from three fire engines were moving very fast toward the ashram door when they heard Franklin's instructions. Incredibly they all stopped. One man ran back to the closest fire engine and grabbed some plastic runners. Four firemen then raced together to the front door and opened it by its handle. Inside in the pitch dark, they laid down the plastic runners and did the best they could not to step on the rug!

When the firemen were sure the fire was extinguished, they allowed us to enter. Franklin led us inside. There was a hole in the meditation wall and some scorching around it, but the fire had been contained on the other side of the wall. A little soot was on the rug near the hole, and the smell of smoke was everywhere. The firemen had followed Franklin's instructions so well that there was only one partial footprint on the rug! No books in the bookstore were damaged other than being exposed to smoke. The impact of the explosion on the ashram was slight, but the shop next door was destroyed.

In the midst of the chaos generated by the crisis, seeing Franklin appear so calm settled us down. I felt He was Working Spiritually to protect the ashram from the fire, and He also protected it from any harm the firefighters could have caused. It was a miraculous intervention in every way.

The next day Franklin asked where we all were when the fire started. One man said he was in the meditation hall, actually sitting against the wall when the explosion next door blew the hole in it. No doubt, our Beloved Guru responded, he experienced the explosion as his first spiritual experience! Franklin's laughter healed our leftover distress about the fire and we all praised Him as Hero of the ashram fire.

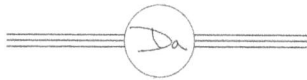

His Blessing Touch

I had just returned from a difficult sales day and was standing outside the back door of the ashram feeling wiped out and stressed. Feeling my state, Franklin came outside and asked me how I was doing. Still locked into my extremely contracted state, I started telling Him about my day as if He were just my friend. In a moment, He pressed His thumb against my forehead, between and above the eyebrows. Immediately, I stopped talking. My attention turned to the touch of His thumb and its pressure on my forehead. I didn't feel any additional movement of energy. There was no sense of a "magical eraser" happening. He maintained the thumb pressure for about a minute. In that time, my entire condition changed from being stressed, disturbed, and turning inward, to feeling free of all of that by turning attention to Franklin. As a result, everything changed; I simply felt happy.

After that minute, without a word spoken, Franklin just walked away, back to His desk inside the ashram. My impression was that He had felt my disturbance and come to help.

Left to my own devices, I might have found a remedy for my uptight condition. There are countless remedies for the infinite variations of the self-contraction. But with any such solution, the underlying problem of "self" dealing with "self" only supports the self-contraction. Instead of addressing problems with "self"-effort, Franklin instructed us to turn our feeling-attention to Him instead. With attention on feeling His Free State in the deep heart-bond with Him, problems dissolved.

The only awareness I had during that minute was of His thumb pressing on my forehead. Everything I was feeling before Franklin's touch got completely washed. I had no stress. My bodily energy was back in balance, I felt happy to see my Guru. Simply, it was a miracle, whatever Spiritual means may have been involved—a Blessing Gift and sign of His unlimited ability. Yet, the gesture was as simple as just helping one of His students.

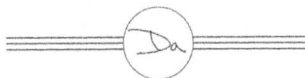

The Vision of Love

OCTOBER 1972

One day I was sitting in the meditation hall feeling full of love for my Beloved Guru when the most wonderful thing happened. Franklin came into the room and sat on the floor next to me with His shoulder touching mine. I was so happy to see Him and to feel His closeness that I spontaneously responded to Him and began to praise Him.

After I'd only spoken a few words, Franklin leaned forward to face me directly. His face was right in front of mine, just inches away. His deep brown eyes looked so soft, seeming to overflow with feeling. As I looked into His eyes, His pupils grew wider and wider. I was overcome by a sense of His profound vulnerability, even deeper than an innocent infant's. He showed no protection, no defense, no sense of being a separate person. His absolute vulnerability was all there was, and it was pure Love. It was Love without limit—Bliss. He was Radiating the Divine Condition of Love-Bliss.

In that moment everything changed. His Presence and Heart-Power overwhelmed "me" and removed any sense of separation between us. I was no longer looking at Him as if He were a separate person. The sense of being a separate "I" was removed. There was only the awareness of His Love-Bliss. Franklin Revealed His State of Divine Reality and it was perfect. It was perfection far beyond the deepest love I had ever previously experienced: complete non-separate intimacy, everything and every condition washed in His Divine Love. "I" wasn't having an experience. The one who would have had an experience was gone, dissolved in Franklin's Brightness. He Blessed me with the utterly transformational gift of His Divine Condition.

It was so blissful, tears of overwhelming joy poured down my face. There was no sense of time, but after a seeming eternity Franklin smiled and softly said, "You should see what you look like." He laughed and I laughed with Him. My Beloved Guru then leaned forward and enveloped me in His Embrace. That marvelous hug felt like I was "falling into" Him.

On that day I not only felt Beloved Adi Da's Divine State of Love-Bliss, but "I" was transformed by His freely given glimpse of Divine Reality. It was clear that He was and is not a separate person. He is Divine Reality appearing in human form, here to Reveal and Awaken all beings to the Divine Truth prior to the ego's illusion of separation. On that day I saw the Divine Master's capacity to Awaken all who would open their hearts to Him. That was the day my heart was changed forever. Blessed by that Revelation, I truly became His devotee!

Avatar Adi Da Samraj:

Those who fall in love with Me, Fall into Me. Those whose hearts are given, in love, to Me, Fall into My Heart. Those who are Mine, because they are in love with Me, no longer demand to be fulfilled through conditional "experience" and through the survival (or perpetuation) of the ego-"I". Their love for Me grants them Access to Me, and (Thus) to My Love-Bliss—because I Am the Divine Love-Bliss, in Person. ("What Is A Greater Message Than This?" *The Aletheon*, 2009 edition, 1945.)

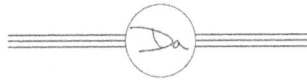

Two Gifts:
The First Gift

NOVEMBER 3, 1972

One day Franklin was talking about prayer beads and said that the best oil to use to keep them polished and prevent cracking was sandalwood oil. I mentioned that I had worked for a company that imported the finest sandalwood oil from India. I had saved a small bottle of the very best, and when I asked if He would like to see it, He said yes.

The next day I brought the special vial of oil to the ashram. Franklin placed a couple of drops on His index finger then rubbed it with His thumb for a moment to feel the consistency and release the fragrance. He obviously knew how to test fine oil. After the test, He asked if He could use it to oil His rudraksha bead mala. Of course I said yes. Then, feeling how much my Guru appreciated the fine oil, even though it was a treasure I wanted to keep, I gave it to Him as a birthday gift on November 3, 1972.

Franklin received my simple gift graciously, as He did all gifts. He accepted the bottle, then, as before, He opened it, rubbed some oil on His fingers to feel the consistency, and inhaled the fragrance. Then He looked up with a soft smile and said, "Thank you." So vulnerable and loving—those two simple words reached the depths of my heart.

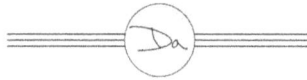

A Fate Escaped

NOVEMBER 1972

One day three men from the ashram where the Om Bar candy was made arrived at the Melrose Ashram to talk with me about sales. Franklin suggested I meet with them in the back room. He was about to leave, but before He left He looked through the curtain and saw them.

When Franklin returned after they left, He made a few observations based on their appearance. He said they were a good example of people in religious and spiritual groups. He observed that they were wearing all white clothes, had beards, and seemed to try to speak slowly and softly. "They are spiritual seekers!" He said. "Under the white clothes and behind the beards are people just like everyone else, with all the same tendencies."

He explained that spiritual seekers conform to a lifestyle, and/or a discipline, as well as a social order, all enabling them to avoid dealing with their tendencies. Instead, they assume a superficial state of happiness. But they're still seeking True Happiness as much as everyone else. Then He said, "Oh well, to each his Om."

Along with His humorous word play, there was a bright twinkle in Franklin's eyes. Remembering that, I know now what was unspoken beneath His playful words. He Came to Awaken all beings beyond superficiality and all forms of seeking. He is here to offer the Way beyond all limited approaches to Divine Realization. He is here to show that Divine Reality is prior to the ego-"I" and all of the ego's doings.

After that short conversation with Franklin, I thanked Him for drawing me to Him, beyond my own spiritual seeking.

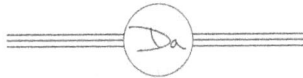

Thanksgiving Dinner

NOVEMBER 23, 1972

Franklin accepted an invitation to have Thanksgiving dinner at a student's home and invited a few other students to join Him. When He arrived, He greeted each of us with a smile and a big hug. His hug pressed His Love right into my heart. I had the feeling that, to Him, we had never been apart.

There weren't any formal dietary disciplines at this time, so the hosts went all out to set the table full of the traditional foods for a Thanksgiving feast. When the large roasted turkey was brought out, it was placed directly in front of Franklin. He stood up holding a carving knife in one hand and the matching fork in His other hand. With a soft smile He said, "When I was a child My father always got the drumsticks, so now I'm going to take them." He neatly carved and placed the two drumsticks on His plate, then He looked up again and, still smiling, continued carving and serving the rest of the turkey, asking each of us which cut we preferred. I felt completely embraced by Franklin, as if I were part of His family.

After the meal, we all moved to the living room where Franklin stayed for a while talking with us. His engaging conversation was never superficial, always inspiring us to consider things more deeply, to find Truth at a more profound level. His Divine Humor was uplifting, heart-brightening, and totally delightful. And when He sat quietly, His equanimity was infectious.

The meal and the rest of the day may have looked like a typical Thanksgiving dinner among friends, but this occasion was so much more. Franklin's Liberated Presence and His Free Happiness were obvious in every movement and gesture—everything about Him.

When Franklin left at the end of that Thanksgiving day, I was left having fallen into the heart's prior place of Bliss. And I could see by the shining faces of my friends that they were there too.

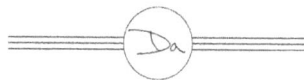

PART TWO

Stories from 1973–1974

The First San Francisco Darshan

JANUARY 1973

Once *The Knee of Listening* was published in the summer of 1972, Franklin Blessed all the books and sent them to a distributor to be sold at bookstores throughout the country. Soon the ashram began getting inquiries asking how to find out more about Franklin Jones.

Many of those inquiries came from the San Francisco Bay Area. Franklin suggested the people in that area should get together and study His Teaching, then once they were ready He would send a representative to talk with them. In about a week we were told they had arranged to meet together as Franklin suggested and looked forward to having a representative come. Soon Franklin sent someone to meet with them.

The report on the first visit was very positive. So Franklin had me facilitate their weekly meetings and I also made regular visits to San Francisco. Each time, before I went, my Beloved Guru instructed me to tell them all about Him. Each time I returned He asked for a full report on their response. A typical report went something like this: *They are all studying and considering Your Teaching together. They all feel the truth of it. They really want to meet You in person. They are asking if You will ever come to San Francisco, or can they come to Los Angeles to receive Your Blessing Darshan? They are all getting involved in the Teaching and feel their relationship to You is growing.*

Franklin was pleased to hear the weekly reports and their continued requests to receive His Darshan, and He said they should continue studying and considering His Teaching together.

When He felt they were sufficiently prepared and serious about meeting Him for the right reasons, He said it was time for Him to meet them. For this great Blessing occasion, the new San Francisco students rented a spacious room at a motor lodge in Palo Alto, just south of San Francisco.

My Beloved Guru invited me to travel and attend Him. We flew to San Francisco and drove directly to Palo Alto. When we arrived, some students were in the lobby. Franklin seemed to know which people in the lobby were His new students, no doubt because they were so happy to see Him.

Franklin entered the room that had been rented and put His overnight bag away. He briefly refreshed Himself and then went to the seat prepared for Him at the front of the room. Noticing the abundance of beautiful flower arrangements all around His seat, He said, "It was done right." His new students had fully cleaned and prepared the room and lit incense to refresh the air. He was obviously pleased with their preparations.

Franklin sat silently in the room. It seemed to me that He was Purifying the room so that nothing would interfere with the reception of His Spiritual Transmission. Franklin had said His Regard affects all beings, all things, all space, even the door knobs and the walls. Nothing is beyond His Blessing Influence because nothing is separate in His Realization of Divine Reality. When He was ready, He nodded for the door to be opened and the students were invited in.

After everyone was seated, the Divine Awakened Guru sat silently granting His Holy Darshan for about forty-five minutes. Visible signs of everyone's response were obvious. Some people were swooning, some were slightly swaying back and forth, and some were so heart-moved they were drawn into meditation. Everybody seemed deeply absorbed in Franklin's Divine Siddhi. His requirement that they study His Teaching before allowing them His Darshan had prepared them to be in His Company and to be available to receive His Blessings.

After the formal Darshan, Franklin invited each student to come forward and receive a big hug. He hugged each one for at least a full minute. When Franklin would hug you, He would press close and hold you firmly. After a time you might want to let go, but He would keep holding until you were willing to stay there forever. Then He would let go. It was a capsule version of the entire Way of the Heart! It was obvious that everyone was greatly moved by His Embrace, and overwhelmed by His heartbreaking Gifts of Divine Love that washed any sense of separation. After His Embrace, each student left, with visible reluctance, without a word spoken.

The next day all the students were invited back. Again, Franklin granted Darshan, again filling the room with His Divine Siddhi. And this time He also spoke with them, deepening their understanding of the Way of the Heart.

Over the years, the students who sat with Avatar Adi Da on those two sacred Darshan occasions have often said that He entered them Spiritually on that occasion, revealing the Prior Reality of Divine Love. They all have said that feeling the Heart's True Happiness prior to the self-contraction changed their lives.

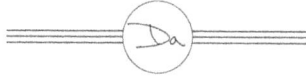

Palm Springs

Our Beloved Guru invited three of His male students, myself included, to accompany Him for a day at Palm Springs, a desert resort in Southern California. He said He wanted to get some sun and relaxation, and also enjoy the healing waters of a spa. On the trip, Franklin talked about the development of the ashram culture and the need for cultural leadership.

Once we arrived at the Palm Springs Spa, Franklin put on His bathing suit and relaxed in the sun by the pool. After a while one of the men noticed a ping pong table nearby and asked our Beloved Guru if He'd like to play. He agreed and they played several games. Franklin was very good at ping pong.

I really wanted to play with Him, since I had played a lot in the Army. After Franklin wiped out His first opponent, He asked if anyone else wanted to play. I spoke up and got my chance. We played a very close game until I got the winning point, which made me happy. Feeling my aggressive play and fully understanding all my emotions behind it, my Guru knew more than I did why I was so happy to win. He started laughing out loud. He put His paddle down on the table and said, "Now what are you going to do—go to Swami Satchidananda?"

How funny and what a perfect reflection! I didn't fully understand any underlying reasons why I wanted to win, or why I was happy in winning, other than knowing that the ego likes to win. Franklin showed it all to me with His Humor and His laughter. I beat my Beloved Guru in ping pong! Did that mean I was better? Did that mean He wasn't the one to teach me? Should I go to another guru to see if I can beat him too? The ego-"I" in its self-glorifying act was revealed again.

Commonly in those early years, whenever Franklin directly addressed and revealed something of the ego-act to one of His students while they were actively engaging in it, then, in recognizing their ego-act, the student would say, "I'm busted"!" Franklin's way of serving self-understanding and self-transcendence with His Divine Humor was perfect. I was "busted" and happy to confess it, for my tendencies and motives were obvious and I was able to laugh at them.

After a little more sun, Franklin invited us to join Him in the hot baths in the basement of the spa. We entered a large steam-filled room. As we felt our way to two small hot baths, sounds of our movement echoed off the walls.

I shared one of the baths with Franklin. The only sound was of dripping water. Franklin was silent. His Radiant Divine State saturated the water and transformed the space, awakening Blissful Equanimity. His Free Love-full Presence made me feel very open and vulnerable. In spontaneous response to the given sacred intimacy, I began to softly chant a Hebrew prayer that I had learned in my childhood. It was full of feeling and felt entirely appropriate in this pristine circumstance with my Beloved Guru. The soft chant echoed throughout the chamber.

I stopped chanting after a few verses when Franklin began to chant. He started softly with an ancient Sanskrit chant, "Om Namah Shivaya". His voice was sweet and full of feeling. We all listened closely to His chant and were initially moved to be perfectly silent. After a few verses we all spontaneously began chanting with Him. We chanted for about fifteen minutes. The intimacy with Him in this occasion was more than great. It was sacred. It was holy.

Our chant carried throughout the spa, yet being with Franklin, we had no concern about others hearing us. In fact, no one at the spa made any comment at all.

Later, Franklin led us to the exercise room to see if we could do hatha yoga. He showed us a few poses, which He did perfectly. When we showed Him what we could do, He said, "Someone is going to have to teach yoga in the ashram, but it's not going to be any of you!" He shook His head as if to say, "Too bad." Then He laughed.

On the way home He talked more about the need for cultural leadership. At the end of the trip, we thanked Him for the Blessed day in His Radiant Company.

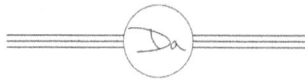

Bowing

Franklin began talking about bowing as an essential devotional practice. He explained that bowing is an acknowledgment of the sacred, and that, when directed to Him, bowing is the recognition of Him, as our Heart-Guru, and of His egoless Divine State. Thus began the lesson that the seemingly simple act of bowing is vital as an expression of real devotion.

Franklin said that, as His students, we had been devotionally recognizing Him to some degree, but now we should begin expressing devotional recognition by bowing. He talked of different forms of bowing. He said bowing is also done as a respectful gesture, such as is common in Japan. In India they bow to acknowledge the Divine in each other. He said, "Those kinds of bows are more respectful than a hand shake, but they are still basically a social gesture." He said, "You should understand what bowing is all about, then bow with devotion."

Franklin explained that He is our Divine Heart-Guru, no matter where He might be, or what He might be doing. He said that in order to undermine any social familiarity and casual approach, or non-recognition of His Awakened State, we should acknowledge our heart-relationship by bowing. Franklin said we should bow when He comes into the meditation hall, and also to bow again when He leaves the hall. Bowing should be done whether sitting or kneeling. He suggested we try the different forms of bowing and feel the bodily surrender in each form.

Our Beloved Guru then instructed that if He was not physically present in the meditation hall, we should bow to His Divine State and Person via His photograph (Murti) placed on His seat as a statement of His Omnipresence. So we then began to include bowing to our Beloved Guru via His Murti.

We also learned that if we were standing we could acknowledge our heart-recognition of Franklin by placing our hands over our heart while looking at Him and receiving His Darshan.

111

In later years Beloved Adi Da described the "full feeling-prostration" bow, emphasizing "feeling". In the full feeling-prostration the full body is surrendered face down on the floor, with arms, hands and fingers extended forward, pointing to Him. The fingers and palms should be touching, but not folded as in common conventional prayer. In this way the entire physical body is turned to Him, including the legs. The feet could be touching or not.

One time, years later, while Beloved Master Da was seated in a meditation hall, I approached and devotionally bowed with the full feeling-prostration. While I was prostrated, He asked, "Who are you bowing to?" I looked up from the floor and said, "To you, Master." He said, "No you aren't. You're bowing to the vase. You are pointed directly to it." His raised eyebrow also told me He wasn't just making a humorous comment. There was an important message in it for me and for all who bow to the Divine.

I understood that Heart-Master Da was addressing the need to bow to Him directly, not casually, and not just in His general direction. It was about directness between the devotee and the Divine Heart-Master, direct bodily turning by laying the body down at His Holy Feet with full feeling surrender. To bow to Him is to recognize that His Person is Divine Reality, not a separate person at all. To bow down whole bodily to the Divine Heart-Master is an acknowledgment of the devotee's heart-recognition of His Divine State.

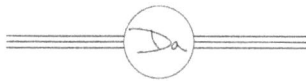

The First Fast

Franklin had been talking about the advantages of dietary discipline and fasting. He asked us to consider the different approaches to it all. When we brought Him Paavo Airola's book *Are You Confused?* He said it was not a new approach to diet; Airola addressed different diets that had been tested over many years and he recommended what had proven to have beneficial results. Franklin said Airola's approach was the right approach and we should follow it.[5]

Franklin said that while right diet will support optimum health, the real purpose is devotional response and ego-transcending discipline. He said periodic fasting should be included to allow the elimination of toxins. He said fasting would also serve to loosen our dependent grip on food and its consolations.

Our Beloved Guru had us fully study *Are You Confused?* and take on the lacto-vegetarian diet. Most of us weren't thinking about fasting yet; the new diet was enough to deal with. Then one day He suggested we all should begin a fast. He said a ten-day juice fast would be best. He directed us to refresh ourselves on the details of such a fast, so we all started reviewing the fasting rules that night.

The fast began two days later. Each day of the fast, Franklin was at the ashram helping us to gain the maximum benefit from it. He always asked how the fast was going. The next question He typically asked was about our favorite foods! Franklin also talked about His favorite foods. He had someone bring cookbooks to show us full-color pictures of great dishes from many different cuisines. He showed full-color spreads of different desserts. He talked about the tastes, fragrances, and textures of different foods. As He spoke, He animated His body to exaggerate smelling and

---

5. Over the years, Avatar Adi Da would consider many different approaches to diet, and His Instruction was progressively refined. While His consideration of diet with devotees started with this lacto-vegetarian approach proposed by Paavo Airola, Avatar Adi Da's final general recommendation was the "searchless raw (fructo-vegetarian) diet" described in *Green Gorilla: The Searchless Raw Diet Given by His Divine Presence . . . Avatar Adi Da Samraj* (Middletown, CA: The Dawn Horse Press, 2008).

swooning over food delights. Franklin's Divine Humor helped us let go of our concerns about not eating, concerns like *"I'm hungry"*, *"I'll die if I don't eat"*, *"I'm getting too skinny"*, or *"I don't have any energy"*.

One day during the fast, Franklin had someone actually buy some food at a nearby restaurant and bring it to the back room of the ashram for us all to smell. It was agonizing, yet His Play was also pure delight! During this fast, unlike typical fasts, our food desire wasn't being ignored, suppressed, or avoided in any way. On the contrary, due to Franklin's delightful reminders, we felt our food desire much more! His Humor about our desires made fasting so much more useful. Franklin used the fast to serve our self-understanding and strengthen our capacity for self-transcendence by seeing that we didn't have to live from the point of view of a separate one in need. We saw that by turning feeling-attention to Him, our desires faded, obscured in the Brightness of the Heart's Prior Condition.

Franklin totally engaged us throughout the entire ten days. On each day, Franklin asked how many days we had done so far. Then He would enthusiastically make the point that we only had "x" days left! His daily Play allowed us more contact with Him and that contact awakened more love and more devotion to our great Open-Hearted Guru.

After the fast had ended, Franklin heard that one of us had violated the fasting rules by juicing bananas. He said that, since someone had violated their fast, "I guess we are going to have to do it again," and He called for another ten-day fast for all of us, which began two days after the first fast ended.

What a letdown! He Laughed and made fun of our reaction to His suggestion to do it again. He said, "You shouldn't have violated the fast!" When we protested, saying we didn't all violate it, He said, "Well, maybe not all, but you should have been responsible for each other's integrity during the fast. Besides, it will be good to do it again." Then He commented on our fantasizing about food and how, thinking the fast was over, we were planning what to eat first. He addressed how quickly we were ready to indulge ourselves. He pointed out how the body-mind always goes for consolation. He asked, "Why do we need consolation? What's wrong?" It was another way He showed us the core self-contraction and its eternal need to be consoled or distracted.

At different times during the second ten-day fast, Franklin would project how things would have been had we not done the second fast—such as what we would have been eating on that day. He kept giving us the gift of feeling that we don't have to be committed to fulfilling our desires and addictions, but that we can turn to Him and let that turning undermine our automaticity.

To this day, all those who participated in the two consecutive ten-day fasts agree that the two fasts with Franklin were not mere periods of abstinence; they were periods of liberating self-observation and self-transcendence in which we saw how the turning of feeling-attention to the Divinely Realized Guru freed us—not just from desire, but from the egoic patterning of the self-contraction.

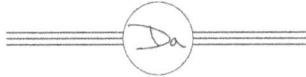

The Knee of Listening Study Meetings

MAY 1973

In May of 1973 Franklin chose to help His students deeply study His first published book, *The Knee of Listening*. A group of us were invited into His home and He sat with us in His living room to guide our study. This unique study in His Holy Company continued every night for weeks, taking us through the entire book.

Franklin's Gift of nightly study was a great sacrifice for Him, and a demand for us to stay with Him in His Teaching considerations. Since the meetings continued every night, the demand for continued self-transcendence became intense. Franklin's seriousness about our understanding of His Teaching didn't allow us any space for attention to wander off.

We sat on the floor in front of Franklin in His living room. As soon as we opened our copies of the book He began reading, a few lines at a time. Then He would fully explain exactly what each line meant. Some explanations were lengthy, some very short. His one-pointed seriousness to have us fully receive His Teaching deeply impressed us all. He would look around to make sure we were staying with Him, then read and explain another few lines. His absolute caring attention continued in this fashion throughout the entire book.

Franklin made sure that we felt and understood the truth of His words and that His Teaching was directly and personally addressing each of us. His readings directly addressed the act of self-contraction that we were doing in the present moment, and that we were always doing. His readings and explanations about God not being the creator, but the always present Divine Reality, were obviously His Self-Confessions.

When Franklin felt it was enough, He put aside His book and sat with us silently, allowing us to simply receive His Sacred Darshan and feel His Free State directly, without anything added. Then when it was right, He'd let us know it was time to go. Filled with His Gifts, we thanked Him and bowed down at His Holy Feet.

After spending hours in the Divine Master's living room, we would leave in a state of elevated consciousness. Yet we were not in a position to appreciate the full import of those hours. We were being guided through the autobiography of the Divine Avatar by the Divine Avatar. Absolutely extraordinary!

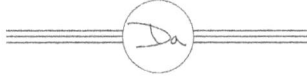

The Preparation

Around April 1973, Franklin began planning for a trip to India. He told us something at the time about the purpose of the trip:

Unimaginable numbers of beings, energies, and processes outside this world generate and cooperate in Spiritual work in this world. Wherever the real Spiritual process is awakened at any point in time and space, it is the product of the Spiritual process that exists prior to time and space and also within all the levels of time and space or manifest existence. So behind our work are all the Siddhas and all the great activities that transcend the Earth plane.

Just as there is a vast Spiritual process behind this work and all true Spiritual work, there are also certain individuals, Siddhas and others, who are very directly involved with our work. Muktananda is the only one alive in the body, and it is very important that I purify My connection to him for the sake of the work itself. There are others with whom My contact is in subtler dimensions— Nityananda, Ramana Maharshi, Shirdi Sai Baba, Ramakrishna. I want to return to the places most intimately associated with these people and ensure My proper relationship to them for the sake of this work.

The real force of this work can move only when I do not exist as an exclusive entity. It is only when the channels for this work are pure, absolutely open, unlimited, that the event can take place without difficulty. So it is inappropriate for someone who is the immediate instrument for Spiritual life among His devotees to appear in any sense as an exclusive, independent source, because there is no such source. Everything is only instrumental. The Guru is not Guru by virtue of being independent, some "guy" who "made it". He or she is Guru by virtue of the Guru-Function, which is to present no obstacle to Truth, and to maintain a "radical" connection to Truth.

There is a stage in this work in which there must be perfect release, absolute surrender, dissolution. It has nothing to do with Franklin's personal Sadhana, Transformation, and Realization. Wherever this Function of Guru arises, there must be this surrender, because the Function of Guru is very different from the State of Realization. One who understands or has realized something is not himself or herself Guru. Guru is a Function in which even Liberation, Realization, and understanding are dissolved. There must be nothing.

During the first year of the Ashram, I needed to be involved in an almost muscular way in formal Satsang, in order to Awaken the internal process. Now My Activity as an apparent individual is dissolving more and more all the time. God Performs this Work. That is what is remarkable about the Guru. The Guru is called "God" and acknowledged as God in the traditional Ashrams, because That is exactly What the Guru Is. But the Guru Becomes That by Disappearing, not by appearing. The Function of Guru exists only where the exclusive individual's life has been turned utterly, made utterly available to the higher life. Then, without the Guru especially doing something, everything the Guru does becomes a Manifestation of the Divine Force, Communicating, Teaching. The Teaching is of no value unless it is going on twenty-four hours a day, at every level, from the solid mass of the atoms to the most sublime Non-manifest Reality.

The Guru is one in whom there is nothing, no obstacle, and all the Divine functions on all levels down into the human become open, active, pure. So My going to India is the necessary discipline that I must observe in order to maintain the connection to all the intimate Spiritual Sources of this work. If that proper connection is maintained, all the Siddhas become active in this work. And they all should. The Siddhas are the functional expressions of God manifesting in the various planes, some in the Earth, some just outside the visible world, and then all the way "up". The individual Guru living with His disciples and devotees is the focal point. Behind Him it spreads out and ultimately includes the Divine in its Perfect sense. (Excerpt from a talk given to April 18, 1973, in Los Angeles, California.)

One day in the early summer of 1973, while I was managing the ashram bookstore, a friend came in and said Franklin wanted to see me at His home (a small house in the Hollywood Hills). I assumed He wanted me to run an errand, but when I arrived, He invited me to sit with Him.

Franklin's Love relationship with me always immediately lifted my heart and removed any possible discomfort about being in His Holy Company. After asking who was minding the store, He began talking about going to India in the fall. I felt sad that He would be leaving the ashram for a while, but as He spoke of His planned trip He made it seem very interesting. Then came the really stupendous surprise: He asked if I would like to accompany Him!

My whole body started vibrating. I felt a beautiful warmth of love in my chest. My eyes began to water. I was smiling an enormous smile, so happy I couldn't speak. He laughed and cracked a joke about the way I looked. Then He said, "Well, can you come with Me?" Still unable to speak, I hugged Him in response. The prospect of traveling with Franklin, my Beloved Guru, was miraculous. Being invited to serve Him 24/7 felt absolutely wonderful!

Franklin talked about some of the holy places He was planning to visit, but I was so overjoyed I didn't have much attention for the details. He told me that the trip would be good for my spiritual practice, and that I would carry the bags and handle the practical things, like making reservations. He said I should learn to use a camera so we could have good photos of all the holy places and important people He would be visiting.

My Heart-Guru explained that He had important work to do in India. He didn't want to be disturbed by people's questions or curiosity. He instructed, "Tell them about Me and about the ashram; if they're interested, refer them to the books." (The two books by Franklin that had been published at the time were *The Knee of Listening* and *The Method of the Siddhas*, later titled *My "Bright" Word*). As Franklin drew me into the upcoming trip, the expectation of serving Him full-time became my focus.

The entire wonderful incident at my Beloved Guru's house was overwhelming and greatly inspiring. I went home and told my intimate partner about this incredible turn of events. She cried with joy at the great opportunity of service to our Heart-Guru.

I had no idea what the requirements serving my Guru full-time would demand. It would be a constant requirement of self-transcendence, extending to every aspect of life. For example, Franklin said when He had visited Swami Muktananda at his ashram in the past, Baba (as Swami Muktananda was called) was impressed that Franklin could comfortably sit with His legs folded in the yogic full-lotus position. Franklin said He expected me to learn to sit comfortably in the full lotus too—it would be embarrassing if His devotee had to sit on a chair while everyone else sat on the floor. I immediately intensified my attempts to find some comfort in that cross-legged agony.

Suddenly I was being given more and more responsibilities at the ashram. I had sheets of paper filled with things to do and Franklin continued to find more for me to do. I began carrying a clipboard; the to-do list was so long. None of my responsibilities were impossible; my list just demanded that I do it. Simultaneously I was feeling my constant resistance to functioning. But, no matter how much the demand to function bothered me, my resistance was overridden just by the Grace of being allowed to serve my Beloved Guru.

One celebration day, held in a devotee's backyard, as I joined everyone sitting on the grass listening to Franklin, a friend told me, "Franklin doesn't ever want to see you anywhere without a clipboard in your hand. You should always be ready to take notes and function." My friend then laughed and said, "You think this trip is going to get you straight. The way I see it, Franklin is going to get you straight before you leave!"

Franklin invited me to keep doing things with Him in preparation for the trip. One day we drove to Malibu where He bought a beautiful conch shell as a gift for Swami Muktananda. Along the way we were speaking about various things, when I asked my Beloved Guru an important question. I said, "Because of my trust and devotion, I feel so close to you, I feel open and very comfortable around you. When I'm around you I'm very happy. But I also respect you very much, so I feel I should be more formal around you. That feeling tends to hold me back. I feel a conflict between these feelings. My question is, Can You help me understand which is correct?"

Franklin said, "Your feeling close to Me is appropriate. But the respect which holds you away is how you protect yourself from deeper feeling." It was clarified. I understood that it was appropriate to be fully open and let devotion be my focus. I also understood that true respect would not reduce devotion; it would be a result of devotion.

My Beloved Guru said I had to be especially humorous and free on this trip if I was to do my service well, and that He expected me to do it thoroughly. For the entire three months prior to departure, I was constantly working through my assumed limitations on my ability to fully function and really effectively serve my Heart-Guru.

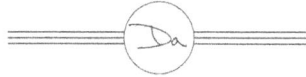

Late for the Flight

When it was almost time to leave for India, Franklin went to New York to visit His parents. Meanwhile, I took the opportunity to visit my parents in Boston. We planned to meet at Kennedy Airport in New York to catch our Air India flight.

On the day of our flight, I felt I had plenty time, but my flight from Logan Airport in Boston to Kennedy in New York was delayed and finally arrived really late at a domestic terminal far from the international terminal where Franklin would be. After arrival, there was another delay at baggage claim. It was already past the time we had arranged to meet and my plan had been to help check in my Beloved Guru's bags. My stress level was building rapidly.

No taxis were available, so I started running. Soon the weight of the suitcases and camera bag slowed me down while my mind raced with all the negatives. The hot, humid weather pressing down only added to my stress.

Finally I made it to the international terminal. Now with muscles aching, red-faced, pouring sweat, exuding stress, I rushed to the counter to meet Franklin; a very wrong way of beginning an international trip of service to my Guru!

As I turned the corner, Franklin was standing there, talking with His father. He was so calm, relaxed, simply Happy, and very Bright. He looked at me and I immediately felt the chaos I was bringing to Him in that moment. Effortlessly, the Divine Guru's egoless Condition reflected me back on myself. I could feel how out of relationship I was, how completely self-concerned I had become. In that same moment, I saw Him, my perfect Loving Master, happily enjoying time with His father.

Franklin's obvious equanimity and Presence transformed me on the spot. My entire dilemma literally dissolved! Utterly changed in that instant, I approached, so happy to see Him, in the calm disposition of the heart, as if fallen to my knees. He hugged and kissed me, then introduced me to His father. I checked in and confirmed our seats, then took some pictures of my Beloved Guru and His father, so happy to be in His Transforming Company.

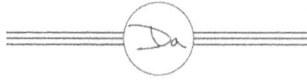

On the Plane

Once we were seated on the plane, Franklin started to up the ante on my functionality. His way of dealing with me was to come up with one thing after another to do. He kept telling me He didn't like this or that, and He expected me to change whatever it was. At first His Play was pure joy. In time, I could see He was doing everything to show me my "good guy" strategy of not wanting to bother anyone or make demands on people.

My Beloved Guru said the plane was too small, and that we may have boarded the wrong plane. I should check it out.

He didn't like the location of His seat. I should find better seats.

He looked at the menu and said there was no food on the menu that suited Him. I should find a new menu.

He asked for the movie schedule and after reviewing it said He had already seen all of them. I should get more movies.

Since nothing got changed, He laughed and said, "The service is lousy." His raised eyebrow directed at me communicated that it wasn't just the airline service that was lousy. And we hadn't even left the ground yet!

Once we began flying, Franklin said He was sure we were going in the wrong direction. I should talk to the people in charge.

He looked concerned when He said the plane wasn't flying high enough.

We had just been in the air a short time when He said He didn't like how long the flight was taking!

Each time my Guru criticized something, I spoke with our stewardess to try to change it—like the seat locations, the videos, the food, things that seemed possible to change. Every time I returned to Franklin to tell Him something couldn't be changed, He raised His eyebrow: That wasn't service!

My Beloved Guru's Play was so full of Humor; it made learning the lessons easy. The test was to understand and stay in relationship.

When I asked if the plane was flying in the right direction or flying high enough, I tried to be serious, but the stewardess was obviously irritated. Then she started to completely avoid me. I had to make my unreasonable demands of another stewardess or steward. Eventually, no matter what I wanted to talk about, they all acted too busy to listen. Each time I returned to Franklin and told Him they were too busy to talk, His body language let me know that my service had fallen short again. Finally He told me to sit down and be quiet.

Franklin's Play with me wasn't over. A little while later He said, "They aren't listening to us, we will have to take over the plane! Once they serve our food, hide the plastic knives and forks, we'll use them. On our way to the cockpit, see that lady up there with the large hat? Have her remove it!"

It was obvious Franklin wasn't going to stop requiring me to do things I absolutely didn't want to do. His Play on the plane was preparing me to serve Him in the coming weeks, months, even forever—showing me that real service thrusts one into the fire of transcending tendencies, habits, and patterns.

A bit later on the flight, Franklin said, "You must take a bite out of life. You shouldn't be afraid to use your emotions. They're a part of life and when used rightly, they serve life." He said I should learn to deal with people strongly, when necessary. "Even anger is fine, and there is no need to contract because of it." He said I should be free to use all emotions and live freely. Then He told me to complain again and have another situation corrected by requiring someone else to function even though they didn't want to.

The plane made one stop in Lebanon, which was at war with Israel at the time. As we started down the stairs to the tarmac, Franklin noticed several armed Lebanese military guards securing the area. Before we reached the ground, knowing I came from a Jewish family, Franklin jokingly whispered, "Jerry, quick! Cover your nose!"

One thing that surprised me on the flight was that my Guru ordered several glasses of milk. I knew He normally wouldn't drink milk, but I didn't ask Him about it. However, once we returned to the Melrose Ashram, He was talking about the trip and when He mentioned the Play on the plane, I did ask Him. He said, "You wanted the milk, but since it wouldn't be good for you, I drank it."

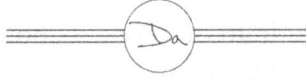

Bombay

AUGUST 1973

Once we checked in to our Bombay hotel and dropped off our bags, we headed out into the city. Mingling on the city streets were people dressed in clean, attractive clothes and also beggars wearing rags. There were people living and sleeping on the sidewalks. We came across a dead man lying on a sidewalk. There had been a great drought, which had caused food shortages and the signs of famine were obvious. There were many sick and crippled people. Cows roamed freely through the streets, while families with babies and small children were sleeping under a sheet of metal or had a tent made of a few rags as their permanent home. Many beggars were missing body parts and always made it a point to call attention to their condition. Franklin didn't comment about all this, but I could see, by His bodily Response, that He was Magnifying His State, Transmitting His Blessings in relation to each and all of these despairing people.

We met a beggar with one eye, who spoke a little English. He was also a little crazy, often speaking in riddles. Franklin asked Him if he knew where we could find a good harmonium and a pair of tabla drums. The beggar asked us to follow him and Franklin agreed. Even though the beggar had a bad limp, he was able to lead us down side streets, through alleys, over a fence, into a friend's home to see some art for sale, and in and out of two taxis. Every time the taxi stopped, a beggar came to the window asking for money. Several times men with leprosy showed their horrible scars, hoping to get some money.

At one stop a young girl pushed her live cobra, fully coiled in its basket, through the open window, right in Franklin's face. I yelled and she immediately removed it. Franklin didn't comment about the girl and her snake. He said that the heartbreaking condition of the Indian beggars was enough to make a person sick. "What karma," He said as His face showed signs of His total Compassion and Love. "And our people back in the Los Angeles ashram think they have it rough." His obvious Freedom allowed Him to completely feel their condition and Bless them at heart.

In all these different, even unusual, circumstances, Franklin was always in a State that was indescribable. In my limited understanding, I saw Him always balanced, free, and humorous. He just kept on flowing from one thing to the next, never giving me time for my mediocrity. He told me I always had to be right there with Him, even out the door before Him.

Some places seemed more dangerous than others. Some of the people we came in contact with in these side streets and alleys hadn't eaten a good meal for a long time, if ever. We were foreigners dressed in clean white clothes and I was carrying a very expensive camera in a new camera bag. Whenever Franklin noticed my concern, He would indicate if the circumstance was okay, or not. At one place He said the circumstance didn't feel safe, so we should leave. When we finally got to the harmoniums, they weren't what He wanted. Later on the trip we did find a well-known harmonium shop and Franklin did order a beautiful harmonium for the ashram.

On this very first venture into Bombay, Franklin saw a rack of canes and walking sticks in a clothing store. One of His legs, damaged by polio as a child, had flared up as a result of long hours on the plane in a cramped position. He bought a cane and carried it with Him for the rest of the trip. After returning to America He commented, "The cane has touched the ground of every holy place in India."

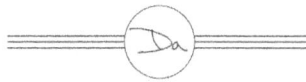

Swami Muktananda

AUGUST 1973

After spending the evening in Bombay, early the next morning we hired a taxi to take Franklin to Swami (Baba) Muktananda's ashram. Franklin was quiet during most of the drive to the ashram. He only spoke a few words, such as when He pointed out the numbers on a very long line of trees, saying with a chuckle, "The reason each tree is numbered is so it won't be stolen."

His Humor was always there even in the midst of His intense Blessing Work. He said He was active on a subtle level and that was the nature of much of the Work He had come to do in India.

I felt the significance of Franklin's meeting with Baba Muktananda. Franklin had said He had certain karmas to resolve on this trip, so His Work could be purified. Baba Muktananda was the only remaining living guru from the time of Franklin's Sadhana. Even before Franklin left for India He told me that if Baba could prove that his Realization was superior to Franklin's, He would turn His ashram over to Baba Muktananda. That was the test Franklin was placing on Baba Muktananda, His way of resolving karmas.[6]

As we approached the ashram from the distance, we could see a large impressive building surrounded by acres of open fields. Franklin commented on how the ashram had grown since His last visit in 1970. Outside the ashram entrance flower malas were being sold. My Beloved Guru suggested purchasing a mala for me to give Baba at our meeting. Franklin had brought a large conch shell, which He had purchased in Malibu as His gift for Baba.

Entering the ashram front gate, we were greeted by some devotees who lived there. They directed Franklin to the courtyard where Baba was sitting. Franklin approached Baba and bowed at his feet, then gave him the conch shell and a rudraksha bead mala. He then stood to the side. When I gave Baba the flower mala he asked if I had been there before. (We were speaking through a translator.) I

6. For more detail regarding this meeting between Swami Muktananda and Avatar Adi Da Samraj, please refer to *The Knee of Listening*, Standard Edition, 2004, 524–3.

said that I hadn't. He said I looked familiar and was sure I had come previously.

Franklin stood by Baba as more people came to offer him gifts. Baba made a comment about something and Franklin laughed. That was the only outward contact between Franklin and Baba during that time. After about fifteen minutes Baba got up and went through a small door behind him into the ashram building.

Franklin said hello to a few people He knew, and then He was directed to a room on the third floor where we could stay for the duration of our visit. The room had two single cots and mattresses, a small dresser, and a ceiling fan. Franklin unpacked and rested for a few minutes. When He was ready we walked to Bhagavan Nityananda's ashram, about twenty minutes down the road.

Each morning Franklin walked from Baba Muktananda's ashram to Bhagavan Nityananda's ashram and stayed for an hour or two. At the time, Bhagavan Nityananda's ashram, on the dirt road in the village of Ganeshpuri, was made up of two buildings and a natural hot mineral bath.

Bhagavan Nityananda was Baba Muktananda's guru. Avatar Adi Da had had a direct Spiritual relationship with Bhagavan Nityananda for many years. Bhagavan Nityananda left the body on August 8, 1961.

His devotees told us that Bhagavan Nityananda had been accustomed to washing in the hot bath and would often tell his visitors to use it. Outside the ashram were several wooden stalls where pictures, trinkets, and flower malas could be purchased.

Franklin visited all the rooms and sat quietly for a while, filling each room with His Blessing Presence. He commented that He liked the chair with extending leg rests that Bhagavan Nityananda had used during his lifetime. I noticed that the platform where Bhagavan Nityananda would rest during the day was very firm, since it didn't have a mattress. Occasionally children, laughing or singing, ran in and out of the main hall, and once while we were there a bird flew through. The hall doors and windows were always open. It was a happy place for everyone, a part of their village.

On our second visit, a bright-faced, skinny old man wearing only a loincloth was standing at the front steps to the main entrance. Greeting Franklin, he smiled and bowed, and when Franklin went inside and sat down, the man sat near Him. Every day after, the old man was there, happy to greet Franklin and to sit close to Him.

"Bhagavan Nityananda's ashram has lost some of its force," Franklin said, "because people aren't using it exclusively as a place of spiritual practice." He asked if I had felt any force there. I said no.

He said, "The force can be felt in the vital.[7] Bhagavan Nityananda was a yogi. Although he transcended the limitations of yoga, his force and movement can be felt in the seat of yogic work, in the vital. His work was involved in purifying the vital."

After the first visit, when we returned to Baba Muktananda's ashram, Franklin followed the ashram schedule and attended the chanting and meditation occasions in the main hall. The first couple of days He attended all four chanting occasions each day. After that He only attended the scheduled mandatory ones. By the end of His stay, Franklin had stopped going to any chanting occasions. He said the chanting was simply "crowd control", rather than "an external representation of the internal practice of feeling-attention to God."

The first morning my Beloved Guru asked me to get some bananas for breakfast. I went to the banana stall outside the ashram. Once there, I noticed another stall selling sandalwood malas. Knowing He particularly liked sandalwood, I felt that a mala would be an appropriate gift for my Beloved Guru. So I got the bananas and a beautiful sandalwood mala. It was my first opportunity to truly thank Franklin for the unique and wonderful service He was allowing me to perform—a service that was anything but ordinary, or even extraordinary, in a conventional sense. I bowed at His Holy Feet and gave Him the mala. He smiled as He looked it over. Franklin carried the sandalwood mala in His shoulder bag until He arrived at Ramana Maharshi's ashram near the end of the five-week trip. Once there, He placed it on Ramana Maharshi's Murti in a small hut called Skandashram near the top of the sacred Arunachala hill.

---

7. "The vital" is the navel and abdominal area.

At the tea house next to Swami Muktananda's Ashram, 1973

One of the first nights in our small room, as I was falling asleep, my mouth became unusually moist, causing me to swallow a lot. Each time I swallowed I made a clicking noise caused by my tongue moving off the roof of my mouth. Franklin turned to me and said, "You don't have to do that anymore—that was from another life!" No further explanation was offered.

After a few days at Baba Muktananda's ashram, I began to feel bored and unimpressed. I told my Guru how I felt. "Every time I try to muster a little religious reverence, it shows itself as a mediocre strategy, a phony emotion. Also every one of my attempts to get with these ashram functions is frustrated and seems to fall flat. I'm really bored. There doesn't seem to be anything happening here, and I feel kind of numb, while I'd expect the ashram to make me feel happy."

Franklin said, "Most of the time people distract themselves in high or low states, excitement or mediocrity. Boredom is just another distraction, because right behind that feeling is an enormous fear, an enormous dilemma. The dilemma must be experienced, rather than the distraction. And it must be understood and transcended."

The majority of participants at the ashram were Westerners, many from America. Baba Muktananda's staff was mostly comprised of Indians. Franklin saw many people at the ashram who reminded Him of His own students in Los Angeles.

Franklin said there are mainly two types of people in the world: those who never get the message of life and walk around in a daze, and those who see a message in everything and become so serious and concerned that they can't do anything freely.

One day we visited the Vajreshwari Temple, just twenty minutes down the road. It was a popular temple, honoring three different forms of the Devi (Divine Goddess).

When we arrived, there was a man lying on the ground in great pain from broken bones. We learned that he had just tried to commit suicide by jumping from a tall tower next to the temple.

Franklin had said that there is no such thing as a coincidence. The man had tried to take his life just as the Divine Master arrived.

Franklin had also said that His Pure State feels everything without limit. I could see by His facial expressions that He was deeply feeling the man's suffering.

He said that the man would continue to suffer—most likely no one was going to take care of him—but eventually he would be taken to a hospital. Franklin's Regard for the man Blessed him beyond the limits of his body.

Once we entered the temple, Franklin gave His Blessing Regard to the Devi deities, and then to the entire temple. The main temple was surrounded by a large patio; Franklin sat on one of the benches, continuing to do His Blessing Work. This was the first time in India it was very obvious to me that Franklin was working at a depth to Empower a holy temple. His Silent Regard was beyond conventional reality.

When He was done, we returned to Baba Muktananda's ashram.

Franklin spent part of every day and evening writing in His notebook. He was quite concentrated, though also often present with His Humor. His Freedom didn't change, no matter what He was doing.

One night when we returned to the bedroom, I laid out the camera equipment to clean it. Just as I began, Franklin asked me to give Him a foot massage. I hesitated, wanting to finish what I was doing. He said, "You must be as functional as a chair, at all times."

The massage seemed to go on and on for a long time. While still massaging His Feet, I kept looking back at my camera equipment, considering how to clean it all. As I did that, my Beloved Guru would say, "Stronger, deeper! Now the other foot." I was wondering when the massage was going to end. When I felt it wasn't going to end soon, I finally stopped turning away and focused my attention and feelings into the massage. As soon as that happened, Franklin said, "That's enough massage." The lesson was clear.

The next morning Franklin asked me to get the camera and the tape recorder. Professor Jain, Baba Muktananda's interpreter, had arranged a personal meeting with Baba in his private room and it would start right away. In anticipation of this most important meeting, Franklin had written down questions He wanted to ask Baba. He had two copies of the questions, one for Professor Jain and one for Himself, so no misinterpretation could be made.

The meeting began with Franklin giving Baba a safari-type hard hat with a fan built into the front, brought from America. Baba and others laughed at the built-in fan. Baba gave Franklin an orange cap. Meanwhile Amma (Baba's assistant) and I were setting up our tape recorders on the table, and I also took a few photos.

The meeting started with some light comments by Baba. Franklin gave Professor Jain a copy of His questions, so He could translate to Baba. Then Franklin began asking each question. I felt the questions were to see if Baba's Realization agreed with Franklin's Realization. Baba addressed the first few questions from his point of view, which was clearly not in agreement with Franklin's Realization. In fact, I felt his answers belittled just about everything Franklin asked, and then he changed the subject of the meeting entirely. I personally felt offended by his disrespect for the seriousness of Franklin's questions.

The meeting ended with Baba leaving through his door, back into his private quarters. As we stepped outside the meeting room, in reaction to Baba Muktananda's responses to my Beloved Guru's important questions I asked, "Are we going to stay here?"

Franklin paused a moment, then smiled wide and said, "Here's my plan: find the first bus out of here. Let's get packing." Within a very short time He was packed and headed for the bus. As Franklin walked through the courtyard toward the ashram front gate, where the bus was about to arrive, His dear friend Amma called to Him from the other side of the courtyard. He never turned around, just raised His arm and waved to her as He walked on. This visit was the last time Franklin ever physically saw Baba Muktananda or Amma.

Franklin said that Baba Muktananda was a yogi and that his teaching was the way of the search. He had shown that he hadn't transcended that limitation. Franklin said that He was very happy about the meeting turning out as it had. Everything was out in the open, and the karmas of relationship with Baba had been purified and broken clean. I could see Franklin was pleased with the resolution that the meeting had provided. He said that this freedom was very good for His Work.

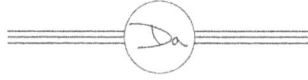

The Lesson of Jelly Toast

AUGUST 1973

We returned from Baba Muktananda's ashram to Bombay and checked into the Taj Mahal Hotel. The contrast between the hotel and the ashram was impressive. I thought: *I have to do sadhana no matter where I'm at, so maybe living in a luxurious environment is best.* It was certainly more comfortable, and a lot less demanding! I could see how the consolations of comfort and luxury could undermine the will for self-transcendence.

In the morning we went to the hotel dining room for breakfast. The table was set with white linen and shiny silverware. There were large attractive plates and sparkling glasses—a glaring contrast to the ashram's banana leaves and eating with fingers.

Franklin ordered and I asked for the same. The waiter brought a platter of butter and assorted jellies. As soon as the toast arrived, Franklin spread some butter on toast and ate it. I noticed He didn't use jelly, but I felt maybe it's okay for me. I spread some butter, then added jelly to the toast and ate it. The sweet taste of jelly toast was refreshing. It had definite nurturing and somewhat consoling qualities. Absorbed in pleasure, I ate the jelly toast.

Once we returned from India to the Melrose Ashram, when devotees asked about the India trip, one of the first things Franklin told them was, "In India, Jerry would be sitting down at breakfast, having his jelly toast, and I would be Instructing Him. All he wanted to do was to eat this jelly toast and drink his sweet tea. That was really the smack for him! So I would usually find some way to aggravate him at breakfast. Here we were in some of the greatest spiritual centers that exist on Earth, and he would have no experience whatsoever. But at breakfast I would be sitting across from him, and he would be intensely, absolutely absorbed in this jelly toast! This was the appropriate time for Instruction."

For the next year or so, and on and off in later years as well, my Beloved Guru gave me the name "Jelly", which everyone used when addressing me. It was a humorous reminder from my Beloved Heart-Master of my tendencies.

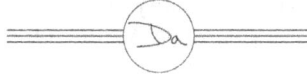

Shirdi Sai Baba

AUGUST 1973

Franklin traveled from Bombay to Shirdi Sai Baba's ashram. He was quiet the entire way. When He arrived He walked directly into the temple without any delay. He obviously felt this visit was important.

Shirdi Sai Baba's temple was oriented around his Mahasamadhi Site.[8] His body had been laid to rest in a white marble tomb in the center of the temple. A larger-than-life white marble statue of him stood facing his tomb.

There was a crowd of people standing around the shrine. Some people were sitting around the edge of the marble tomb, chanting and placing beautiful flowers in different patterns all over it, occasionally sprinkling water on the flowers to keep them fresh.

Franklin stood directly in front of the shrine until He was given permission to approach. He approached and bowed, touching His head to the marble at the foot of Shirdi Sai Baba's statue. He then placed some flowers on the tomb. After standing still and giving His full Blessings to re-empower the shrine, He moved aside so others could approach. Soon after, the priests began waving flames and incense around the statue, then passing out Prasad (blessed gifts) to everyone while the chanting continued.

Franklin said, "Some of the priests were good men. They knew what they were doing. They had a devotional relationship to Shirdi Sai Baba, so it wasn't just ceremonial."

Whenever Franklin said someone was a "good person", it was an acknowledgment that the person was doing the sadhana of devotional self-transcendence. The priests' devotion was obvious to me in their faces and in their devotional feeling when they passed out the Prasad.

Franklin stayed in the temple for less than an hour, then said, "Let's go." He said Shirdi Sai Baba's temple was "good"—it had a lot of force. He said that Shirdi Sai Baba was a saint, his work was

8. Mahasamadhi is the passing of a great Realizer.

the purification of the subtle vehicles, and that he had transcended that limitation. His force could be felt in the sahasrara (chakra at the top of the head).

Franklin was always Working; He never lingered anywhere after He finished His Blessing Work. He always made a point of making contact with the main shrines and holy places at each temple. He never spoke specifically of what He did at each temple, but it was obvious He wasn't there to receive something; rather He was there to Purify, Bless, and Empower each place.

Later in the trip He said, "The reason a place remains holy is not because a saint once lived there, but because people are doing sadhana there. The responsibility of saints and holy people is to visit these places periodically to purify them. This keeps the force alive."

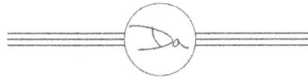

Lessons

After leaving Shirdi Sai Baba's ashram, we visited a few more places on our way to Pune in southwest India. One such place was the home of Sri Pantsachiv (the Raja of Bhor), an elderly and wealthy devotee of Narayan Maharaj. Franklin had formed a relationship with Sri Pantsachiv through correspondence, which was also how the invitation for Franklin to stay with him while in India was received and accepted. We stayed as his guests for a couple of days and visited different temples while there. It was a joy to see the respect Sri Pantsachiv had for Franklin, even providing his car and driver for Franklin's use.

Throughout the trip, people would show that they were very aware of Franklin's Presence. Wherever He walked people would look at Him. Some tried to approach Him. It seemed a lot of people just wanted to be near Him. When we went into temples the priests would acknowledge Him by smiling or reverently bowing their heads. They would make room for Him to walk through crowds and give Him space to sit down. Wherever He went, you could pick Him out of the crowd immediately. There was a physical Radiance about Him. At one point He explained that He was wearing sunglasses to cover His eyes because He felt they must look strange, as He was dealing with matters of great intensity.

One morning while at Sri Pantsachiv's house, Franklin awoke, washed, and was out the door, with me struggling to catch up. He told me, "You must sleep consciously. When you wake up in the morning there is no time to be wasted regaining consciousness. There is only time to 'brush tooth' and run." I never learned how to sleep consciously, but I did learn to wake up and run. Franklin said, "You should always be a few steps in front of Me when walking out the door. No resistance, just do it!"

Another day at Sri Pantsachiv's home, after I showered I threw the wet towel under the sink, intending to bring it to be laundered later. When my Beloved Guru noticed the towel, He told me to fold it and place it neatly in a corner. I said, "But it's dirty." He replied,

"That's no reason for it to be messy."

Next we visited Tukaram's tomb. Franklin told me Tukaram was a holy man who called his wife "Sadhana Murti" because she was a real disturbance that motivated him to do sadhana. Each day he would leave home and walk to a mountain a few miles away, stay there all day, and return in the evening. Once at home, his wife would complain about him being gone all day. Tukaram used his tendency to react to his wife as a goad to self-transcendence.

Franklin was told about a man named Diling Yogi and decided to visit him. Diling Yogi served us tea in his large living room. Just as he was about to start telling Franklin the truth as he experienced it, my Beloved Master told me, "Give him the book." (I carried copies of *The Knee of Listening* with me at all times.) I handed him the book and explained that Franklin had come to do certain Blessing Work in India. I told him about Franklin's devotees and His ashram, and gave him time to look through the book. As soon as he could see that Franklin was not a seeker coming to him for help, he put the book down. For a few minutes Franklin sat silently giving Diling Yogi His Divine Regard; then He said it was time to go. I thanked Diling Yogi for his hospitality.

Franklin heard of another yogi who was adept in raising the kundalini in people, even over long distances. When we got to his house we were informed that the yogi was ill, but we would be allowed to see him for a short time. We went upstairs to his bedroom where he lay attended by servants. We sat to one side of the room for only two minutes, when Franklin whispered, "He can't even raise his head, never mind the kundalini. We had better leave before he dies in front of us."

The next day we went to a very famous large temple at Pandharpur, dedicated to the Lord Vithoba. There were long lines of people waiting to enter. It seemed everyone was coming to get something—health, happiness, success, more male children, and so on. I felt blessed to have been taught about understanding seeking and the nature of true devotion by my Beloved Guru. I think Franklin was the only person there whose purpose was to give something: the Blessings of His Divine State and His Spiritual Force to keep the Divine Presence in the temple alive.

We left the Lord Vithoba Temple and headed for Bombay. I spent many hours in taxis with Franklin throughout the trip. When He didn't speak for long periods, I felt uncomfortable. I was always so happy when He related to me, but when He didn't for extended times, I felt unloved. So I kept seeking ways of releasing my concern. But that only magnified the intensity in my stomach, in my chest, and in my head. Being in His Holy Company I felt a real pressure pushing me to surrender. I would read, or write, or just think, constantly involved in working out my understanding of the Teaching.

Franklin was always doing His Divine Work, which apparently also included having me see that I was always self-watching. *How do I stop avoiding relationship?* I kept trying to figure it out. My failure to understand and always live in relationship was becoming an obsessive concern. Then I confessed my quandary to Franklin. He said, "How many times do you have to see the avoidance to know that you are suffering? To put your attention there isn't this Teaching." He told me that I had always done that my whole life. He said, "To turn in relationship and live relationship is the Teaching."

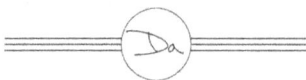

Narayan Maharaj

AUGUST 1973

On the way back to Bombay the Raja of Bhor's driver reminded Franklin of Narayan Maharaj and said that his ashram was only twenty minutes down a dirt road he was pointing to. Franklin told the driver to take us there.

Narayan Maharaj's ashram had a large open-air temple for Lord Dattatreya at the entrance and his shrine and living quarters were behind it. As Franklin entered, He was warmly greeted by four elderly male devotees who had been with Narayan Maharaj when he was alive. They invited us to sit and refresh ourselves from our travels with warm tea.

I told them Franklin was my Guru, that He had a large ashram in America, and that He was traveling in India for a few weeks to bring His Divine Blessings.

They were pleased that Franklin had come to visit their guru at his ashram and were very responsive to Him. Wherever Franklin sat, the four men gathered around Him. At times, two lady devotees joined the men. When the opportunity arose, they were all happy to sit on the floor in front of Him, as they had done with Narayan Maharaj. It felt like they were hoping He would talk Dharma with them.

The men proudly showed Franklin through the upper rooms where Narayan Maharaj had lived. Franklin said Narayan Maharaj had taken on the role of a raja. He commented how much He enjoyed seeing Narayan Maharaj's wonderful personal belongings so well preserved. His beautiful hats had real gold threads interwoven into the fabric. His ornately embroidered vests and tailored outfits were regal. His decorative shoes with turned up tips gave Franklin a laugh. They were well kept, all on display in glass cases. Franklin especially liked the full-size silver palanquin inlaid with jewels. The devotees had great pride in showing Franklin everything about their guru, taking out albums of old photographs and telling many stories.

The entire time my Beloved Heart-Master was at the ashram, the four men stayed with Him and kept offering more ways of serving Him. They loved answering His questions about their guru and were truly happy He was interested. They obviously felt a devotional response to Him.

Franklin called them "good men", saying that Narayan Maharaj had done his work with them, but hadn't finished because he had died too soon. (Narayan Maharaj died September 3, 1945, at the age of 60.)

Franklin said He could stay to live in that ashram; He would have Work to do there. But it wasn't a serious consideration. With His ever-present Humor He pointed out that since He already had an ashram established in Los Angeles, maybe we could just put these men in vegetable crates and ship them back to Los Angeles where He could further serve their spiritual growth.

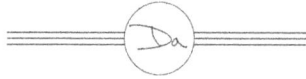

Self-Understanding

From Narayan Maharaj's ashram we went to the Meher Baba ashram, staying only a short time. We also met an Anandamayi Ma disciple, whom Franklin sat with in silence for a short time. Then we returned to the Taj Mahal Hotel in Bombay. The next day Franklin remained in the room while I traveled by taxi through Bombay looking for a film-processing lab. I also felt the need to get some space and be alone. My mind was filled with thoughts about the Teaching of "relationship" and "avoiding relationship". I still couldn't come to a clear understanding of exactly what relationship was. I had thought of it as a big event, something to be accomplished, even though Franklin wasn't talking about any such thing.

My anxiety about understanding was greatly exaggerated by the intensity of having been in my Beloved Guru's Company non-stop for twelve days. The profound Blessing of His Presence was a constant pressure requiring true devotional recognition, and to *wake up—right now!* But my willingness to constantly surrender was falling short.

In my exaggeration of thoughts and emotions I felt lost and alone. And I felt angry. I hated the taxi driver. I hated everything I saw through the taxi window. Still, in that contracted state I kept trying to understand something of my activity and apply the Teaching. But I only saw my problems and possibilities for fixing them, so my dilemma only intensified.

Then, by Grace, with <u>real</u> heart-feeling I enquired, "Avoiding relationship?"[9] Immediately I understood! The question directly revealed the relationship I was avoiding. Feeling my Beloved Heart-Master, my stress spontaneously vanished. All that was left was heart-Communion, the love of my Guru. And in that heart-Communion my entire contraction ended. The enquiry "Avoiding Relationship?" penetrated and undermined my internal automaticity, my crisis, my

9. "Avoiding Relationship?" was a form of "enquiry" practice Avatar Adi Da had given to His devotees at the time. In His final Teachings, the practice of enquiry is no longer to be used.

<u>doing</u> avoidance—the core of the self-contraction, the turning away, the turning inward. In a moment of deep feeling, my Beloved Guru revealed that relationship is my true state and that is Who and What He Is. What a profound gift!

Everything changed for me in that taxi. I was happy. I laughed a lot, out loud. The taxi driver must have thought I was crazy. He kept looking back at me via the mirror. Instead of hating him, now I loved him and happily smiled at his image in the mirror. I even felt connected to what I saw through the taxi windows.

Later, I mentioned the incident to Franklin. He laughed and said something like, "It's about time." He said I could mention something about it to the ashram when we returned, but said nothing more about it.

In the following days, the more I enquired "Avoiding relationship?" the more I saw it yielding heart-Communion and self-understanding. And the more I enquired, the more I saw that Franklin was always Revealing, in every moment, Who He Is, only Present as Consciousness Itself. His State draws you to Him like a magnet and Awakens the heart.

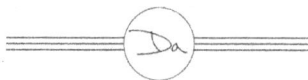

The Avatar of the Age

During one week of the trip, Franklin was playfully reflecting the spiritual seeking of the time, specifically the many claimants to the status of "Avatar". One morning He said, "See that man over there, I recognize him—he's the Avatar of the Age!"

The next day He said, "Jerry, I just saw the Avatar of the Age—he's right over there behind you!"

On another day, "Don't turn to your left. Don't move at all, but behind you, there's a big stone. Under that stone is a rat, and that rat is the Avatar of the Age!"

The last time it was, "See that man over there? Don't stare."

I said, "Wait a minute, <u>You're</u> the Avatar of the Age!"

"No, Jerry, relax. That man over there is the real Avatar of the Age!"

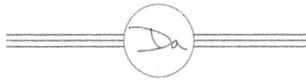

Sathya Sai Baba

AUGUST 1973

The next day Franklin left for Sathya Sai Baba's Prasanthi Nilayam ashram near Bangalore. When we arrived we joined about two hundred people forming a semicircle on the grass in front of Sathya Sai Baba's temple. It still amazes me how, throughout the entire trip, Franklin would submit to join the crowds and all the gurus and yogis in order to Bless them, through His supernormal Functioning, far beyond ordinary consciousness.

After a short time Sathya Sai Baba came out from his private rooms by his temple. I looked at Franklin and noticed He was very intensely concentrated on Sathya Sai Baba, who walked in front of the crowd and occasionally stopped to touch someone on top of the head, or to place his finger on their forehead. He also gave some people fabric shawls, which were carried by his attendant walking behind him. Occasionally someone would give him a written note, asking for his blessings for a person who was not able to be there.

At one point Sai Baba stopped walking and materialized vibhuti.[10] I watched closely as he moved his right hand and fingers around circularly a few times. Soon white ash began to fall from his fingers. Then he stopped its falling, allowing the ash to cover his fingers. He then placed a little of it on several people's foreheads.

I was very impressed. I used the close-up lens of my camera to watch for trickery. His sleeve was loose and wasn't covering anything unusual. I took several close-up photos for historic proof. It was very impressive and the crowd praised God for the miracle.

Sathya Sai Baba kept walking, not acknowledging Franklin's Presence in the crowd.

That night, my Beloved Guru asked how I felt about seeing the vibhuti. I said, "I was impressed."

10. Vibhuti is the ash from a ceremonial fire used in religious worship in Hinduism. Considered sacred, it is commonly placed on the forehead.

Franklin responded, "It's magic. It's real magic, but it's only magic. When you see it, do you notice that you don't change?"

I said I wasn't changed. He continued, "If it didn't change you, what good was it?" Then He poked further at my amazement by joking that the next day I should ask for the manifestation of a hot dog.

He further said, "Sathya Sai Baba doesn't actually create anything. He has a room where vibhuti and other things are kept. When he wants something, he transports it from that place to where he is through subtle spiritual powers."

Sathya Sai Baba had been dressed in beautiful orange robes, which were well tailored and of fine silk and other luxurious fabrics. Franklin said, "I like the way Sathya Sai Baba dressed. His tailor was a good man."

One day I was on the porch outside our room, trying to take a photo of a hawk in flight. As it moved, I kept refocusing the camera. Franklin was standing behind me watching. After a few minutes, with still no picture taken, He asked for the camera. With complete confidence He raised the camera, pointed it at the hawk and took the picture without looking through the viewfinder. No hesitation. He said, "This wishy-washy oscillation is a waste of energy. Just do it." Franklin's photo came out perfect, as expected.

Franklin told me prior to leaving Los Angeles that during this trip He didn't want to have to deal with people generally, other than the ones He chose to see or had special reasons to see—and He noted that most of them had already left the body. There were a few Americans at Sathya Sai Baba's ashram and some of them had heard of Franklin. A particular girl kept asking me if she could meet Franklin. I told her that He wasn't there to Teach, or meet with people, but that I would ask Franklin for her. This didn't satisfy her; she simply wanted to meet Him.

Franklin had noticed the girl and told me He didn't want her bothering Him. But one night I returned to our room from a trip to the local store to find the girl sitting with Franklin in our room. Without hesitation, I escorted her outside. Once on the porch I asked her again not to bother Franklin and reiterated that if she had something to say to Him, she should tell me. Removing her was abrupt, but it felt necessary, given Franklin's instructions to me. Franklin didn't comment about it. Franklin requested a meeting with Sathya Sai Baba through his assistant but the request was denied. Furthermore, Sai Baba did not look at Franklin in the crowd anytime during the days He was there, which was surprising since the Divine Master stood out in the crowd and had been identified to Sai Baba as the Western Guru wanting to meet him.

Another day while on the porch in front of our room at Sathya Sai Baba's ashram, Franklin said, "We will have to have a name for the university we will incorporate some day. What do you think of *Sri Hridayam University?*" (*Sri Hridayam Siddhashram* was the name of the Melrose Ashram.)

I hesitated, then said, "It's too Indian."

The next day, Franklin asked, "What about *Free John University?*"

I thought awhile and said, "It certainly is American."

"Do you like it?"

"No."

He seemed displeased and said, "Well, that's the name!"

Later that day I was writing a letter to my intimate partner when Franklin interrupted and said, "Tell her to tell the ashram to call me *Bubba Free John.*"

I laughed and wrote, "And call Franklin '*Bubba Free John*'." I thought it was very funny. But then I realized He was serious.

He said, "I want you to call Me 'Bubba Free John' from now on," and He told me to write a letter to the ashram in Los Angeles and tell them of His new Name.

I began calling my Beloved Guru "Bubba" from that time on. However, a few days later I slipped and called Him "Franklin". In response, the tone of voice was enough to remind me. He said, "Franklin is dead. I am Bubba Free John!"

Another time I said "Frank—" and caught myself before "lin". He said nothing, just raised His eyebrow.

I didn't realize the profound significance of His Name change at the time. It wasn't clear to me until sometime after our return to Los Angeles. Franklin Jones had "died". As my Heart-Master later said, "Franklin Jones was a fictional character" and now those karmas had been purified. His new Name was a sign that Bubba was free to do whatever was necessary to serve the Awakening of His devotees. It was the beginning of what He would call His formal "Teaching Submission". *Bubba Free John* was the Heart-friend—Bubba, "brother", Free in God. It was also word-play on *Franklin Jones*, His birth Name; therefore *Bubba Free John* carried the connection from Franklin to Bubba, including everything from His past into His present service as Heart-Friend to all beings.

While we were at Sathya Sai Baba's ashram several people mentioned Neem Karoli Baba's name and asked if Bubba would see him. Before we left Los Angeles, Neem Karoli Baba's address was the only one He didn't have. However, a person at Sathya Sai Baba's ashram gave me the address. Bubba said, "See how things always work out? . . . Sometime later in the trip we may visit him."

But in the morning Bubba said he didn't need to physically go to Neem Karoli Baba's ashram since He had contacted him during the night. He said, "I went through some very strange experiences with Neem Karoli Baba. It occurred during sleep, but I was fully conscious and apart from the physical body. I met Neem Karoli Baba on the subtle plane, and we dealt with one another in a very odd way. We immediately embraced one another and then started throwing one another away. We started discarding our own forms in the face of one another and became ridiculous, singing and laughing and throwing ourselves to smithereens, until there was nothing but that very Bliss. It wasn't a vision, it was actual, not just a dream, but a completely conscious, direct meeting with him. Afterward, I thought at first that I would still go see him physically, but it has since become clear that that is not necessary."

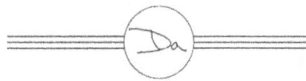

Bubba Free John

Bubba Free John

"Free John" is a rendering of Avatar Adi Da's born Name, "Franklin Jones". "Bubba" was an affectionate nickname for Him in His family, meaning "brother". Avatar Adi Da did not assume this Name casually. It was, as He says in *The Order of My Free Names*, a "Divinely Self-Revealed Name" that came to Him in August 1973, as the real Sacrifice of His Teaching Work was beginning. As "Bubba Free John", Avatar Adi Da became the "brother" of His devotees, extending unreserved friendship to those who came to Him in Los Angeles and later at Persimmon, His ashram in the hills of northern California, established in January 1974, which would come to be known as the Mountain Of Attention Sanctuary.

During His years as Bubba, Avatar Adi Da passionately involved everyone around Him in the most profound evaluation of every aspect of human and spiritual life, always asking them in one form or another: Who, what, or where is happiness? Always Radiating in His own irresistible Humor and Love, Avatar Adi Da was waiting patiently for His devotees to understand that their attraction to Him, their Beloved Heart-Friend, was their only source of lasting Happiness.

Adapted from *The Order of My Free Names.*

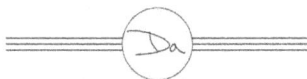

Avatar Adi Da Samraj:

During the Years of My Divine Avataric Teaching-Revelation, I Submitted Myself to My devotees, and I Took On and Suffered all the limitations of My devotees. During the Years of My Divine Avataric Teaching-Revelation, I Became exactly like My devotees. During the Years of My Divine Avataric Teaching-Revelation, I Submitted Myself to My devotees Completely, and I Became more like My devotees than they were themselves. During the Years of My Divine Avataric Teaching-Revelation, I Became exaggeratedly what My devotees were—I Submitted Myself to them, Such That I Became what they were altogether, while My devotees remained only what they could express in the midst of their limitations and their egoic "self"-consciousness. Thus, by Becoming exaggeratedly like all My devotees, I Reflected them to themselves at depth—and, So, I Taught them, and Moved them To Me As I Am.

During the Years of My Divine Avataric Teaching-Revelation, I Became My devotees Completely, by Submitting Myself to them As to God, in order to Demonstrate to them how to likewise turn to Me and surrender to Me and (Most Ultimately) Realize and Be Me.

To Completely Become My devotees Was the Unique Form of My Divine Avataric Teaching-Work. Realizers in the past have spoken about coming down a little into the body while still being somehow above the body. I Am Always Already Infinitely Above and Perfectly Beyond and Prior to This Divine Avataric Body of Intervention here. Nevertheless, during the Years of My Divine Avataric Teaching-Revelation, My Manner of Teaching was to Submit Myself to Coincide With This Body (and all of Its relations) Completely, to Become This Body (and all-and-All) Completely.

By (Thus) Becoming This Body and all of its relations, I Became the body of each and all of My devotees. This Was How I Meditated "others". This Was Why the Divine Avataric Accomplishing-Powers Associated with My Most Perfect Divine Enlightenment Were As They Were during the Years of My Divine Avataric Teaching-Revelation. ("Then and Now and You and The Bright", *The Aletheon*, 2009 edition, 1869–70.)

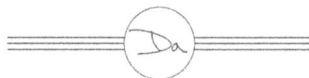

STOP IT!

AUGUST 1973

One day, almost three weeks into the trip, my Beloved Guru came close to my face and said in a strong, loud voice, "STOP IT!"

I had no idea what He was referring to. I didn't feel that I had been doing anything inappropriate.

Later that same day, as I passed Him in a corridor, He strongly repeated, "STOP IT!" Again, it left me blank.

When I came into His Company a few minutes later, it was, "STOP IT!" Several more times that day He would say the same thing. And several more times. I would have no idea what He was talking about.

Stop it! Stop what? I didn't feel I should ask because the way Bubba said it suggested that I absolutely knew exactly what He was talking about. So as not to sound dumb, I didn't ask and my Guru never explained what I should stop doing.

Back in Los Angeles when reviewing notes about the trip, I came across my entries from that day. "STOP IT!" What was He Addressing? I considered unconscious behavior . . . superficial reactivity . . . But nothing clicked.

Then one day while studying His Teaching, I read His words, "The ego-'I' is an activity, not an entity." In that moment, it suddenly became clear: Bubba had been directly Addressing the body-mind activity that is my egoity. That was what I was doing. "STOP IT" was Addressing the fact that, since I am doing the contraction, I can also stop doing it.

Of course, later my Heart-Master also often said, "You can't pick yourself up by your bootstraps." In other words, "stopping it" is not a self-improvement gesture or a technique to distract yourself. Rather, "stopping it" is the shift from feeling self, and all the forms of contraction that come with it, to feeling communion with His un-contracted Free State of Divine Reality.

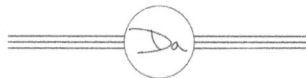

157

Ramana Maharshi

AUGUST 1973

We arrived at Sri Ramanasramam (Ramana Maharshi's ashram) after a full day of travel. While Bubba stayed in the taxi, I told the man in the office that Bubba had come to visit and had reserved a room. The man was very pleased He had arrived and went right outside to meet Him. He immediately showed appropriate respect by offering his assistance with any of Bubba's needs. We were shown to a private room across the street; Bubba set His luggage down, and immediately left for the main temple, the place of Ramana Maharshi's Mahasamadhi shrine, where his body was laid to rest.

The temple was quite large, with a beautiful black marble shrine at the front. A white marble platform indicated where Ramana Maharshi's body was laid to rest. Bubba walked around the shrine three times as is the custom, then bowed in front of the shrine and sat on the floor. He stayed for about an hour, and then returned to our room.

Bubba said the Mahasamadhi shrine was a very powerful place. As soon as He had entered, He was taken over with incredible force. He said Ramana Maharshi was the Heart and his force could be felt in the heart on the right side of the chest. Bubba said Ramana Maharshi's Realization about "the Heart on the right" was the same as His, and that at the shrine He also directly felt the ascension of force from the Heart to the sahasrar.[11]

The next morning we were greeted by a guide who had come to lead us up Arunachala hill, headed for Skandashram, a small one-room hut built into the hill, where Ramana Maharshi had lived for many years. Because Arunachala was a holy hill, Bubba told me to take my sandals off for walking on it, as this is the custom. Looking ahead at the rocky climb, I mentioned it and asked if we could possibly wear sandals to protect our feet. Bubba said,

---

11. Avatar Adi Da later wrote at length about the similarities and differences between Ramana Maharshi's Realization and His own. See *The Knee of Listening*, 2004 edition, 345–61 and 449–58.

"You wouldn't wear them in the Satsang Hall." This steep hill was clearly a holy place.

The path was set with stones of all sizes, some smooth, some not so smooth. Bubba showed no sign of discomfort when stepping on the rough rocks. The day was very hot with too many gnats and mosquitoes, but they didn't seem to bother Him either.

When we reached Skandashram, Bubba went directly in and placed the sandalwood mala He had been carrying with Him on Ramana Maharshi's murti at the front of the room, then sat in front of the murti on the floor. I prepared the camera, and entered to take a few photos. After about half an hour Bubba got up and walked outside. I picked up the camera bag and followed, but I was moving too fast, hoping not to keep Bubba waiting. Due to the intensity of that room and not paying attention to the low door casing, I smashed my head against the casing. I stumbled out, seeing stars before my eyes, and almost fell down. Bubba asked if I was okay. I told Him what had happened and He told me to sit until I regained my balance.

Later, Bubba said Skandashram was one of the most powerful places in the world. Because I couldn't conduct the force of such power and purity, I had almost knocked myself out! One has to be properly prepared to conduct the force of true holy places. Through Bubba's Work of submitting to His devotees' general lack of preparation, He taught us about the responsibility for conducting great spiritual force.

We walked down the hill by way of a cave where Ramana Maharshi had spent some time. Inside were an old man and an old woman who had devoted their lives to caring for the cave. They both looked like prehistoric cave dwellers. Their gray hair was very long, never combed but twisted into long unkempt strands. Their faces were dusty and their minimal clothing looked like rags. They were cooking something over a wood fire. I asked permission to take a picture of these two priests choosing to live as austerely as possible in a holy cave, keeping devotion alive for their guru. But photos were not allowed.

The rest of the day we spent visiting the different rooms where Ramana Maharshi had lived and spent time with his devotees.

Bubba really enjoyed integrating with those places. It was obvious He wasn't just curious; rather He was re-Empowering each room.

All the devotees at the ashram acknowledged Bubba with real respect. Whenever He passed any devotees, they would bow to Him. It was more than the usual Indian salutation—they would stay in their bow after He passed, continuing to feel Him. There was a real sensitivity to Bubba by all the Ramana Maharshi devotees.

One day Bubba wanted to see some photographs of Ramana Maharshi and one of the ashram staff was happy to oblige. While Bubba was looking at various photographs, gnats began to bother Him. I got a hand fan and waved them away, the moving air cooling my Beloved Guru at the same time. This was the first of many times that I would fan my Beloved Guru. The physical gesture of serving Him so directly was a heart-felt, joyful feeling.

Another day an elderly bedridden devotee sent word asking Bubba to please visit him, just so he could meet Him. In the man's room, Bubba asked about his experience with Ramana Maharshi while he was alive. After a while, Bubba just sat silently, Blessing Ramana Maharshi's devotee. When Bubba left his room the man was sitting up, looking bright, obviously enlivened by the strength of Bubba's Divine Presence.

Since it was the custom to walk around holy places, one morning Bubba told me we would walk around Arunachala hill. He said "only once, though," as this walk was eight miles long. He told me to take the camera bag. I lightened the bag as much as possible, since it was heavy when full.

The walk was quite easy, allowing Bubba to give His Blessing Regard to Arunachala hill from all sides. Halfway around the hill was a famous ancient temple. As Bubba entered, He asked me to take some pictures inside. I told Him that I couldn't, because I had left the heavy flash equipment at the ashram.

He said, "Who told you to do that?"

I said, "I didn't think I'd need it."

"Don't think!" He said. "Whenever a person only uses his mind to decide on something he always tends to make the wrong decision."

This was true for me. Throughout the trip, whenever I would decide something on my own, it eventually turned out to be wrong.

On Arunachala hill at Ramana Maharshi's Ashram

Bubba said, "You have to begin to doubt your mind and live from the point of view of intuition."

Each night Bubba climbed a little way up Arunachala before sundown to sit on some rocks and enjoy the natural beauty. It was a very beautiful place, overlooking the ashram and the distant villages. Those evenings on Arunachala were particularly enjoyable to me, for the intensity of the day's activities had slowed down and we could just relax and talk. Bubba was showing such a simple and fully enjoyable aspect of His Love.

I took a lot of photos of Bubba on that holy hill. At one point as I was focusing, Bubba kept moving. I asked Him to please stay still so I could get the best photos. He humorously answered, "I don't pose."

Bubba said Ramana Maharshi was a sage, the third type of teacher, along with yogis and saints. He said, "Ramana Maharshi's

In the courtyard of Arunachaleshwara Temple
near Ramana Maharshi's Ashram

work was the purification of the Heart—the Self—but he, in fact, transcended even that limitation. His force could be felt in the chest to the right. Ramana Maharshi lived as the True Self to his devotees."

We stayed at Sri Ramanasramam for three days, then we left for Sri Aurobindo's ashram and Auroville.

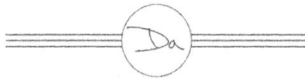

The Great Banyan Tree

On our way to Sri Aurobindo's ashram we visited the Theosophical Society in Madras, where reputedly one of the largest banyan trees in the world was still growing. It was recorded as being 450 years old with aerial root coverage of 60,000 square meters. When the Divine Master, Bubba Free John, stood approximately at the middle, the tree was so large that the extended edges of the root system were too far away to be seen. Standing within the tree's root system felt like being in a forest with hundreds of trees.

Bubba commented on how magnificent the tree was and showed great pleasure as He walked around some of the central roots, seeming to be very impressed by the grandeur of life the tree expressed. He kept touching the roots with His cane, obviously Blessing and Empowering this magnificent life-form for all who would come to see and enjoy its natural splendor.

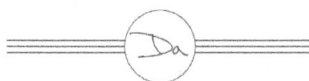

Sri Aurobindo

AUGUST 1973

We traveled to Sri Aurobindo's ashram. When we arrived a few ladies were placing multicolored flower petals in beautiful, delicate designs on Sri Aurobindo's tomb. Sri Aurobindo had dropped the body some years before (December 5, 1950), and his successor, known as "the Mother", was now near death, so Bubba didn't have a chance to meet and directly Bless either of them. A devotee representative of the ashram was our guide for two days. He was a nice man, very enthusiastic about his guru, but he didn't stop talking about Sri Aurobindo's teaching for a minute, one quote after another. Bubba didn't feel the man expressed real understanding, just that he exercised his memory, remaining immune to the requirements of self-transcending spiritual practice.

Our guide took us to Auroville, a futuristic self-sustaining community, and expounded on the principles of that lifestyle. To enter, a person would have to surrender all material possessions and would then be provided with all the practical necessities of daily life from the community. Bubba said the concept of Auroville was correct as long as the purpose of being there was God-Realization. He said He didn't feel that happening at Auroville.

The last day of our trip our guide came to our hotel to say goodbye. He joined us for breakfast, but didn't stay, because when he began quoting his gurus, Bubba would have none of it and stopped him in his tracks. Bubba told him directly that he had not been changed by his gurus, or by their teaching. All he had were quotes that made no difference. He told the man that Sri Aurobindo and the Mother's teaching was based on seeking rather than Realization. Bubba addressed the man's protective stance and what he needed to do to go beyond the limits of his gurus. He said, "There is no genuine relationship to God in a community of seekers."

Our guide had become our friend, but he was shaken up by Bubba's criticism, and had no quotes to respond with. At his first chance, he made his apologies and told us he had to run. Bubba was direct and straight with him. His comments could have served our friend, but I don't think he understood any of it.

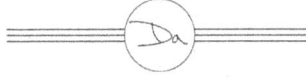

Sri Ramakrishna

AUGUST 1973

In Calcutta we visited Sri Ramakrishna's ashram. As soon as we arrived Bubba headed directly for the bedroom where Sri Ramakrishna had slept. As we approached, Bubba said it was very important to take a photo of this room. However, a large sign outside the bedroom said "No Photos Allowed" and an attendant at the door was obviously there to make sure everything that happened inside was honorable and appropriate.

Bubba entered with several people. He bowed and then sat on the floor in front of Ramakrishna's bed. I knew it was very important to Him that I take a photo, so I hid the camera under my shirt, entered, then sat at the rear of the room. The room filled with about fifteen other people. Everyone sat quietly on the floor.

As I sat I remembered another time when I wasn't able to take photos because I had left the flash equipment in our room, and how disturbed my Heart-Master was about that because of its effect on His ongoing Blessing Work. So I felt: *I have to take this photo without fail.*

While Bubba was doing His Blessing Work with Sri Ramakrishna and everyone else was meditating, I had a functional mission to accomplish. I secretly set the manual settings on the camera, then waited until it felt like everyone was in deep meditation. My plan was to sit upright, quickly lift the camera above the heads of those in front of me, and without delay I would press the button. To cover the noise of the camera shutter I felt I had to cough loudly. Then immediately I would have to pull the camera down and hide it under my shirt. I thought through the plan in detail, even visualized the angle the camera had to be pointed to get the full view of the room.

When it felt right I took the photo, coughed, and immediately sat quietly again. No one, not even the attendant at the door, did anything that suggested they noticed anything other than my loud cough. Apparently the sound of my cough covered the sound of the camera shutter. As to the flash attachment, which was necessary, maybe the bright flash of light felt like a spiritual experience.

Since I had to just point and shoot—it would have been too noticeable to look through the camera viewfinder—I wondered if I had got the camera angle right. I decided I had done it too fast and may not have gotten both beds in the shot. I felt I had to do it again.

The second time I concentrated on the angle of the camera and repeated the procedure. Again, no one seemed to notice anything other than my loud cough. But I had done it the second time so fast, I still wasn't confident that the camera angle was right. My challenge was that this was a photo my Heart-Master really wanted. I understood something of the great importance of Bubba's relationship with Sri Ramakrishna so I decided I had to get the photo right, therefore I needed to do it again!

The third time I addressed everything: *This has to be right!* Imagine meditating in a sacred space and someone is loudly coughing. Every time I coughed everyone in the room got disturbed and moved a bit. After the third time, many of the people turned to look at me. I'm sure they felt I could have covered my cough, that I was being totally insensitive.

As soon as we left Sri Ramakrishna's bedroom Bubba asked, "What was all that loud coughing about?" I said I was taking photos. "You were?" He asked, smiling. But I could tell He was wishing I could have done it without disturbing everyone. My attitude was to serve my Beloved Guru, do whatever it took, to put Him first, while taking everything else into account as best I could.

From there we walked past Sri Ramakrishna's Kali Temple and left for the Ramakrishna-Vivekananda Mission at Belur Math where Bubba visited the tombs of some of Ramakrishna's devotees. Bubba said that Sri Ramakrishna's ashram was a great place. He told me that Ramakrishna's Realization was that of a saint; his qualities were love and devotion. But, Bubba said, he had transcended a saint's limitations. His force could be felt in the crown chakra.[12] To his devotees Ramakrishna was a devotee of God.

---

12. Crown chakra is the subtle energy center at the top of the head.

Outside Sri Ramakrishna's bedroom

After leaving Ramakrishna's ashram, Bubba said His Work on that trip in India was over and the rest of the trip would be for pleasure.

As to the photos, all three shots turned out. It seemed that the camera lens had a wider exposure than I realized. And the important thing was I had done the service my Guru had asked of me.

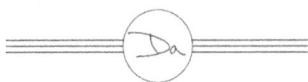

Two Malas

AUGUST 1973

As we left Sri Ramakrishna's ashram heading for our taxi, I noticed a flower stand. I wanted to give my Beloved Guru a gift, and a flower mala was perfect.

He was walking quickly. I told Him I'd be right there and ran to the flower stand. As it turned out, they didn't have any flower malas already made. So I chose to stay and wait for them to make me one, hoping it would be fast. But it turned out to be a slow process.

By the time I got to the taxi with the mala, my Beloved Guru had been waiting for quite a while and asked, "What took you so long?"

I gave Him the mala and said, "I was waiting to get this for You."

The incident revealed my superficial attitude that the object must be the gift, rather than the gift of my feeling sensitivity to the Master and my focus on serving His needs. Bubba's response to my "gift" was Instructive. He threw the mala on the shelf behind the back seat and told the taxi to leave. By the time we arrived at our hotel, the sun through the rear window had been baking the flowers until they had become mush, completely decayed. I removed the pieces and threw them away.

This incident was in sharp contrast to the gift of the sandalwood mala I gave my Heart-Master at Baba Muktananda's ashram. He had carried that mala in His shoulder bag throughout the trip until He placed it on Ramana Maharshi's Murti in Skandashram on Arunachala hill.

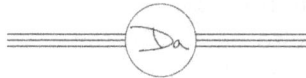

Benares and the Ganges

AUGUST 1973

We continued from Sri Ramakrishna's ashram in Calcutta to Benares. Upon arriving, Bubba said to get two bicycle-driven carriages to take us to the Benares house of the Raja of Bhor. Bubba's carriage went first and mine followed. I really enjoyed seeing His orange cap bobbing above the back of His carriage. He kept looking back to make sure I was still there, smiling each time.

At one point Bubba stopped at a traffic junction and my carriage pulled up next to His. He gave me a sly look, as if leaning out of a car window to say, "Pretty good lookin' buggy you got there! Ya wanna drag?" I raised my hand as if holding a stick over my driver and said, "Let's go." We both laughed as we raced down the road . . . naturally, with the Heart-Master in the lead!

At one point, a small Indian boy, about thirteen or fourteen, approached me and in broken English asked where we were from. He said he welcomed us to his town and offered to show us around. I didn't know Bubba's plans, so I declined and the boy disappeared. But Bubba's bike driver was faster than mine and after a few more turns I lost sight of Him.

The streets were crowded; it wasn't a good place to be lost! Then to my great surprise, the boy appeared again and said, "Your friend went that way," and he led me to Him. I felt my Divine Master's influence watching out for me, and I was also very grateful to the boy.

After a while it turned out our two drivers didn't know where the house was. Again the boy appeared and this time brought us directly to the house. Bubba told the boy to meet us there in the morning before sunrise to take us to the Ganges River. The boy was pleased and said he would.

The Raja of Bhor's room was quite bare, with only two mattresses on the floor and a couple of pillows stacked in a corner. There was no shower, but we could wash with a bucket of water. The day had been very hot and dusty, so at the first opportunity Bubba washed. While kneeling by a bucket of water, with soap on

On the Ganges in Benares

His face, He laughed and said, "The two best things in the world are Darshin and washin'."

Early the next morning the boy came and led us down narrow winding streets to the edge of the Ganges. On our way we passed a small temple. There was practically no way of telling it was a temple because its walls looked like every other wall in the narrow street. Bubba stopped for a moment and said, "This is a good place." Then we continued our walk to the Ganges. Later He said, "That temple was the best spiritual place in Benares."

Bubba had the boy arrange a boat to take us on the river. The boat moved slowly down the Ganges while the sun was rising. The Divine Master seemed so content. He fully enjoyed the ride, Blessing the river, everything around it, and everything about it.

The next day the boy returned as Bubba suggested. He brought us to two famous temples, the "Golden Temple", with its golden dome and the "Monkey Temple". The boy then took us to his uncle's and his sitar teacher's homes, where Bubba bought some antique paintings, thankas, and some fabrics. He knew what to look for, always able to separate the real from the fake.

One day when we returned to the room, I wanted to work on my camera and needed to open a metal container. It was stuck and wouldn't open! I tried and tried. Then in my frustration, I smashed it against the floor, both to force it open and to vent my anger. Bubba was standing nearby and immediately after I smashed the box, He kicked me hard in the butt.

171

I turned fast without thinking and spontaneously said, "What did You do that for?" Then I immediately realized I was out of line and swallowed a few times. My Beloved Guru said, "You must deal with karma as it arises. You shouldn't let it accumulate."

His kick was the consequence that relieved the karma of my action. Immediately I was shocked out of my reactivity over the unopened can. Frustration and anger vanished; the karma was resolved. I thanked my Beloved Guru for the lesson.

We spent three days in Benares and the boy helped every day. During the second day I asked if he expected something from us for his help. He said he just wanted to show us around and was totally unconcerned about money. I took his response to mean that he was a good-hearted person spontaneously responding to the Divine Master, Bubba Free John. But then at the end of the day he asked, "Could you give me some money for my day?"

I gave him a little in gratitude for his service and he said, "Tomorrow I'll show you around, and you shouldn't give me any more money; you've given me enough."

The next day the boy said, "I don't want any money, but maybe you'll give me something of your personal possessions, by which I can remember you." His colors were beginning to show. Anything we had from America was worth much more than the few rupees I would have given him. So his request for a personal possession was a practiced strategy.

When I told Bubba, He said, "Give him a handshake." He wasn't interested in reinforcing the boy's con. Instead of money or possessions, Bubba gave him a lesson, as the true Guru always does.

That evening was unbelievably hot. Bubba didn't sleep at all. In the morning He said, "That was the most uncomfortable night of My life." He said He had felt that His skin was turning inside out and that He could barely breathe all night. But as He was telling me this, He was laughing. He always showed He was free of attachment, even to His own bodily suffering.

He said, "The pores of My skin were closing during the night."

I asked, "Did You do something to stop it?"

He said, "Since I am the body, I felt the closed pores and opened them."

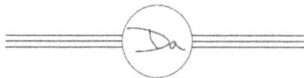

Gautama Buddha

AUGUST 1973

From Benares we went to Sarnath, where Gautama Buddha established his ashram. We went to the grand stupas (stone mounds), where Gautama met his disciples and gave his first sermon. We also visited the famous "Deer Park" where deer were still being cared for.

In the main temple at Sarnath, Bubba's Enlightened State Blessed the Buddha shrine. Outside the temple was a Bodhi tree, which supposedly was grown from a cutting of the original Bodhi tree at the site of Gautama's Realization. And on the ashram grounds were the ruins of the main building where Gautama's monks once lived.

Enclosed in a protective shelter, a sign explained that the four foot section of the marble pillar on display was part of the main pillar in one of the earliest Buddhist temples. The words on it were carved during Gautama's lifetime. The alphabet was ancient and no longer in use. When Bubba saw the markings He said that earlier in His life He had been spontaneously moved to write in an unfamiliar alphabet. He said, "These markings were of that same alphabet!" Beloved Guru Bubba laughed and raised His eyebrows, seeming to suggest, "Could it be?"

Though Bubba was playful about recognizing the unfamiliar alphabet, the fact that He did recognize it was proof, in my view, that He was there when the pillar was in use during Gautama Buddha's lifetime. Considering Bubba's Divine State, He wouldn't have been a devotee of the Buddha. He would have been Gautama Buddha Himself. (Bubba had said that He had appeared in the form of all great Realizers over all time. He had said that He is the Consciousness they Realized.)

Before we left the ashram, we visited a museum of Buddhist statues and paintings. The first statue ever made of Gautama was on display. Bubba considered another statue in the museum the best image of the Buddha He had ever seen. The statue expressed something of the Enlightened State of the Buddha.

One of the rooms in another temple was painted with images of Gautama's life, covering all the walls and the ceiling, depicting all his important Leelas. Bubba liked everything about that room and said of the wall, "Someday My devotees will do one like this of Me."

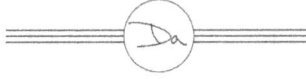

At the base of Dhamekh Stupa at Sarnath

Kathmandu, Nepal

AUGUST 1973

From Sarnath we traveled to Kathmandu, Nepal. We arrived on a festival day and everyone was dressed in their celebration clothes. Red, the dominant color everywhere, was a very popular color for ladies' saris and Bubba commented on the beauty of the Nepalese women. It was impressive how, wherever I looked, people were crowded into the many temples and hundreds of people were sitting on all the temple steps.

Tibetan Buddhism is the main spiritual tradition in Nepal. Each temple had many prayer wheels that one should turn prior to entering, sending prayers with each turn. Each temple steeple had two "eyes" that gave me the feeling that a greater Reality was present and watching.

At one temple we met some monks and Bubba purchased a few rudraksha bead malas that had been previously used by now-deceased monks.

We also met with a Tibetan refugee who had been assigned by the Dalai Lama to establish a carpet weaving business in Nepal to support Tibet. Bubba liked many of the carpets, especially the tiger rugs, which are a traditional sign of the guru's fierceness regarding the ego-"I". (In later years our ashram purchased carpets from that source.)

The following morning we rose early and hired a taxi to take us to a special hill where Bubba could view the Himalayas and see Mount Everest. We were told there would only be a few minutes to see Mount Everest before the morning clouds would cover its peak. On the way there, the taxi had a flat tire. We still had plenty of time, so Bubba walked up the hilly road and around a bend while the tire was being replaced. While He was gone, a passing car stopped to help.

After a few minutes, the Divine Master Bubba Free John reappeared walking down the road toward us. It was before daybreak on this remote road heading into the Nepalese mountains. He was wearing white clothes, as He did throughout the trip, to reflect the

176

Sunrise on mountaintop in Nepal

hot sun. When the woman from the other car saw Him, she excitedly exclaimed, "Look at Him! He looks just like a guru coming out of the Himalayas!"

"He is!" I told her. Her spontaneous impression was absolutely correct.

The driver took us to the hill and pointed out the path to the top. From the summit, Bubba had a panoramic view of the fantastic mountains and beautiful countryside. The sun was just rising, Bubba was facing it, and as it washed over His body, it illumined His Sublime Blissfulness. He was sitting on top of the world facing Mount Everest and the rising sun, Transmitting His Divine State to Awaken everyone and everything, everywhere. The hilltop felt like a Heavenly domain. I took many photos of the Divine Master's ecstasy that morning.

Bubba only saw the peak of Mount Everest for a few moments before the morning clouds covered it, though He did see much of the great mountain looming below the high cloudbank. While there, a Nepalese peasant came and began to play his bowed instrument (which looked like a simple violin) and chant softly. It was a beautiful form of honoring the new day. It was fully appropriate that soft, happy music was being played and sung as the world received the Divine Master's Transcendental Regard.

Soon a French couple arrived. It turned out that hill was actually a popular tourist spot and we were fortunate to have arrived before others came. The French couple fully enjoyed themselves. They probably attributed their pleasure to the environment and the music, but I have no doubt that Bubba Free John's Radiant Presence was a big factor in their delight. As they were leaving, they asked the man if they could purchase his violin in remembrance of the wonderful event on this beautiful hill.

He seemed to hesitate to sell his personal instrument. So back and forth the conversation went until he agreed to part with it, reluctantly (for a higher price than the couple originally offered). After the couple left, to my surprise and amusement, he took out another violin and began playing and singing again! He was a violin salesman with a good business on this beautiful, remote Nepalese hilltop.

Bubba was concentrated in His Sacred Work and didn't see the interaction between the musician and the couple. When I told Him what had happened, He was greatly amused.

Originally Bubba had planned to stay for a few days in Nepal, but when we returned to our hotel room later that morning, He said, "Now, here's My plan . . . "

We left the hotel within twenty minutes and caught a flight just before it pulled out.

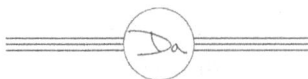

The Taj Mahal

SEPTEMBER 1973

From Kathmandu we headed for Agra and the Taj Mahal.

The Taj Mahal, one of the great wonders of the world, is the finest example of Mughal architecture. The white marble structure with its four pillars, round domes, and intricate design is a wonder to behold.

A long pool leads to the entrance steps. The white marble walls are finely inlaid with precise designs of beautiful colored stones and carved with intricate patterns. There are beautiful corridors designed for aesthetic effect only, ending at delicately carved marble screens. The high-domed main room gives a feeling of open space within the marble structure. On a lower level, the white marble tombs of Shah Jahan and his wife Mumtaz Mahal are surrounded with more wonderful marble screens. To walk within the Taj Mahal is to be within a structure of profound beauty.

At the Taj Mahal

Leaving the Taj Mahal

Bubba's appreciation of the Taj Mahal was very noticeable. It was also obvious that the Divine Master was giving it His Blessing Regard, as He did the temples and ashrams throughout India.

Bubba said, "The Taj Mahal deserves its reputation—it is one of the most beautiful buildings in the world." He went on to say, "While it's built of marble and is impressive in size, it shows no weight. Its overall lines and balance are free of any heaviness."

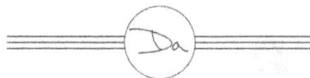

Tapas in India

Often during the trip, Bubba would be quiet for long periods. I knew that His primary purposes on this trip were His Transcendental Blessing Work and the purification of karma. Even so, in my self-contracted state I tended to take His silence personally. My pattern was to feel rejected, then He would say something, or smile, or somehow relate to me, and immediately I felt loved and happy again.

One day this cycle kept happening over and over: I kept feeling rejected, then loved. However, finally I saw the upside to all this. I realized that my pattern intensified my attention to the Divine—He was my focus whether I was happy or unhappy.

Being that close to the Divine Master every day I constantly felt a strong intensity, one aspect of which was the reflection of my self-contraction. His egoless Presence constantly reflected me to myself. At times I felt anxious or troubled. At other times His intensity increased my love for Him, which transcended my disturbance, allowing me to more deeply feel how happy I was to be with Him and serving Him. My state fluctuated according to my emotional reactions to His absolutely unwavering State of Being.

Bubba said, "Tapas, or the heat of spiritual demand, is caused by the friction of the internal resistance to relationship." He said that His intensity is part of His Gift. "If a person keeps resisting, eventually he will have to leave. The intensity will become too much for him to bear. On the other hand, if a person surrenders to the guru, he will be shown the Divine. Mediocrity, which is everyone's strategy in life, only breeds mediocrity. It's all inappropriate in the face of God and is unacceptable. It must be seen and understood from the point of view of Truth."

Near the end of the trip we were in a taxi when, once again, I became unsettled by His constant intensity. Bubba addressed my disturbance, saying, "When I relate to you and act friendly, like a nice guy, you are happy, but when I give you something of My quality, you react. You must allow yourself to relate to all My qualities. My intensity is there to serve you."

After having returned from India, on one of the occasions when Bubba was telling His devotees about the trip, He said, "There were a few days on the trip during which Jerry was getting very upset. For a few days, I had hardly said anything. He thought there was something wrong, something negative in all that. He began to react. And Jerry is not extraordinary. He is a good example of how everyone tends to relate to the process of spiritual life."

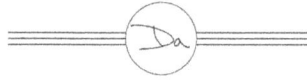

Back to Los Angeles

SEPTEMBER 1973

At the airport in Bombay, as Bubba approached the plane to return to the United States, He commented, "Look at this big Boeing 747 airplane. For what it cost to build this airplane, the entire peasant population of Bombay could be fed for a year."

Once on the plane, I felt exhausted. My exhaustion surprised me, since I hadn't felt tired until I took my seat. I had been so focused on serving my Beloved Guru throughout the trip that I hadn't made rest a priority. Now, with the trip basically over, I deeply relaxed, immediately fell asleep, and slept for the entire flight.

The flight took us to New York, where we briefly visited Bubba's parents. Bubba's father made me feel like I was part of his family, and I felt so comfortable with His mother, Dorothy, that I immediately began calling her "Mom", as Bubba did. She said that Bubba had always been a happy child and told me amusing stories about His childhood.

Upstairs in their house there was a mural on the wall of His sister's bedroom that Bubba had painted as a child; Dorothy wanted to make sure I saw this. It was a city panorama of French streets and cafés, not the least bit childish—stylistically mature and quite detailed. I was very impressed that, as a child, Bubba's art had been so sophisticated. I became immersed in it, feeling heart-joy in seeing His childhood art.

From New York we flew to Los Angeles. When the Divine Heart-Master Bubba Free John arrived at the Los Angeles airport, the entire ashram was there to greet Him. It was definitely the most moving experience of my life. In the presence of His devotees, He became even more Radiant. He once said, "My devotees are the God I have come to serve." As He walked down the ramp to greet everyone that day, He was shining like a million suns. The outpouring

Arriving at Los Angeles International Airport

of love for their Beloved Master by all of His devotees made me cry with joy.

When asked by His devotees about the purpose of the India trip, Bubba said, "Well, one of the reasons for going to India was to purify the karmas of this Work. In the past, I've gone to India for the sake of sadhana in My own case. My purpose for going there this time had nothing to with that. It was entirely for the sake of the Work. There were certain contacts that needed to be made, certain sacrifices that needed to be made, certain things that I knew had to be done for the sake of this Work, and until they were done, I could not be full in My Teaching function. But those things are done now, and many of the qualities of My Teaching Work that I suppressed before will become manifest."

And so His Work as Bubba Free John began—the Teaching Revelation characterized by His Submission to unprepared devotees. In His Master-Work, *The Aletheon*, He wrote of this time:

In the entire history of the Great Tradition of humankind, there are no complete precedents for My Divine Avataric Work of Teaching-Revelation—because the Moment had not previously existed for an Adept to Work As I Did. All the Adepts, each in his or her time and place, have Worked as they should have. However, My Divine Avataric Work of Teaching-Revelation Coincided with a unique Time—and, therefore, the Accomplishing-Powers of My Divine Avataric Self-Manifestation, and (Thus and Thereby) My Divine Avataric Teaching-Revelation, were Required and Enabled to Be Uncommon and Unusual. ("Then and Now and You and The Bright", *The Aletheon*, 2009 edition, 1871.)

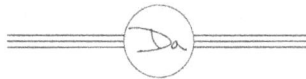

Fill It Up

When my Beloved Master invited me to accompany Him and attend to His needs during His India trip, He had said, "It will serve your practice." And so it had. The entire time was a constant demand to keep surrendering, through self-understanding of my act of separation, to deeper and deeper recognition of His egoless Enlightened State.

During those five weeks of serving my Beloved Guru, He never gave me time for myself—no time to hang out, to be mediocre, to be lazy and do nothing. His demand for service based on devotional recognition was for me to be attentive to Him and keep turning to Him, contemplating Him twenty-four hours a day, seven days a week, while also fulfilling practice requirements. Thus all my actions could become service. This great lesson profoundly intensified the devotional relationship to my Beloved Heart-Guru.

I also learned how such constant turning and service allowed for self- transcendence, while at times bringing up the heat of self-resistance (tapas). It all served greater self-understanding. His lesson given was vividly clear: The ego-act is a perpetual-motion machine and will not stop on its own. Only His Free Attractiveness, His constant requirement that I give Him my devotional attention, His clear, straightforward Word of Instruction, and His profound Gift of Spiritual Transmission kept turning my feeling surrender to Him instead of staying locked into the addiction of self-absorption.

Once we returned to Los Angeles the circumstance dramatically changed, since all of His students were now there to serve their Beloved Guru and be served by Him. I no longer was the only one. While in His Blessing Company day and night in India, His egoless Presence carried me. He was a constant demand and, at the same time, being with Him made my deeper response possible. I definitely missed that intensity and the assumed exclusive intimacy. On the other hand I also felt the opportunity to relax and sit back, out of His direct demand.

Before we left for India, the Divine Master had decided that the Melrose Ashram was too small, since the gathering of devotees around Him had grown to over sixty. He confirmed that a larger location on La Brea Avenue, just one block away, would be a better site. While we were in India the devotees had moved the ashram from Melrose Avenue to La Brea Avenue.

Shortly after we returned from India, Bubba was talking about the trip with a few students in the new La Brea Ashram. I was hanging out, lazily listening from a distance. When Bubba noticed my mediocre preference, He picked up His car keys and tossed them to me saying, "Go fill it up."

I was surprised. I had been enjoying just hanging out. His demand was a wake-up call. As I left to put gas in His car, I understood that He was calling me to always engage the same intensity of practice that the India trip had required.

Over time it became perfectly clear that everything Bubba Free John did in India, including Teaching me how to respond to His Divine Presence, was not just for me, but for the sake of all beings, by establishing His egoless State in this ego-based realm, and revealing what is truly required for self-transcendence.

Divine Consciousness, Radiant as Love-Bliss appeared in the bodily human Form of the Divine Heart-Master to Accomplish the realignment of humanity with the True and Prior Reality of everything and everyone.

Two Gifts:
The Second Gift

NOVEMBER 3, 1973

Bubba's birthday was soon to arrive on November 3, 1973. My intimate partner had found a beautiful antique box to give as a birthday present. But for a while I was stymied: *What could I give my Beloved Guru?*

Then it came to me: While serving Bubba in India, I had a beautiful rudraksha seed mala made at Baba Muktananda's ashram. It had small, very high-quality beads strung with gold wire. My intention was to use it in meditation for the rest of my life. But then I felt, *My Beloved Heart-Guru is my meditation. The mala is just a tool.*

In heart-gratitude for His Blessings I placed the mala in one of the three drawers of the antique box and we gave our Beloved Guru the box with the mala enclosed as a gift from the two of us.

The next day Bubba told us the gift we gave Him was "the best gift I got all year."

What an immeasurable gift to us!

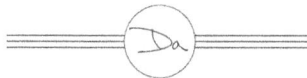

Lunch Righteousness

NOVEMBER 1973

Bubba said that we should follow His Instructions as devotional, ego-transcending discipline, bringing self-understanding and a heart-surrendered disposition to whatever resistance we might feel. But after the second ten-day fast back in May, as we got back to our vegetarian diet, we misinterpreted our Beloved Guru's Instructions regarding diet. Instead of bringing self-transcendence and self-understanding to the eating of food, we became purists, fanatical about food.

Feeling we were conforming to our Beloved Guru's Instructions, we started holding on to dietary rules as if they were the law. No food was bought without a detailed scrutiny of the label. If there was any salt or sugar in a product, even in bread, that made it unacceptable. When we went out to eat, certainly there couldn't be any meat, poultry, or fish, but did the vegetables have MSG, pepper, sugar, or salt? Whoever waited on us was even asked about the spices; we considered if they were tamasic, rajasic, or sattvic (depressing, stimulating, or balancing). If not sattvic, we asked to have the spices changed. Did the drinks or desserts have sugar or synthetic sweeteners? If the answer was "yes" the chef was asked to make our food without those ingredients. If the chef couldn't or wouldn't agree to our request, we simply had to leave.

Since we were righteous vegetarians, we started criticizing others for killing living things other than fruits and vegetable for food. We became quite self-righteous about our diet. And proud of it—after all, what could be more holy than following Bubba's direct Instructions?

At different times during this period, we mentioned things to Bubba about how we were completely honoring His Instructions, proudly giving Him details about our food saintliness. For many weeks, He didn't say anything. Eventually, however, in His exquisite timing, He addressed our fanaticism in a talk He called "Lunch

Righteousness". The two paragraphs below are from a later talk where He also spoke about this time:

Devotees, just as people anywhere else in the world, tend to take on the point of view of "lunch righteousness". Right away all kinds of goals for diet and physical life become very fascinating. For a period of several months when I first spoke about this vegetarian diet and we began to use it every day, practically every time a devotee came to Me, I was asked some questions about the diet. All everybody wanted to talk about was the diet. The questions were endless! People had become obsessed with it—yet it was only lunch!

Just as you must be free of self-indulgence and all its goals, you must be equally free of the cult of discipline, the form of righteousness that appears whenever you fulfill a discipline. Feeling self-conscious and modest while drinking a little mint tea with friends who are drinking coffee is so small, so narrow and tacky. It is the product of that motivated cult of discipline in which there is no freedom, no fundamental humor, no real comprehension of the importance of daily events—just foolish concerns for purity of diet when people are murdering one another with every movement of their minds. All that obsessive concern for diet is inappropriate. What is appropriate is just a natural, fundamental awareness of what you eat. ("Diet Is Not the Key to Salvation", *The Yoga of Right Diet*, 2006 edition, 31.)

It was often Bubba's way to let us fully establish and demonstrate our patterns in response to His Instruction, as He did regarding food. Then when He revealed how self-involved we were, we could fully feel the criticism. His Words about "lunch righteousness" addressed something we clearly felt, and they directly served our self-understanding. Dietary discipline is an integral aspect of Adidam, but Beloved Adi Da also always calls for the tendency to "lunch righteousness" to be observed and understood.

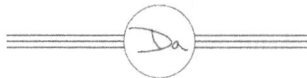

Balboa Island

NOVEMBER 1973

One of our Beloved Guru's students invited a few of us to join her for a weekend at her family's summer home on Balboa Island, which is part of the city of Newport Beach in California. We all happily agreed and began looking forward to an enjoyable time together. When we told Bubba of our plans, He asked, "Who is going?" We told Him the names of the four couples and He responded, "Have a great time, I'll see you all on Monday."

We left midday on Friday and arrived at the Balboa house a couple of hours later. Once there, we considered where we'd sleep, and then we relaxed in the living room enjoying good company. That evening we got a call from one of Bubba's attendants. She said, "Bubba wanted to know if you are having a nice time." We told her to tell Him it's great, the house is very nice, and the island is beautiful. We could hear her relaying our comments to our Guru. A moment later she said, "Bubba wants to know if He can join you." We were thrilled and extended our enthusiastic invitation.

Early the following morning, to our total delight, Bubba and His attendants arrived. Two more students, whom He had invited, arrived soon after. It was still early in the morning, so one of the ladies began making pancakes for everyone, using a healthy buckwheat mix. When Bubba tasted a sample of the pancakes, He said something like, "If we are going to have pancakes, I'd rather have good ones. This one turned out like a piece of leather." The cook and everyone else laughed. He asked if someone would go buy some Aunt Jemima pancake mix. The lessons about "lunch righteousness" were taking a new turn! (In fact, His manner of Working altogether was changing in ways that would become more obvious in the coming month.)

When it arrived, the lady who had started making the buckwheat pancakes started to mix the Aunt Jemima batter instead. But then Bubba took over as the master pancake chef. Watching Him cook pancakes was a real delight. He actually tossed them high in the air to flip them on the pan. When they were done cooking, He placed them on a big pile. As He did that, He placed His open hand above each one, clearly Giving His tangible Blessing. After breakfast Bubba suggested the ladies do some shopping for lunch, and invited the men to play touch football with Him in the street. To begin the touch football game, our Beloved Guru defined the rules. He clearly identified the boundaries and the goals. But during the game, when it was to His advantage, He ran outside the stated boundaries to avoid being touched. When challenged, He simply declared those were not the boundaries! The boundaries always changed to fit His Play. He changed the goal posts too, explaining that we all misunderstood where they were.

His Play was such a delight. Spontaneously and arbitrarily, it seemed, He changed the rules to His team's advantage. It was hilarious. No one believed His explanations about the changed rules, but that wasn't the point. Clearly this game wasn't about winning. For me, it was about enjoying the relationship to the Divine Being and submitting to His Play, even though it was outrageous from a conventional point of view.

In His early "Teaching-Submission" with people, Bubba did things to reflect us to ourselves. He thus initiated the process of self-observation, which led to self-understanding, and the essential ground for self-transcendence in the Free State prior to separation. Bubba's Sublime Love-Bliss-State was the constant counterpoint to our observation of our egoity. His confrontation with "John" illustrates the point.

Apart from changing the rules, Bubba also challenged many calls. For example, when someone on His team was touched with two hands as the rules required, He contested saying only one hand had touched. Those on His team always supported His challenges. But at one point, "John" on the opposing team got quite disturbed that none of the rules held. In his reaction he came up close to Bubba and yelled at Him.

We all stopped in our tracks, stunned by our friend's angry, aggressive reaction. It was shocking that he was yelling at our Beloved Guru. But Bubba gave his disturbance no support. He simply laughed and said, "A rule is a rule. Who's got the ball?" With no support for his dramatization, all "John" had was a sense of his own contracted state.

When the ladies returned from shopping, the football game ended. Bubba suggested we all go to the beach. We walked on the beach with Him and enjoyed watching our Guru looking and commenting about creatures in the tide pools. Then we followed Him to the swings at a playground area where He swung for a while. From there we all went with Bubba into town. He wanted to see if there were any shops of interest. While walking down the main street He passed by an ice cream shop. We were all close behind. He stopped in His tracks, back-stepping without turning around to look in the ice cream shop window. Then He turned to us and asked, "Does anyone want ice cream?"

We all modestly ordered single scoop ice cream cones, but when Bubba got to the counter, He ordered an ice cream soda. Immediately we cancelled our cone orders and ordered ice cream sodas, hot fudge sundaes, and banana splits!

While eating the ice cream, Bubba commented about the consoling taste of milk and sugar. We all had been studying diet and knew the negatives concerning dairy and sugar. But we were so happy being with our Heart-Guru, it felt like more than just an indulgence.

When we returned to the cottage, Bubba suggested we all play touch football, this time the men against the women. The light of day was changing, but there was still time for a game. At one point, when it was getting dark enough for the street lights to be on, Bubba threw a long pass to one of His teammates. The pass went up above the street lights and out of sight into the darkness. Bubba was yelling, "Run!" and the intended receiver kept running as fast as he could with no idea where the football was, his arms extended. To the amazement of all, the ball came right down into his arms. A perfect throw! Or was it a miracle? The night was setting in and the game was over. Bubba brought us into the cottage to sit around the fireplace. We sat quietly, immersed in His Divine Presence while gazing into the fire.

Later in the evening Bubba offered another form of physical contact: He challenged us all to leg wrestling. In the competition,

His strong, grounded stance was unbeatable. It was very impressive how He secured His Energy to the ground and couldn't be moved. Those who tried wrestling Him ended up on the living room floor, while the Divine Guru was still standing strong.

The following morning Bubba and His attendants left early. We were all profoundly affected by the heart-felt time with our Beloved Guru.

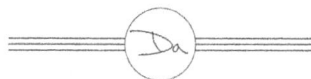

The Book Inscription

When Bubba Free John's recently published book *The Method of the Siddhas* was first in our hands, my intimate partner asked Bubba if He would sign my copy. In response, the Divine Guru wrote the following:

> Dear Jerry,
> I have come into this world
> for the sake of my devotees,
> those who are mine. The
> highest responsibility of men
> is Satsang, to live in the
> condition of relationship, the
> condition of the Heart, the
> company of the Self, the Guru.
> The essential responsibility of
> the Guru is Satsang, to live
> the Heart to his friends.
> The highest responsibility of
> those who live this Satsang
> is to make it available to others.
> > Love,
> > Bubba
> > Christmas 1973

I was overwhelmed and surprised by the generosity of His Gift. In those few words, He expressed the essence of the Way of the Heart. The words He penned in my book were a perfect example of His commitment to all beings: "I offer you a relationship, not a technique."

A copy of His holy handwriting is shown on the next page.

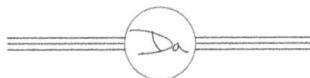

Dear Jerry,

I have come into this world for the sake of my devotees, those who are mine. The highest responsibility of men is Satsang, to live in the condition of relationship, the condition of the Heart, the company of the Self, the Guru. The essential responsibility of the Guru is Satsang, to live the Heart to his friends. The highest responsibility of those who live this Satsang is to make it available to others.

Love,

Bubba

Christmas 1973

The 70-Year Party

Bubba once said, "No one ever came prepared for spiritual life." Therefore, while in India—in preparation for what He would call His "Submission-Work" of Teaching that would commence after His return to California—my Beloved Heart-Master took the name "Bubba Free John", meaning "Friend who is Free in God". It would be "Submission-Work" because He had discovered by His early time of Teaching that to write, speak, and embody "high Dharma" did not "work" with us unprepared Westerners. We were not "getting it"—that is, we were not understanding and changing accordingly. We were being intoxicated by the depth of His Wisdom, astonished by His Discourses, overcome by His Humor, we were swooning in the delight of His Enlightened Presence . . . but we were remaining basically unchanged.

Submission-Work meant that He would deal with our egoity on our life-level in order to prepare us for real spiritual life. Metaphorically, Submission-Work was rolling up His sleeves, grabbing a shovel, and getting down in the trenches with us. And at times He would Teach in the likeness of the ancient Avadhoot or Crazy Wisdom traditions, characterized by using unorthodox and surprising means to prepare us beginners.

As mentioned earlier, He explained His Way of Working by saying, "I offer you a relationship, not a technique." The relationship He offered allowed us to participate in His Divine Revelation while He created Teaching incidents for us in familiar human terms. He was clear about what this familiarity was about, explaining, "What I Do is not the way that I Am, but the way that I Teach. What I do is not a reflection of Me, but of you."

The series of events He would call "The 70-Year Party" were a dramatic example of Bubba Free John's heroic Way of Teaching. It began on Friday, December 21, when, to our surprise, Bubba came from His office to sit with us while we were having lunch at the La Brea Ashram.

In the midst of conversation, He commented that most businesses were having Christmas parties on that day. We agreed, but didn't think any more about it. Then our Master and Heart-Friend Bubba suggested we could also do something. He asked if anyone would like to go out to get coffee and donuts. On our strict diet, coffee and donuts were in the "off limits" category called "accessories", and were only to be indulged, if at all, on a special occasion, such as a birthday.

Someone ran out and returned in just a few minutes with the coffee and donuts. While enjoying the sweet treat and the stimulating drink, Bubba asked about other devotees who weren't with us. When He was told one of them was at a company Christmas party, Bubba had us call him to see how it was going. When He heard the devotee was having champagne at the party, Bubba opened an even more surprising celebratory vista. He said, "If he can have champagne, we can at least have beer—since champagne is too expensive for our budget!"

He asked if someone would go get beer and cigarettes. And while out there, they should bring back some Pink's hot dogs! (Pink's was a well-known hot dog stand just next door.) We all gave our requests for the condiments we wanted on our hot dogs and someone left to fill our orders.

At that time we had been studying Bubba's Word about True Happiness and the error of seeking for it, which He would later summarize in saying, "You cannot become Happy, you can only be Happy." Bubba's suggestions of all these "accessories" definitely aroused our self-indulgent tendencies. It was a perfect example of the value of a Teaching incident to create the opportunity for self-observation: How "happy" we got with the release of discipline and the opportunity to indulge, clearly not celebrating from the freedom of Prior Happiness in the Divine Reality. Bubba stayed right there with us in the middle of it all, reflecting us to ourselves, serving our observation of our tendencies of active desire and self-indulgence.

Each time a devotee called on the phone, as they would do daily to stay connected to their Heart-Master, they were told we were having a party with Bubba and asked to come as soon as possible. Soon there were about twenty-five devotees in the lunch room, all in a celebratory spirit, drinking beer, eating hot dogs and smoking cigarettes with our Loving Guru and Heart-Friend, Bubba Free John. At the same time, working in His heroic way, Bubba constantly Revealed His Free Divine State.

After a while, Bubba started talking about the way we all were dressed. He very humorously explained how our personal limitations determined the clothing that we were wearing. His descriptions were perfect portraits of the basic self-protected, insecure, fearful, seeking aspects of each of us, and there were a lot of jokes and laughter from Bubba about our reactions to His comments. His Humor loosened our defenses and helped us laugh at our self-images and our reactions to the revelations about them.

Bubba said instead of trying to present an image, why not just relax all our self-imagery? We were willing but didn't know how to just do it. He then said if we understood His comments about clothing as forms of self-protection and self-imagery, why not see what difference it would make by doing something about it? We agreed; but what could we do? We could take off some of our clothing, Bubba suggested. We laughed at first. But then we began to seriously consider the proposition: What if it would be a really good opportunity to gain additional self-understanding? Gradually, then, we all took off clothing until eventually we were undressed.

Bubba made a lot of jokes regarding our concerns about being undressed. He said, "By the way, you were born naked—you just started adding clothing as you got more uptight." This reference to "uptight" was an indication of what was most important about the occasion: Stripped of the self-projection of clothing, we were feeling exposed and vulnerable.

Of course, there were sexual innuendos involved in being naked in mixed company. But we didn't get undressed to get sexually involved; the sexual energy simply seemed normal. The incident released huge, complex energy, but there was nothing erotic about it. Our Heart-Master pointed out that covered and decorated bodies were a lot more erotic than having it all hang out, secrets exposed for all to see. Being in Bubba's Enlightened Company, full of His Divine Humor, our attention was drawn to the Prior

Happiness of His Divine State, away from mere physicality. Any difficulties connected to nakedness were minor in the Brightness of His Presence.

In fact, once we took off our clothing and looked at each other, by the Grace of our Heart-Master we were enabled to return our feeling-attention to Him in His Divine Freedom, instead of getting complicated by mixed feelings and mental projections. His laughter and His Enlightened State of Being carried us beyond our self-concern. With our attention on Him, we simply sat undressed on the floor around our Heart-Master considering His great Wisdom-Teaching and enjoying His wonderful stories. It was so amazing to be with Bubba in His heroic creation of this occasion—beer, cigarettes, hot dogs, nakedness—that being naked lost significance, except that in the sublimity of the occasion there was something liberating about it.

We stayed in the lunch room with Bubba for a couple hours. He spoke on several subjects, then talked to us about sex and intimacy and the taboos society establishes to control people. He explained the main social taboo is basically about preventing ecstasy. He said, "Ecstasy is uncontrolled Bliss," beyond the limits of the self-contracted ego. Someone who is ecstatic is only interested in ecstasy, not concerned about social conformity. When ecstatic, the person is uninterested in being productive in society; thus society's taboos to prevent ecstasy have been established and are so deeply entrenched that we don't recognize them for what they are.

By this time a phone tree message had been sent out for all active devotees to come to the ashram. In the earlier message we said we were having a party with Bubba. This time we didn't say what was happening so we could enjoy the surprised look as they arrived. As they came into the room and saw all their friends sitting naked with their Beloved Guru, their facial expressions were totally hilarious—frozen in disbelief and the whole gamut of astonishment!

Everybody immediately realized if they wanted to stay, they also should take their clothes off, which everyone did voluntarily right away. The newcomers didn't have to go through as much self-concern as the first group about taking off their clothes. But everybody had to go through the process of letting go. Ecstatic submission replaced entrenched patterns of behavior as people fell into celebrating Freedom in the Company of the Divine Person.

When just about everyone was there—about sixty of us—Bubba suggested we all move into the large meeting room. We set up a comfortable couch for Bubba to relax on. He then had us turn dance music on and we began dancing. The party was a great celebration of the happiness of letting go and staying in feeling Communion with Him. He proclaimed it as the beginning of "The 70-Year Party". Once it started, it continued nonstop every day and every night from the weekend before Christmas to the middle of January.

Bubba was there all the time, laughing, talking, and explaining the details of His Teaching of the Way of the Heart, His Gift to us and the world. Devotees also spent a lot of time with each other considering Bubba's Teaching Instructions, inspired by the profound Compassion of His Sacrifice for our spiritual growth.

At night the celebration included dancing and singing in celebration of the Divine Person's Presence in our lives. After the first day, clothing was optional—whatever we felt would serve our fullest availability to Bubba's life-changing Siddhi was taking real effect in our lives.

People went to work when necessary, but then returned to be in Bubba's Blessing Company as soon as possible. Many called in to their jobs giving reasons why they couldn't be there. At night people slept on the floor, on chairs, or anywhere they could, including on my office desk. Bubba was Transmitting His Free Divine State, and in so doing, He was showing that His Enlightened State was not at all affected by His embrace of this new Teaching method. His Divine Freedom carried the celebration. In fact, His State of Being was really what we were celebrating!

One day a devotee gave Bubba a big-brimmed cowboy hat. Bubba loved it and wore it many nights. Seeing Bubba with that hat was a statement to everyone that He was not only our Beloved Guru, and our best and most intimate Heart-Friend, but He was, in truth, one with us, celebrating His Free Nature as each and every one of us. That was the mood of the entire celebration.

Bubba's genius of having the celebration continue unending for so long allowed both negative and positive feelings to come up. It was easy to feel happy around Bubba; His Humor and laughter filled our hearts and drew us close to Him. Simultaneously, the demand for self-understanding and vulnerability was always present. And as the party continued night after night for weeks, staying vulnerable wasn't always easy. In time, everyone got to see that they had a lot of self-concerned emotions and reactive feelings still coming up.

Bubba constantly repeated His Instructions about self-understanding and surrendering everything arising to awareness of the Prior Happiness of Divine Communion with Him. As we did, our concerns fell away. Feeling our self-contraction over against Bubba's profound Presence and Wisdom Teaching and directly addressing what we were feeling were the main dynamics of "The 70-Year Party".

Bubba never gave any support to the dilemma in everyone's life; instead, He gave Instructions on how to transcend it. He explained that the enquiry "Avoiding relationship?" He gave for devotees to use at the time, when used properly, directly turned feeling and attention to His Divine State and transcended the act of self-contraction. Every day of the celebration Bubba explained the importance of self-understanding and serious application of His Teaching.

"The 70-Year Party" was an unimaginable Submission of the Divine Being to seekers unprepared for real spiritual life. Bubba Free John was "in the trenches" with us, Teaching us to observe the self-contraction, to understand and transcend it, and to commune with His Love-Blissful Presence. It was a totally wild, ecstatic, and transformative time. He drew us out of the patterns of our ordinariness and Awakened in us the intuition of our prior state of Divine Happiness.

"The 70-Year Party" continued until Bubba interrupted it by moving the entire ashram to Persimmon, His new Sanctuary in Northern California (now known as the Mountain Of Attention Sanctuary).

Bubba emphasized throughout the celebration, and repeated it many times since, that His Gift is the Awakening to Divine Reality.

The True Way of Liberation sometimes required His "heroic" Teaching, reflecting His devotees to themselves for the sake of self-understanding, surrender, and self-transcendence. It was never about self-indulgence for its own sake. He said of this mode of Teaching, "I was not merely indulging in anything. I was Reflecting and Addressing people relative to their bondage to these things." He demonstrated that His Way was not buttoned down, or puritanical, that He would do whatever was necessary to take us beyond our limits to true spiritual life.

In later years Divine Heart-Master Adi Da Samraj said of His Submission-Work:

No mere "technique"—is going to deal with those illusions. No formulas, prescriptions, idealisms, no ceremonialism—nothing in the mind is going to deal with illusions.

Thus, I necessarily became associated with the characteristics of [My devotees'] bondage, their addictions, their illusions, because of the Unbounded Nature of such Submission. I entered into . . . their "world" of bondage . . . for the sake of Waking people up to the Reality That Transcends conditionality. ("Waking People Up To The Reality That Transcends Conditionality", *I Am Here: A Revelation-History, in Form and Word, of the Divine Avataric Incarnation of Conscious Light,* 2014 edition, 81.)

The Divine Heart-Master's years of Teaching-Submission radically changed in many ways over the years, and came to an end in April 2000. In those twenty-eight years from 1972 to 2000, He Submitted completely, until His Submission Work and Teaching Demonstration fully allowed the Incarnation of His egoless State to be eternally established. That's when His Submission-Work simply ended. From April 12, 2000, to His Passing on November 27, 2008, the Divine Master continued to serve His devotees through Darshan, while calling all to respond in devotional recognition and devotional surrender to His Divine Revelation.

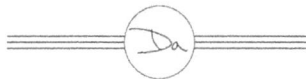

PART THREE

Stories from 1974–1979

Guru Enters Devotee

T he extended time in Bubba's Blessing Company during the "70-Year Party" allowed us more exposure to His egoless Free State, and greatly served our devotional recognition of His Divine Person, our self-understanding, and our self-transcendence. It also was "good company", all of us getting to better know each other and, through mutual devotion to Bubba, strengthening the devotional culture of the ashram.

Bubba said:

The function of the Guru is first of all to make the student a devotee through the process of understanding, until he comes to the point of surrender. Then the Guru enters where he surrenders, and that one becomes a devotee. That is the entire yoga of this Way. There is nothing to do from that point except to surrender to the Guru, surrender to the Lord night and day, receive the Lord in your body and in your cells . . . , not as a technique, but as a woman receives her lover. ("Guru Enters Devotee", *The Bodily Location of Happiness*, 1982 edition, 38.)

A perfect demonstration of the Divine Guru facilitating the transition from "student" to "devotee" occurred one particular night in early January. The evening began with everyone receiving Bubba's silent Darshan while gathered around Him in the large meeting room of the ashram.

Once the formal Darshan ended, Bubba sat quietly on His couch. His face was soft. His eyes were closed. His fingers were extended. His intensified Spiritual Presence was felt as greatly magnified, profound happiness. Overwhelming Divine Joy rushed through my body and mind, saturating my entire being in Divine Love-Bliss.

Bubba's Spiritual Presence descended into each body through the head from above, removing any sense of separation and drawing each person into blissful meditation. I don't know how long we meditated; the sense of time was entirely gone.

Eventually everyone spontaneously began to express their ecstatic state of happiness. Some started laughing in total delight, others cried. Some began singing praise of our Beloved Master, still others started dancing ecstatically. Suffused in the thickness of Bubba's Divine Siddhi, we all hugged each other over and over. Some moved close to sit at Bubba's feet, directly thanking and praising Him for His Great Gifts. Free in God, we all were "gone" in our Heart-Master's profound Blessing Regard. There was so much of His Divine Radiant Presence in the room it almost felt as if the walls would blow out.

The Divine Master remained relaxed on His couch, freely relating to everyone, serving our heart-reception of His Spiritual Blessing. We celebrated our Beloved egoless Master late into the night, praising Him and singing and dancing in the ecstasy of His Radiant Company. We truly felt the profundity of Bubba's Submission-Work that night. It is still being referred to over forty years later as a spiritual experience that we will never forget. We all refer to it as "Guru Enters Devotee".

Yet, over time, the Divine Avatar would make it clear that spiritual experiences, no matter how profound, indicate "someone"— an egoic presence—having the experience. Even though the incident served the awakening of devotional response it was not really a matter of my ego being subsumed by Bubba's egoless State, beyond all presumption of separateness. Rather, I enjoyed the effect of His Presence, which registered in my body and mind. But I did receive some delightful clues about what it would be like if I were to be completely "entered" by the Divine Guru, and thereby freed from egoity.

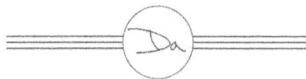

Persimmon

JANUARY 23, 1974

As early as 1972, Bubba had had people looking for property outside of Los Angeles, where He could more fully establish His ashram. Many properties were found, but none had enough of the right qualities. In October 1973, however, a property in Lake County, California, three hours north of San Francisco, was found that seemed promising. Accompanied by some devotees, Bubba drove north to see it.

The property was beautiful. It had previously been used as a hot springs resort. Before that, it had been used sacredly, the locale of several Native American holy sites. It had fresh water wells, flowing streams, hills, meadows, untouched areas, great rock formations, and grand old oak trees. There were several active natural hot springs, even a bath house fed by hot spring water. There were many buildings, and it was located in the mountains, secluded and private. Bubba was very pleased and said, "This is the one!"

Bubba moved to the property and established His residency on January 23, 1974. We watched as the Divine Master established His Living Presence all over the property. It was becoming His Sanctuary, but it didn't have a name. The devotees living there called it "the property". Those still in the city called it "the land up north". Bubba asked us to propose names. Weeks went by, many suggestions were offered, then a devotee came up with "Persimmon" (there were several Persimmon trees on the property). Bubba liked it immediately and the Sanctuary was officially named "Persimmon".

As Bubba was Empowering various sites, His devotees were working on cleaning and repairing the Sanctuary. Each night Bubba invited us to gather with Him. The gatherings took place in the largest room of the Sanctuary, the former resort dining hall. Later, Bubba moved the gatherings to His newly renovated house, but that space soon proved to be too small for everyone. Bubba then began to invite a smaller group of devotees, mostly those who had taken on services within the ashram, explaining that He works with all His devotees through His work with a few.

One day I saw Bubba as He was walking by the cabin I was living in. I asked if He would like to come in to see it, and He accepted the invitation. As He walked in, I said, "Welcome to my humble abode." He smiled and said, "And you have a lot to be humble about." We both laughed. The informal words of the Guru are as true as the most esoteric Teaching.

The early days at Persimmon were a wonderful time of directly feeling that Bubba's Way of the Heart is a Love relationship between Guru and devotee. Bubba constantly revealed the Divine Process by allowing us into His Blessing Company day and night. He called for us to always cultivate our love for Him through increased devotion, through which we would receive His Divine Love that opened our hearts, allowing us to respond with even deeper devotion. At Persimmon, Bubba' established specific holy sites and identified significant places, giving them appropriate names. In time, the name "Persimmon" would give way to "The Mountain Of Attention Sanctuary". But other names He gave, starting in those earliest days at Persimmon, are still intact, each expressing something specific about the sacred place and its use. Some of the site names (and their uses at the Sanctuary now) are:

The Manner of Flowers (His residence)

Bright Behind Me (library and archives)

Huge Helper (sacramental service room and storage)

Plain Talk Chapel, Temple Eleutherios, Land Bridge Pavilion (indoor temples)

Here I Am, Earth-Fire Temple, Skyway Temple, Holy Cat Grotto, Red Sitting Man, Lithia Springs, Chanting Springs, Seventh Gate (outdoor temples)

Pile of Poles, Spirit Vase, Goat's Wool Blanket, Huey, Dewey, and Louie (residences and dormitories)

Ordeal Bath Lodge (the hot springs bath house)

Humpback Whale (the large bell)

Home Dance (retreat facility, formerly the laundry)

Fear-No-More (park and facilities for non-humans)

Tall Animals Land (the field and forested area across the road)

Mother's Bed (the lake across the road)

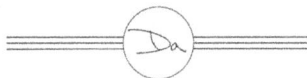

Ecstatic Gatherings

MARCH 1974

Bubba had accepted Persimmon as His Sanctuary in late January 1974; devotees began moving there in February, and soon began a period of time humorously called "Garbage and the Goddess", which lasted off and on for a number of months. It was named later, after an important talk called "Garbage and the Goddess" that Bubba gave on April 15, 1974. In that talk Bubba emphasized we should not hold on to spiritual experiences—no matter how exalted and blissful they are—because they are all "garbage". The spiritual experiences are the Goddess. He would prove this point to us during the "Garbage and the Goddess" period by using His Siddhi to *create* exalted and blissful experiences in us, after which we found ourselves still bound by our egoic patterning. The experiences did not free us, did not produce Enlightenment; ultimately, no matter how "high" the experiences were, compared to Enlightenment all of them were "garbage".

Bubba invited us into His Blessing Company night after night. Each night began with the Divine Master granting His Darshan, allowing us to surrender our attention to His Divine Condition and State. After the period of silence, He would begin what was called a "consideration". In Bubba's Company, to consider a topic was to investigate it from every angle with full thought and feeling until reaching the point of ultimate clarity. He brought us fully into each consideration, drawing out our emotional reactions and intellectual responses, opening us to deeper self-understanding, greater heart-Awakening, and real Wisdom.

Not just in the "Garbage and the Goddess" period, but throughout all the years of His Submission-Work with devotees, the Divine Heart-Master made Himself available for consideration. From personal hygiene to life after death, no topic was taboo. Working with us in this way, our Beloved Master always opened a greater conscious awareness that not only addressed the topic at hand, but always placed it in the context of Divine Reality and the

Gathering with devotees on Guru Purnima, 1974

foundational Teaching of "no seeking" (Divine Reality cannot be realized by seeking because It is always already the case).

Throughout all of this, the Divine Master was calling His devotees to be ecstatic, to go beyond our assumed limits on happiness by surrendering into His Divine State of Prior Happiness. Each night the Attractiveness of His Divine Freedom and the awakening power of His Divine Siddhi opened our hearts to the True Reality prior to our egoic act of separation. The Divine Master never related to us as separate egos. He never supported our self-contraction. Every night was sacred Darshan in His Blessing Company. We were being Instructed in Spiritual Reality even though we still interpreted all His Blessings Gifts via the mechanisms of the self-contraction, separate self-sense intact.

During "Garbage and the Goddess", we received the great Gift of Bubba's ecstatic confession of His Divine Condition on many nights. With tears rolling down His Radiant face, He would confess His Love of the teachers and gurus that had Served and Blessed His Spiritual path. He confessed His Love of His devotees, including all who were yet to come.

Late in the evenings, when we were no longer able to fully receive the profound Grace of His Siddhi, Bubba would say, "I guess we've reached the crossover point." At that point the dancing and singing would begin. We danced and sang ecstatically in the Company of the Beloved Heart-Awakener. It was a time of opening up, turning to His Being of Divine Happiness, going beyond the separate self-sense, joyfully surrendered into His Sacred Presence.

These ecstatic gatherings in Bubba Free John's Blessing Company continued off and on for about a year. His commitment to "offer a relationship, not a technique" could not have been demonstrated more fully.

Several of the following stories took place during the "Garbage and the Goddess" period.

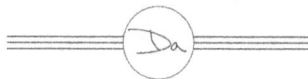

The Anniversary Present

MARCH 1974

I had mentioned to a couple of friends that my first wedding anniversary was coming up and asked if they had any ideas of how to celebrate it. They suggested that they and their intimate partners join us for a group celebration. The idea sounded like fun, but the ashram had changed to a period of strict discipline. The party was temporarily over. No "accessories", a strict diet, meditation, study, and service were the rule of the time. No one felt Bubba would approve the idea of a group celebration.

It was about 8:00 p.m. on a Sunday night when I impulsively brought the idea to Him. Sunday nights were especially set aside for Bubba's private relaxation, but I trusted my relationship to my Beloved Guru and felt I could ask Him anything at any time.

As I arrived at His door, I improvised a strategy to get past any attendant who might answer the door. I thought, *I had better make my request to see Bubba as strong as I can, even <u>demand</u> to see Him.* The devotee who came to the door said she was surprised that I knocked so late, and that no one should bother Bubba unless it was an emergency. I told her it was! She said, "Are you really sure?" while looking me straight in the eyes, trying to validate my assertion.

Just then Bubba called from the living room, "Who's there?"

She said, "Jerry."

"What does he want?"

"He says it's an emergency."

"Send him in."

The Divine Master Bubba Free John was lying on His couch looking completely relaxed. A few devotees were sitting on the rug in front of Him, seemingly enjoying a quiet night of TV. He had them move a bit to make space for me to sit close to Him. I think He already knew it wasn't a true emergency. He asked in a soft voice, "Now what is this?"

Holding on to what I felt would be some humorous play I said, "I have a demand."

He asked with a slightly stronger voice, "A what?"

I said with a slightly softer voice, "A demand."

His voice got stronger and a bit louder. He asked, "A what?"

This was my Spiritual Master, my Divine Guru. I could suddenly see my casual friendly assumption in our relationship was entirely in error. He showed me the self-reflection that I had felt I could present myself to Him in a loving yet friendly way but ended up interfering with His clearly established privacy.

Now with some trepidation I said, "Well, a request."

He asked again, but this time in a more inquisitive and softer voice, "A what?"

My totally self-absorbed approach was completely finished by His Heart-Mastery. I touched His hand and asked softly, "A question, please?"

He said, "Now that is more like it."

I was happy that the inappropriate gaming was over, that my Beloved Heart-Guru had put me back in my devotional place. I kissed His hand. As He rubbed my head, He asked, "What's your question?"

I described the anniversary celebration idea and He said, with a twinkle in His eyes, "First of all, tell them they're not going anywhere. They have a lot of studying and meditating to do. Ashram conditions are fully in effect and they should not be looking for ways to get out of them.

"Now as far as your anniversary . . . Well, you and your intimate should go alone to celebrate. After all, it is your celebration and not anyone else's."

Then even though ashram discipline was strictly on He made a concession by recommending we go to the Blue Fox, which in those days was a fine French restaurant in San Francisco. Having been there before, He even suggested what we could order from the menu according to what He had liked. He talked about their wine list and recommended a couple of fine wines, depending on which entrée we ordered. He said, "Be sure to have the waiter take you downstairs into the wine cellar. It is very impressive."

Since it was a long trip to San Francisco, Bubba thought we should consider staying in a motel for the night, and then return the following day. Before I left, my Beloved Master gave me a big hug and a soft smile. My heart was overflowing with my Guru's Response to my blatant disrespect and unconscious actions. I was back in devotional alignment and heart-relationship.

I directly returned to the cabin where my friends were waiting. As I entered, they immediately demanded to know what had happened. Did He Approve us going? "No," I told them, "you all have to get down to the conditions of ashram living, but my wife and I will be going." Then I told them everything Bubba had said and we all laughed at the skillful means He had used to realign His devotee.

I learned a big lesson from Bubba dealing with my palsy, casual approach. My feeling of heart-intimacy with Him led me to feel I could interrupt His relaxation time with my request. Such casualness was part of what He had to confront during the Submission of His Teaching Demonstration. But I didn't have the heart-intimacy because He was a "good guy" and I was His "buddy". I was Blessed to be His devotee. The Spiritual Love between Master and devotee is beyond any other form of human love. It is the non-separate Prior Reality of Divine Love. Surrender is the only appropriate response to the Heart-Master's Divine Attractiveness.

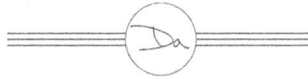

God-Possession

Bubba had called for a gathering in the meeting room at Persimmon for a Darshan occasion. In advance, He had sent two devotees to talk about what had been transpiring at His house. The first speaker described intense Spiritual Transmission occurring over the preceding week.

The second speaker began to speak, but he couldn't continue. His body started shaking and his head began jerking back and forth. His body was overwhelmed by energy that he couldn't conduct. Instead, he was throwing it off in spontaneous movements (kriyas). Then all of a sudden we all felt a great surge of Bubba's Divine Blissful Energy rushing through our bodies, and in response everyone began having kriyas. Some devotees started breathing fast and loud in blissful intensity (pranayama).

I was sitting near the door and I saw and felt what happened next, when Bubba entered the room. Another great surge of Blissful Spiritual Energy rushed in, but, unlike the first wave, this was like a hurricane. And it didn't stop! As Bubba walked toward His seat, His Spiritual Presence and Siddhi were absolutely overwhelming. His intensified Presence caused many to scream even before they saw Him. The Divine Heart-Master took over the body-minds of everyone in the room. We all felt His overwhelming Love rush through our bodies with such intensity it was completely ecstatic, but totally impossible to conduct. It was God Possession! We all responded with kriyas—screaming, jerking, twisting, bouncing, crying, laughing. Some of us fell into meditation, others swooned. Like the others, an enormous Blissful Energy filled my body. I felt I had to breathe very deeply or I'd explode.

Still on His way to His seat, the Divine Master stopped by different devotees and placed His hands on their heads to help them conduct His Magnified Transmission. He also looked deep into some devotees' eyes, as if opening the path for His Spiritual

Transmission to be most effective in them. By the time our Heart-Master got to His seat, everyone was totally undone in His Siddhi of Love-Bliss.

Once at His seat, Bubba smiled, saying, "I've gone too far!" and He laughed. He humorously told one of His attendants that He should be reminded not to invite a certain wailing devotee to dinner without making "adequate arrangements". After things quieted down somewhat, we received the Grace of His silent Darshan.

Before He left, the Divine Master reminded us that He intensified His Spiritual Presence in our body-minds for the sake of serving our recognition of and surrender to the Divine as His egoless State of Being. But we were having "experiences" and all experiences are limited in time and space, not the same as realizing the Divine egoless State of Being. Therefore, experiences, while being instructive and perhaps enjoyable, are "garbage"; they are not precious, not IT.

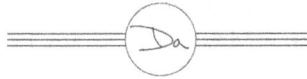

The Hammock

Once the summer weather arrived at Persimmon, Bubba often enjoyed lying in a rope hammock hanging from two trees in the front yard of His residence. He often invited devotees to sit quietly on the grass around Him to receive His Blessing Darshan. To be there with Him always quieted my mind and opened my heart . His Radiant Presence saturated everything in pure Love-Bliss, revealing the Divine Truth of existence as non-separate. Bubba did not swing in the hammock, He just rested there. Some devotees were invited to quietly fan Him. No words were spoken; the only sound was the birds singing and light breezes rustling the trees. Occasionally one of the devotees would bring Bubba a cool drink and, if He was hot, a damp cloth to wipe His forehead. These times were so simple, yet so full of direct heart-Communion in the Divine Master's Radiant Free Happiness. I felt all I ever wanted to do was to be in such simple yet profound intimacy with my Beloved Heart-Guru.

One day, during one of these occasions, I told Bubba, "All I ever want to do is fan You while You relax in Your hammock." He replied, "Tcha," but then continued, "You'll have a lot more to do than that!"

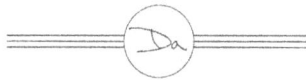

Heaven on Earth

AUGUST 1974

One day, in the course of doing my service at Persimmon, my route took me past the bath house (later named "Ordeal Bath Lodge"). As I walked by, I got the feeling that something was happening inside. So I looked in. What was "happening", I discovered, was absolutely sublime.

The Divine Heart-Master Bubba Free John was in the Plunge (a large warm-water pool) with five or six of His devotees. When He heard the door open, He looked up, saw me, and had one of His attendants invite me inside. I entered and very quietly sat on a bench at the side of the pool, making sure not to make any noise or do anything that might be disturbing.

As He always said, nothing, including doors and walls, was separate from His Divine Siddhi. It was a Siddha-Loka.[13] The scene was full of beauty. No words were being spoken. The fragrance of incense burning at the altar in front of His Murti sweetened the air. Music was playing very softly in the background. The entire room, even the air in it had become suffused by the Divine Being's Presence. Bubba was floating on His back with devotees gently holding Him up under His back and head, while others supported His arms and legs. They moved the Divine Heart-Master very slowly around the pool, united and radiant in the Divine Reality of Oneness. Beautiful flowers floated on the surface of the water and brushed His Body as He was moved through them.

Divine Love-Bliss was the only Reality. Such Love, such Happiness, such purity, simplicity, and intimacy—all was enlivened by His egoless Brightness. Sitting on that bench, my heart was sublimed by what felt like "Heaven on Earth".

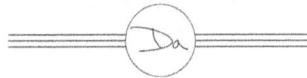

---

13. In Hindu tradition, the Siddha-Loka is a subtle realm where Divine Beings reside.

Andrew's Birthday and More

SEPTEMBER 1974

Bubba had invited a small group of devotees to dinner to celebrate His devotee Andrew's birthday. Andrew was a professional stand-up comedian and comedy writer for television shows. At times throughout Andrew's relationship to Bubba, Bubba asked Andrew to tell jokes. At other times Bubba joined Andrew in joke-telling sessions, where they alternated in telling jokes one after the other. It was totally delightful—they both told very funny jokes and stories, filling the room with great laughter. But there was a difference in the way the jokes affected people. Bubba used the opportunity to Teach us about True Divine Humor compared to conventional humor.

Andrew's jokes made us laugh, but Bubba's jokes brought more than laughter. He Awakened the heart to its True Happiness. Bubba explained that conventional humor comes from the feeling of separation and addresses suffering and seeking for happiness, without transcending the dilemma. Therefore it can make you laugh, but it isn't liberating. He said the source of True Humor is the Divine Reality of Prior Unity, so it is perfectly personal and yet releases the dilemma of separate self by revealing the source of True Happiness as the Heart. All the invited guests came to Andrew's birthday dinner well dressed and excited to be dining with their Heart-Master. The men all wore sport jackets and ties. The ladies wore cocktail-type dresses. The meal servers were also well dressed.

Bubba took His seat at the head of the table and invited Andrew to sit on His left. The entire dinner in Bubba's Company was pure joy. The room was filled by His Divine Siddhi. Everyone was relaxed and feeling Him in this calm, happy, soft-spoken, wonderful evening. A delicious vegetarian dinner was enjoyed by all. When the drinks were served, Bubba raised His glass to toast Andrew. We all joined in His toast, and then we all toasted the Divine Being sitting in our midst, our true Heart-Master and Siddha-Guru!

At the end of the meal a beautiful large white frosted birthday cake was brought out and placed in front of Andrew. On the thick frosting it said, "Happy Birthday Andrew"! The lit candles added a sparkle and festive mood. Andrew was beaming to receive all the attention from His Beloved Guru, a dinner in his honor, and now this great sparkling birthday cake! Obviously, Andrew felt really special, really loved.

Bubba invited Andrew to make a wish and blow out the candles, which he did. Then the candles were removed and the cake was placed in front of Bubba. We all expected Bubba to cut the wonderful cake when—without a word—Bubba lifted the cake in His hands to fully show it to everyone . . . and pushed it directly into Andrew's face! It was like a scene from a slapstick comedy of the silent-film era. It was complete "cake in your face" perfection! Bubba did it so unexpectedly, so completely, we all were shocked for a moment, and then began laughing uncontrollably. Andrew was undone. He couldn't believe it! He totally loved that Bubba, his Heart-Master, actually did that. To Andrew it was perfect over-the-top humor. He couldn't stop laughing, and neither could we. While He helped wipe cake off Andrew's face, Bubba had tears rolling down His face from laughing so hard.

Bubba could make any Teaching demonstration an ecstatic event. It was a wonderful dinner in Andrew's honor. While Bubba did sincerely wish Andrew a happy birthday, the Divine Master had never stopped serving self-understanding and undermining the egos of His devotees while He was there. The cake incident may have been planned, or it may have been a spontaneous gesture in the moment, but in either case it completely served Andrew. As a professional in the comedy business, Andrew depended on positive acknowledgment from others about his comedy writing and performing to support his self-image. Bubba's stunning surprise overwhelmed Andrew's patterned expectations. The Love and Free Humor from his Beloved Guru's Divine Play on this birthday evening made a profound impression on Andrew. He never forgot that evening and always talked about the profundity and freedom of his Guru's Divine Humor.

When everyone finally quieted down, Bubba hugged Andrew. Then He suggested we should all go together to see the others in the ashram dining room. He felt they needed to loosen up, and He proposed the free happiness of a grand food fight with all of them! He immediately left for the ashram dining room, and we all followed. Running behind our Divine Heart-Master, the men took off their jackets and ties, as there was no time to stop and change clothes.

As Bubba entered the dining room, everyone there was surprised and overjoyed to see Him. Without hesitation, He went directly to the first dish of food, took a handful, and pressed it into a devotee's face. I don't think anyone could have imagined the stunned faces of Bubba's devotees when their Beloved Guru started the food fight. But in the next moment we jolted them out of their shock by grabbing some food and yelling, "FOOD FIGHT!" Immediately the entire dining room of devotees jumped up and joined the melee. The first ashram food fight began!

It was such a free, happy event. To have an opportunity to let go of propriety and constraints and completely enjoy something so outrageous was so liberating. There were no holds barred. There was only one rule: if it was food or drink, it was fair game. There was also absolutely no concern for clothing or the furniture or the room itself. The goal was to throw, push, shove, jam, spray, pour, spill, or splash as much food and drink on as many people as fast as possible without any concern, since it was also happening to you. In fact, allowing it to fully happen to you served the fullest enjoyment, so everyone participated without holding back! There were about fifty happy participants in the food fight that night. It was the most unbelievable fun, done with complete abandon, and the Divine Heart-Master Bubba was in the middle of it all.

He went back to His residence once the "fight" was over, completely covered head-to-toe with food. When an attendant from His house met Him with wet towels to help Him clean up, He greeted her with a handful of dessert, which He had hidden behind His back.

Later when we looked at the ashram dining room, it was unbelievable. There was food everywhere—on the ceiling, on the windows and doors, on the light fixtures, on the walls and the furniture, everything was covered. Fifty people had been throwing food and drink at each other for over an hour. The floor was so covered with slippery, sloppy food that it was impossible to walk on.

The food fight certainly released any built-up dryness from living the strict disciplined life of self-transcending practice! Bubba knew exactly how to serve us and, in the complete Freedom of His Divine Enlightenment, the means could be very unconventional. He always said He would serve His devotees in whatever way was necessary to move us out of our heart-deadening social conventions and heart-constricting egoic patterns into greater self- understanding and deeper heart-recognition of His Divine Being and reception of His Divine Siddhi. The ashram food fight was exhilarating. We all loved it! We thanked and praised our Beloved Divine Heart-Master for His ecstatically wild and funny Gift.

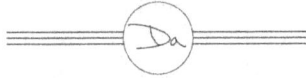

Mysterious Ways

In Bubba's Blessing Company, His Siddhi was almost always palpable, while the accomplishments of His Siddhi were often mysterious. An example of such mystery occurred one day when I was sitting on my cabin porch at Persimmon watching Bubba as He was walking nearby.

When I said "Hi," He stopped and walked over to me.

"How are you feeling?" He asked.

"Fine," I said.

He said, "You are about to go into an episode, and you don't need to do it."

I had no clue about an upcoming "episode"—which was shorthand for a drama or upset about something or other. I had no feeling of an impending conflict. I just looked at my Beloved Guru without speaking as He smiled and walked away.

Nothing else happened. There was no specific Instruction, no Wisdom to ponder—simply His Blessing Regard and His mysteriously accomplishing Siddhi.

What did His Siddhi accomplish in this instance? Specifically, I'll never know—because no "episode" ever happened. And to me that's the point: My Beloved Heart-Master discerned something in my future that His Siddhi prevented from happening because, I presume, it would not have served my spiritual practice. Perhaps it would have even been an obstacle or a setback. His Siddhi is the true root of the saying: "The Lord works in mysterious ways."

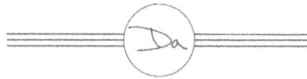

Cloud Dissolving

MAY 1974

Bubba was out for a walk and stopped in a spot where a few of His devotees were talking. Quickly, others saw Him and gathered around their Beloved Guru.

He began talking about Siddhis. He said He had all the known Siddhis, and even some unknown, from the spiritual traditions, but He would not use them to produce miracles. He said that to have a spiritual experience, or to witness a miracle, becomes a form of fascination and only serves the seeking ego-"I". He said, "Spiritual experiences of a conditional kind have a certain oddity about them—they always point to the body, or the body-mind. You are just as bound afterward as you were before."

We understood His point. Even so, we still asked if He could please show us at least one miracle. We promised we wouldn't become seekers of miracles.

In retrospect, I'm very sobered by the naivety and insensitivity of our request. Daily, we had been receiving the Consciousness-Awakening Work of the Great Siddha-Master, but still we persisted in asking for a miracle as if we hadn't already seen one!

I don't know why He relented, but He did by saying, "Okay, I will show you just one."

He directed our attention to some clouds in the sky, then to a specific cloud. He said, "Watch that cloud dissolve and disappear." Bubba raised His cane and pointed it at the cloud. Within a few seconds, right in front of our eyes, we saw the cloud get fainter and fainter and finally, within two minutes, totally disappear. All the clouds around it hadn't changed at all! It was a real miracle—small, but big enough to emphasize His point: We were unchanged by seeing Him do it. We applauded and thanked Bubba. And, even though we understood that seeing miracles had no spiritual significance, we asked for more.

"See, you're never satisfied," He responded, smiling as He walked away.

We immediately tried it ourselves and we actually were able to dissolve some clouds.

At another time Bubba talked about dissolving clouds when He was a boy at the beach. He said, "I did it to not be bored." Then the Divine Master explained what makes it possible. He said, "You have to not feel separate from the cloud. You have to love the cloud." He elaborated about really feeling the cloud and bringing loving energy to it. He said you can't dissolve a cloud if you feel separate from it, so the love has to be full. You also can't assume any limit to the ability to dissolve clouds. Keep bringing loving attention to the cloud and keep seeing it dissolve. "Let it dissolve in your love," He said. "Allow it to dissolve. Eventually it will."

During His trip to India, when we had seen Sathya Sai Baba materialize ash and have it fall from his hand, Bubba had asked if seeing that had changed me. I was impressed, but no, it hadn't changed me. The Divine Master said, "So what value does it have, other than fascination? None!"

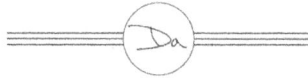

The Family Egg

JUNE 1975

During 1974 and 1975 the Divine Heart-Master Bubba Free John was showing many different aspects of His Divine Person—His Divine Nature, His Divine Condition, and His Divine State. To draw His devotees deeper into the heart-relationship to Him, Bubba was awakening Divine Communion, bringing about spiritual experiences, and calling His devotees to live as love, without "contracts" egoically designed for self-protection. He was also Submitting to His devotees as Bubba, the Heart-Friend, by engaging and laughing with His devotees, creating Teaching occasions with egoless Happiness, and Transmitting His Divine Siddhi to devotees with Free Humor and Divine Playfulness.

A particular example of His Free Playfulness and heart-brightening Humor was demonstrated when Bubba created the "Family Egg occasion". It began when a small group of devotees, in which I was included, was invited to a celebration dinner at Bubba's residence at Persimmon. (The Divine Heart-Master always explained that the few represented the many and that, through those selected, He was in contact with everyone in the world, not just His other devotees.)

During the evening Bubba talked about a tradition His family observed throughout His childhood each year on a particular day. He said He'd love to do it again. We asked what it involved. He seemed reluctant to tell us because of the strangeness of this tradition, but then He said, "Okay, I'll tell you."

This is the "tradition" as He described it: Each year on a certain day, just before dinner, His father passed out hard-boiled eggs to everyone at the table. Each egg was placed on its own separate plate. Then, once everyone was ready, His father would lead everyone by cracking his egg on his forehead, placing the cracked egg on the plate, then peeling off the shell, leaving the peeled egg and pieces of shell on the plate.

Bubba laughed about how much fun it had been as a child to do this. He emphasized that cracking the hard-boiled egg on the forehead was the most important part. He said He wasn't certain, but He assumed the tradition must have come from His ancestors. Then again He mentioned how He'd really like to do it again someday.

Someone asked about the date when it was traditionally done. Bubba didn't answer that but asked if it would be okay with everyone to reenact the "tradition" with Him. We were thrilled to be invited, and I said, "Beloved, if You would like it, we'd love to do it with You."

Weeks later the same group was invited to Bubba's house again. During the evening, Bubba again brought up His family tradition of egg cracking. He talked about how it could be understood as the cracking of the shell of egoity. He said there was something about the way the shell cracked that was important. He related it to stories from different religious and spiritual traditions that told of cracking an egg and its significance. Again He asked if we were actually interested in doing it. We emphatically answered affirmatively, and I started looking forward to the interesting tradition of egg cracking with our Beloved Heart-Master.

Bubba brought the subject up a couple more times over the following months. It was clear that this family tradition was quite a big deal to Him. It also seemed that He only spoke about it when the same group of devotees was with Him. We were beginning to feel a bit special—being invited to participate in such an auspicious event. It was obvious Bubba was really looking forward to the egg cracking. More and more, over the months, as it got closer to the possible day, whenever Bubba spoke about the egg cracking He was like a happy kid waiting to play with a new toy. The anticipation was growing in each of us too.

Finally, after four or five months, Bubba confirmed the date for the egg-cracking event and our group was invited to dinner at His residence. My anticipation had become intense over the many months, and now the time was finally here! We were all excited. Everyone dressed in their best, honored to be in His Divine Company and part of His family egg-cracking "tradition". *Perhaps*, I thought, *it would be some kind of initiation for each of us.*

We expected the egg cracking would begin before dinner, but the meal was served first. It was wonderful—food always seemed to taste better in Bubba's Company. Soft music played while we enjoyed being with our Beloved Heart-Master. There was very little conversation. At the end of the meal, still in that calm, quiet feeling place, Bubba asked again if we would do the egg-cracking ceremony with Him. Having waited months for this very important moment, we were more than ready and all enthusiastically said, "Yes, please!"

And so He asked an attendant to bring in the hard-boiled eggs. An egg on a plate was placed in front of each of us. Bubba lifted His egg, looked at it for a couple of moments, then told us that the secret to success in egg cracking is to hit it firmly on the forehead—very important, since there could not be a second try. Each person had to accomplish cracking the egg on the first try only. He said, "I'll do Mine first, you watch, then you all do yours together right after Me." We said, "Okay," and Bubba firmly smacked His egg on His forehead. The shell fully cracked, and He then neatly placed the pieces on the plate in front of Him.

He then said, "Ready? Go on three. One. Two. Three!"

We all smashed our eggs on our foreheads to make sure the shell fully cracked, but to our astonishment our eggs WERE NOT HARD BOILED! **They were all raw eggs!**

The slimy eggs spread over our foreheads. The shells splattered everywhere. Egg dripped down our faces, onto our clothing, onto the table. We were all stunned! Then realizing what had just happened, with egg dripping down, everyone started roaring with laughter. We couldn't stop laughing, even when we saw a damp towel had been placed in front of each of us. Eventually we wiped off the egg with the towels, but I was almost reluctant to get rid of it. *Too bad*, I felt, *I couldn't keep it as a remembrance of this fantastically funny practical joke.* It was the funniest practical joke ever! And it was set up and pulled off by, of all people, our Heart-Master and Heart-Friend.

Talk about losing face! There can be no "status" face when it is dripping with egg. The feeling of what had just happened in the moment when the egg broke was possibly the most surprising, vulnerable moment I had ever experienced. All I could do was feel it happening and surrender in my love for my Heart-Master, the great Divine Trickster. I laughed so much that the tears rolling down my face helped wash off the egg.

I cannot possibly tell you how much Bubba laughed. He was howling. Tears of laugher were pouring down His beautiful face. He didn't stop for the longest time!

After our laughter settled down a bit and the egg was wiped away, our Beloved Heart-Master continued the rest of the delightful evening talking about how we looked with egg dripping down our faces. Jokes went back and forth between us and Bubba for a long time. The evening ended as all evenings ended in our Heart-Master's Company: with us sitting silently, contemplating His Divine Person, and receiving the great Gift of His heart-opening Divine Siddhi.

Being part of the special group was a set-up for the ego-"I" to build some new layers of self-importance. The "Family Egg occasion" showed me that losing face is a great Blessing, an essential element of self-transcendence. It's humbling to contemplate the great lengths to which I would ordinarily go in order to save face. Egg on my face gave me the opportunity to observe my egoity at work, and to transcend it in the happiness of my Divine Master's Company, all in a few hilarious moments.

Any feeling of status I felt by being invited into Bubba's Company for a celebration dinner, or to take part in His family's egg-cracking tradition, was immediately replaced by feeling humbly surrendered. Also the incident showed me how much Bubba had established His Presence in my life and heart: after the shock of wet egg came the impulse to surrender, not to resist, and that surrender to my Heart-Master, after the moment of feeling out of control and totally vulnerable, was heart-liberating.

The Divine Master had fabricated the entire "family tradition" story, and took months setting us up, and He pulled it off perfectly— the face-losing lesson was profoundly effective. Most of all, His Total Enjoyment was the greatest delight. To see our Heart-Master laugh so loud for so long was supremely wonderful.

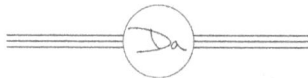

The Chocolate-Vanilla War

AUGUST 1975

This is the story of the Chocolate-Vanilla War, Persimmon, August 1975.

As a way of addressing the source of all conflict in the world, Bubba Free John suggested we should have a once-and-for-all, full-on war between the dark forces, representing egoic separation from God, and the forces of Light, representing the Truth of non-separate Divine Reality. The dark forces would be called "Chocolate" and the Light forces "Vanilla". The battle would be engaged only with food and beverages.

Bubba designated a devotee as the commander of the Chocolate forces, while He stood as the Divine commander of the Vanilla forces. He then assigned each of us to one of the sides. Some of us volunteered to be on a preferred side, but the Divine Master simply placed everyone and we just had to submit and enter the war as assigned. Also a team was designated as the Red Cross. Their job was to make sure no one got hurt and to help soldiers on both sides stay engaged. Altogether there were about seventy soldiers, male and female, opposing each other in the "war".

The Chocolate forces were told to meet at Ordeal Bath Lodge, while the Vanilla forces met at Great Food Dish. Great strategies were being made by both sides. The Chocolate forces, in keeping with darkness, enlisted some spies to infiltrate the Vanilla forces during their strategy meetings. (One of the Red Cross workers was exposed as a spy later in the course of the war.)

The Chocolate forces initiated "hostilities" with a small frontal attack on Great Food Dish, while sneaking in the back door to steal food. The Vanilla forces decided to stay in Great Food Dish, since that was where all the food was stored. They also felt they could protect their Divine commander best in those enclosed rooms. Bubba took His seat in the dining room, intentionally exposing His back to the large windows, showing no concern in His confidence that the Vanilla forces would protect Him and be victorious.

231

The battle began with the Chocolate forces making the first major attack. Somehow they found more food supplies and lots of water to use. Their attack drew some Vanilla forces outside to confront them and the battle was on. Chocolate and Vanilla troops were running at and away from each other everywhere in that part of the Sanctuary. Food and water were flying in every direction! To maintain their food supplies, both sides had trash bags full of food and buckets filled with water.

Eventually the Chocolate forces gained entrance into the kitchen and resupplied, but they could not get back outside. The Vanilla forces had intentionally let them in, so they could be trapped with their bags full of stolen food. That's when the battle moved into high gear in the kitchen and soon spread into the dining room, where the Vanilla forces' Divine commander was seated. The attack required Bubba to move right into battle to help His troops. Since He was the Vanilla commander, He was the main target of the Chocolate forces; therefore, in self-defense He became the most aggressive of all the "fighters".

It was survival of Light over darkness; therefore it required shoving all kinds of food down the enemies' pants, in their pockets, on their heads, and everywhere else. It was necessary to show supreme authority by shaking carbonated water bottles and directing their gushing spray down the enemy's shirts and blouses, all over their backs and down their pants. Yes, the forces included men and women, but a soldier is a soldier, and each had to "suffer" whatever the war between good and evil required.

Bottles and cans of everything were opened: ketchup, mustard, mayonnaise, relish, salad dressing, sauces, soups, carbonated drinks, fruits, vegetables, salad greens, cooked rice, desserts, all were flying in the air. Both forces were throwing whatever foods and beverages they could get their hands on.

Thick layers of food were caking up on the walls and ceiling in the kitchen and in the dining room. People were slipping, sliding, and rolling on the floor, since it was so covered with food. Everyone was saturated with food—literally, totally, entirely saturated! The Red Cross workers couldn't help any of the troops, since they were also covered with food. No mercy for anyone! Bubba was also covered with food. The entire dining room and kitchen, being the main location of the war, was unrecognizable. It looked like a garbage dump. Outside there were major food piles everywhere.

Throughout the entire battle the dominant sounds were of heavy panting from running, groaning and moaning when an attack saturated someone with something, and gales of laughter everywhere. We laughed so hard for so long we reached the point of exhaustion. It was the greatest fun-filled event ever—the food fight to end all food fights!

After about an hour and a half the battle slowed down, primarily because there was no food left. It was then that the Vanilla forces announced that they were the undisputed victors, as declared by the Divine Heart-Master Himself. No one else could have called it—we were all totally covered with food, equally unrecognizable. We bowed to the Divine Master, acknowledging that the ecstatic play had conquered the dark forces with His Divine Humor and Liberating Love.

Later that night after everyone cleaned up, we met with our Beloved Heart-Master. We praised His victory in the battle. The "war" was great fun, but we also noticed our aggression in the midst of the fun. Bubba then explained why He had invited us to play a war game.

He talked about the totally destructive nature of violence—fighting, aggression, killing, all the forms of expressed anger. We had only been fighting with food, and it had been for the righteous purpose of Light overcoming darkness, but it had been fighting nonetheless. Bubba gave us a circumstance where we could feel how our ego harbors dark tendencies even when having great fun. The Chocolate-Vanilla War was exhilarating and no one got hurt. But even in the midst of such extreme fun we felt our usually latent aggressive tendencies as we attacked each other, completely focused on winning. The "war" clearly exposed the source of all conflict—the ego-"I"—and the core purpose of egoic life: survival as the moment-by-moment activity of self-contraction.

The Chocolate-Vanilla War was a great demonstration of the extraordinary measures Bubba Free John would employ to create a Teaching Demonstration. Actually, before initiating our little "war",

He had offered a much more radical suggestion. The best way to resolve world conflict, He said, echoing W. C. Fields, would be for the two leaders of the greatest world powers to meet in a field, each with a sock full of horseshit, and fight it out just using their shit-socks as weapons. That way there could be no victor and the absolutely absurd folly of war would be clear to the whole world.

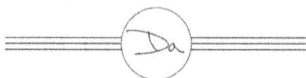

Breakfast with the Divine

L ike the sun, the Divine Heart-Master's Siddhi never stopped Radiating. The mere Presence of the Divine Heart-Master had powerful effects, even when He wasn't seemingly doing or saying anything. He referred to this matter Himself over the years, saying that the true sighting of His Divinely Enlightened human Form should be enough to awaken ordinary beings to immediately become His devotees. Once, referring to beings who weren't so "ordinary", He said, "Leave Me in a room with the Hell's Angels and in a short time they'd be bowing."

What follows is a story about spending time with Bubba Free John over a period of a few days in which, conventionally speaking, very little actually happened apart from His felt Presence. One early morning, Bubba invited four devotees who had taken on major ashram responsibilities to come to His residence on Persimmon. I was one of them, and I expected to speak with my Beloved Guru about my service, since He always wanted to be sure we were effectively fulfilling our responsibilities to properly serve all His devotees. To my great surprise, when we arrived we were invited to simply sit nearby Bubba while He reclined on a lounge chair in His patio sunroom.

As we entered the room, Bubba looked up from a newspaper, smiled, then returned to reading. We all bowed in gratitude for the intimate access to His Blessing Company. It was most unusual to be invited to spend time with Bubba when He was relaxing in His residence. A devotee directed us to sit at a table nearby, where herbal tea and fresh biscuits were soon served. We simply were invited to be there and feel the fullness of being in Bubba's Company, without any words spoken, while He read the newspaper and enjoyed the morning sun.

Peace and quiet Bliss Radiated from Bubba. His felt Presence washed away any movement to speak or do anything other than surrender to His Presence, to His Person. His equanimity and uncaused happiness affected the entire space around Him, which included all of us. I noticed my mind quieted and stopped its perpetual search for answers. This most pristine, simple time in His Holy Company was pure Darshan. This sacred invitation of such intimate access to our Heart-Master was more than wonderful; it was perfect.

Bubba allowed us the same intimate access every morning for several days. At the end of so much pure heart-brightening Blessings, my deep-felt attraction and devotion to my Beloved Guru had been drawn even deeper. I do feel that, after such intimate exposure, even the most macho Hell's Angel would have been heart-melted and sublimed and would have spontaneously bowed to the Living Divine Person.

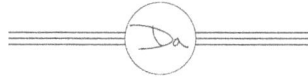

Darshan in Two Settings

JANUARY 1976

Traditionally, it is understood that wherever the guru spends His time is a sacred place, purified and enlivened with his or her spiritual presence. Bubba Free John spent time every day in a room in back of one of the sacred meditation halls to write His Teaching of Divine Truth. Although we casually referred to this sacred space as "His office", the room was set apart, allowing no disturbance, with only an authorized server to clean it daily. Bubba's "office" was the most undisturbed place at Persimmon.

One day, our Divine Heart-Master invited His devotees to Darshan in His office. To be invited into this sacred space was a very special, very rare occurrence.

We all lined up outside His office door. To afford undisturbed intimacy when sitting close to Bubba, only five or six devotees entered at a time. Our Beloved Heart-Master Bubba Free John was sitting cross-legged on a wicker couch. Each devotee would bow, and then sit on the rug just in front of Him.

When I entered, Bubba was sitting still and silent; His eyes were open and at times closed, fully Revealing His Divine Condition. His Enlightened State of Prior Freedom Radiated from His Love-Blissful Presence, available to the hearts of all. I felt the Divine Person, Bubba Free John, as His State of Love-Bliss, embodied by His Radiant Form. Even the room was dissolved and outshined in His Love-Brightness—a profound fullness without any separate self-sense.

After about ten minutes each group left so the next group could sit at the feet of the Siddha-Guru.

Shortly after that sacred occasion I received a message that Bubba wanted to see me immediately at His residence. The message seemed urgent. Self-doubt set in right away. I started to worry: *Had I done something wrong? Did Bubba want to address me about something I did—or failed to do—during that profound Darshan?*

On my hurried way to Bubba's house, I met another devotee who had received a message like mine. He was certain we had "screwed up" during the Darshan and were both about to hear about it.

At Bubba's house we were led into the living room and left alone to wait until He could meet with us. We waited quietly, both feeling something was wrong. As His devotees, we only wanted to please our Heart-Guru with our devotional practice and our service to Him and His devotees. If we had done something that disturbed Him, it would be heartbreak for us. *Why didn't the attendant stay in the room with us?* I wondered, worried that it was a bad sign.

Bubba came in and sat on His couch. We prostrated at His Holy Feet and remained face down on the floor, expecting the worst. Then Bubba spoke.

He said that during the Darshan He had felt that there was another way to bring His Enlightened Teaching to the world. He said He wanted to talk with us about it.

I couldn't believe my ears! This was astonishing. We were about to have a conversation with our Divine Master about missionary work. How fantastic! What a delight! Immediately we both sat up, totally brightened.

Bubba's ideas about other ways to bring His Teaching to the world involved products, including (incredibly) cartoon bubble gum wrappers, collectible cards about all the saints, sages, and prophets, and a line of jewelry. The creativity of His ideas was amazing—wild, free, humorous. And His consideration included ways my friend and I could be involved in developing and marketing these products based on our professional backgrounds.

Whenever the Divine Heart-Master put His Attention on something, He brought such irresistible clarity and energy to it that almost anything could seem possible. He started with the bubble gum wrappers and at first the whole idea seemed very humorous, but totally ridiculous. Then as Bubba kept expanding on His ideas, my feelings changed from dubious to *Well, maybe.* And then, feeling persuaded, I thought, *This not only could work, but could bring the world to Bubba's Holy Feet and make a million bucks doing it!*

Bubba ended the consideration by talking about making a fine line of jewelry and suggesting, "We may just get out of the gum business and get big time into the jewelry business once these designs hit the streets!"

After the consideration was over, Bubba told us to go work it all out and then let Him know what we were going to do. He recommended we use the art department and the editorial department for all the help we might need. We agreed to get right on it, bowed, and thanked our Radiant Heart-Master for the opportunity to spend such delightfully creative time in His Blessing Company and for giving us a way to bring His Divine Humor to the world.

As we walked away from His residence, I asked my friend what he was going to do in working on this project. He said, "Are you kidding? Those things will never sell! I'm not going to do anything at all about it."

I said, "But Bubba asked us to do it."

He said, "Okay, you do it. I wouldn't touch it with a ten-foot pole."

That got me to thinking. If we actually produced these humorous products it would make our Guru laugh every time He'd see them. But who would buy them? Devotees would, but who else? And why put so much energy into the project without making a profit only to have to go out of business?

Bubba never asked either of us about any of it ever again.

Two Darshans in one day—one formal, one informal. I will never forget the humor, energy, and creativity Bubba brought to us about His gum, cards, and jewelry ideas. Only He could know the reasons for serving us with those wild product ideas. What I know is that we were Blessed to see more of the Divine Person and to experience another aspect of His Submission-Work.

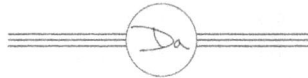

Names for Devotees

Throughout the years, the Divine Heart-Master Blessed His devotees by giving them special names. Some names were related to the devotee's service, some were reminders of their egoic tendencies. All of them were humorous and all had the potential to serve self-understanding.

I was Blessed with several names over many years. First was "Om Bar", relating to a health food candy I had been selling. Then He named me "Bullwinkle Moose", presumably in relation to my Semitic facial features, including a prominent nose. Then the Master named me "Jelly", because I was so immersed in enjoying jelly on my toast at breakfast in India. (Although, once, when asked by others why the name "Jelly", my Heart-Master humorously quipped, "It's Japanese for Jerry.") A few years later, He said I should just use the formal name I was given at birth, "Gerald".

During the Teaching Demonstration called "Indoor Summer", Bubba Free John Lovingly gave all the devotees in His Company new names. We used the names, taking them as a sign of His direct heart-relationship with each of us. Also, identifying with a new name was a way of observing the patterning of one's entrenched self-identity.

When we asked each other about our new names, in most cases we felt somehow that the name served our spiritual practice. However, in a few cases, it was harder to understand how the new name related to the person, such as the name "And The". One devotee was named "God". The next day his name was changed to "Gnat Bug".

A couple in a new relationship was given the names "Jesus Christ" and "The Virgin Mary". For a short time I was called "The Holy Spirit". (It was really amusing when I once made a restaurant reservation for the three of us!)

After a couple of weeks, Bubba changed "Jesus Christ's" name to "Frink Dental" and mine to "J. J. Waterfall". (While Bubba was traveling in Mexico one time, He and His attending devotee got lost. Driving down a desolate dirt road, far from civilization, to their surprise they came upon a sign in English that said "Frink Dental and J. J. Waterfall".)

What amazed me most about all the Blessed names the Divine Master gave His devotees over the years was that He never forgot a new name. From the day it was Given, He always referred to each devotee by their new name. In the case of every devotee, His Understanding completely penetrated the egoic persona. However bizarre the name seemed, it reflected something. His capacity to remember each new name was one more demonstration of the fact that He was the Embodiment of Consciousness Itself.

This long list of Blessed names Given by Bubba Free John in 1976 is still a work in progress:

Actor Bunyan	Cracker Teak	Flower Happiness
After Moon	Dead Pawn	Four Longs
And The	Delilah Falls	Gnat Bug
Aqaba Tryst	Devi Goldfarb	God
Arbor Salt	Diggi Boom	Golden Zones
Aroma Flight	Dolly Napkins	Heaven Chamber
Atlanta Ketch	Doremi Fasolati	Happy Sight
August Sage	Druidor Henge	Hedda Cups
Bad Cowboy	Earner Sharkey	Hephzibah Swartz
Ball Cane	East Rider	Host Veil
Beautiful Land	Either While	Indoor Summer
Beautyway Elizabeth	Elegant Mare	Indra Pond
Big Lids	Emerald Dragon	Inland Whale
Brother Fox	Ever Moth	Island Found
Cadence Head	Fa Dental	J.J. Waterfall
Cardia True	Fair Walking	Jambo Dryduck
Care Salads	Family Pope	Jesus Christ
Casual Rising	Ferris Grande	Jobber Swell
Cicero Keys	Ferule Horseman	Junk O'Cookies
Circa Rest	Fine Sand	Just Seams
Cisco Soda	First Jester	Justine Majorette
Country Woman	Fletcher Rabbit	Katzenjammer Kid

continued:

King Sweet
Lady Cat
Lemon Foal
Lettuce Calling
Mad Hearing
Maid Weather
Mala Friends
Many Too
Marmoset Trophy
Mata Bottle
Mender Clasp
Meridian Smith
Merlin Hats
Messiah Twine
Minneola Tenth
Molokai House
Moses Mana
Mr. Natural
Napa Songs
Near Queens
New Suit
Niagara Falls
Night Bird
Nimbus Dogwood
No Evil
Noah Track
Noble Servant
Northern Wake
Nyoka Reels

Oat Cokes
Odysseus Speak
Omaha Peace
On Patches
Or Phrasing
Palm Springs
Paris Kind
Pasture Shawl
Persia Rings
Pitcher Wye
Pretty Sandwich
Prince Vitamins
Regalia Dahomey
Relief Lamp
Remedy Airs
Remus Hills
Renaissance Glimpse
Romulus Eagle
Ruby Dharma
Samoa Yes
Saucer Aims
September Toe
Singing Cowboy
Sonny Friends
Sounder White Guy
Spacious List
Spirit Gum
St. Lithia
Stately O'Cookies

Sugar Cane
Sybil Stars
Tandaleo Schwarzkopf
Terrible "Terry" Tickets
Topo Strata
Tuka Threads
Tumble Dogwood
Ustad Isa
Valley Wheat
Vector Bench
Venture Lambs
Via La Strada
Viewlois Concept
Virgin Mary
Virginia Wolfe-Pleasures
Visitor Veil
Wag Truthish
Wake Laughing
Water Pear
Whisper Tock
World Trader
Yellow Hand
Young Knot
Zebulon Tree
Zoe Boat
Zuni Balloons
Zuni Roads

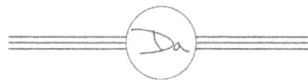

Do the Duck

One afternoon I was invited into Bubba's Blessing Company at His residence at Persimmon while He was relaxing and talking with two attending devotees. As soon as I entered the room and bowed to my Beloved Guru, the devotees mutually and very enthusiastically asked Bubba to please do "The Duck". It seemed that just before I had arrived He had done something really funny called "The Duck".

He said, "No, no, I can't do that." But the other devotees persisted, laughingly pleading with their Beloved Guru, "Please Master, please show Jerry 'The Duck'. Please?"

Finally He agreed to show me "The Duck". Immediately, His entire facial structure started changing. His face scrunched up into a very strange, twisted, distorted, totally exaggerated shape. It didn't look like a duck. In fact, it didn't look like anything that could have felt comfortable to Him. I think all that facial movement was a bit of theater to give me the sense that it was an ordeal to manifest "The Duck".

Then His face stopped twisting and turning and He began to quack and talk "duck talk". That was when it became clear that it wasn't just any duck, it was Donald Duck! Bubba's entire energy had become the psyche and feeling presence of Walt Disney's cartoon character Donald Duck! He wasn't just mimicking the voice of Donald Duck—Bubba Free John had actually become that cartoon character. I was completely astonished at what had just happened right in front of my eyes. I felt His Real Transformation from human to cartoon character. It had actually happened.

The entire room was changed by what He was doing. The room itself became brighter by His Divine Transformative Humor! Everyone laughed and applauded the miraculous transformation. Our Beloved Master laughed with us as the joy of His Divine Humor saturated us all.

That delightful event was a demonstration of the possibilities inherent in the Divine Master's Siddhi. Since He had no "separate self" identity at all, He might seem to become anyone or anything. He showed in that humorous way that He was not in fact the body-mind person I commonly related to as "Master" or "Guru", not an "other" to my ego-"I". He was the Incarnation in bodily human Form of non-separate Divine Reality.

His Divine Confession was, "I (Myself, <u>As</u> I <u>Am</u>) Am the Consciousness Wherein and Whereof every 'I' arises and appears and disappears."

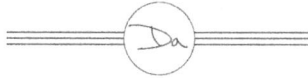

PART FOUR

Stories from 1979–1994

Da Free John
The Mountain Of Attention Sanctuary September 1979

Da Free John

During the spring and summer of 1979, Avatar Adi Da—still known as Bubba Free John—challenged His devotees to find out His real Name. Avatar Adi Da was testing His devotees to see if they understood the true Stature of the One with Whom they had been living with for so long as friend and "brother". In response, His devotees delved into esoteric literature and listened carefully for any clues He might be inclined to Give them. During their research, Avatar Adi Da would sometimes remark, apparently casually: "When you get da name of da god, you get da power of da god!" But no one got the point of His word play. Finally, on September 13, 1979, Avatar Adi Da sat down to write a letter to all His devotees Confessing that His Name is "Da, the One Who is Manifest As all worlds and forms and beings".

"Da" Is A Traditional Name Of Real God, or A Traditional Feeling-Reference To The Ultimate Condition and Power of Existence. "Da" Is An Eternal, Ancient, and Always New Name For The Divine Being, Source, and Spirit-Power— and "Da" Is An Eternal, Ancient, and Always New Name For The Realizer Who Reveals (and Is The Divine Self-Revelation Of) The Divine Being, Source, and Spirit-Power. Therefore, The Name "Da" Is (Since The Ancient Days) Found, Universally, In The Religious Cultures Of the world. (The Dawn Horse Testament, 2004 edition, 863.)

The very Name "Da" is primordial and carries mantric power. Devotees of Avatar Adi Da find His Name "Da" to be the greatest of all mantras, invoking the Love-Blissful Feeling of His Presence directly at the heart. And so the names "Bubba" and "Bubba Free John" were replaced by "Da" and "Da Free John".

Adapted from *The Order of My Free Names*.

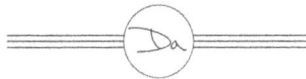

Avatar Adi Da Samraj:

There are two ways to live. We may live as the search for survival, protecting ourselves from change and death, and glamorizing ourselves through the acquisition of relations, goods, and fixed conditions, which we must also then seek to preserve. Such a way of life is not only enacted in the plane of theatre of gross and vital desires, it is also enacted in the subtler and subjective realms, where "spiritual" objects are acquired to our "eternal" selves. But we may freely abandon and be free of that whole adventure, and live as sacrifice, through love, yielding self, in the form of our feeling-attention, into the infinite pattern of presently arising changes and the whole, open-ended field of relations.

The life of sacrifice through love is not opposed to ordinary survival. Indeed, it permits the fullness of ecstatic and intelligent life. But it is free of the illusions and the dramatizations and the destiny of self-possession. (*The Way That I Teach*, 1978 edition, 106.)

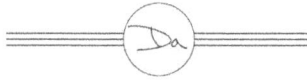

Halloween

For Halloween 1980, Heart-Master Da Free John suggested having a haunted house with ghosts and spirits at the Mountain Of Attention Sanctuary (previously known as "Persimmon"). He asked that several rooms of the Spirit Vase retreat residence be converted to accommodate the event. Devotees went all-out creating scary scenes in each room. The covered porch, which surrounded the building on all four sides, had hanging spider webs with large spiders and creepy insects that seemed to touch everyone who passed. The porch lights were low, which added to the spooky feeling.

We all dressed in Halloween costumes and met on the grass outside the haunted house, laughing at each other's costumes and trying to figure out who was underneath them. When the time came to enter the haunted house, I announced it to the crowd, but no one moved. My voice was drowned out by a cacophony of talk and laughter.

Since they couldn't hear me, I approached a few people just to get things going. I slightly turned each one by the shoulders toward the entrance, while saying in their ear that it was time to enter the haunted rooms.

I noticed a pattern of resistance as soon as each person felt my unexpected touch from behind and the slight pressure on their shoulders. They reacted by tightening their shoulders and firming their stance in resistance to being moved. Then, as soon as they understood what my touch was about, they relaxed and began moving in the direction I was indicating.

There was one exception to the resistance pattern. In response to the exact same approach from behind, and the same turning pressure on the shoulders, even prior to me speaking, I felt absolutely no resistance at all from this one person. He simply turned and moved like a leaf in the wind. He was wearing a Star Wars

"Yoda" mask and a black cape. To my sight, He was completely unrecognizable. But it was obviously Heart-Master Da Free John, immediately recognizable to my touch. There was no separate "self" to offer resistance. No "one" was there! (The Divine Heart-Master described His Divine State as being as vulnerable as an infant, as delicate as a butterfly.)

Heart-Master Da quietly joined the crowd and eased in among us, not speaking even when spoken to. His costume might have given His Identity away since it was "Yoda", the creature of great wisdom in the Star Wars movie. But I think Heart-Master Da's Siddhi kept Him unnoticed. (I observed over the years that during meditation or formal Darshan the Divine Heart-Master would become all-pervading at times, and then at other times He would become virtually unnoticeable.)

Heart-Master Da stood with some devotees in the back of each room, watching and laughing at His devotees' responses to the ghostly play. He continued to keep silent, but once a devotee with Him was recognized, it was obvious who they were with. However, when someone would say, "I think that's Master Da," the attendant would say, "Shhhhhh." His "invisibility" was part of the playfulness of that night.

For us, the Halloween event was all about being someone or something else, then getting scared by ghosts and monsters in the haunted house. To put on a costume and be someone else for a time was actually an interesting release from the self-identity we usually represented. But the release didn't last long; it was just play with the identity of the costume. When we got shocked by some "ghost" or "monster" jumping out at us, there was no doubt of who we were! Over the years, Halloween became more than an unusual and humorous opportunity for us to observe "self" in action. The Divine Master explained that ghosts were beings who had died but had not accepted that reality, so they hold on to the places they knew when bodily alive. Over time, He considered the origin of Halloween, which was thought to be an ancient Celtic festival in which people would light bonfires and wear costumes to ward off roaming ghosts.

Thus Halloween became a specific time of the Divine Heart-Master's Work to release discarnate spirits from their holding on to this realm, helping them move on in their destinies.

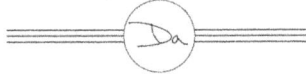

Da Love-Ananda
The Mountain Of Attention Sanctuary 1986

Da Love-Ananda

In January of 1986, the Divine Master Da Free John explained that He had experienced in His body an extraordinary Invasion of His Own Divine Siddhi which brought about a profound change in Him. He was no longer the active Teacher trying to move others, one by one, to the real process of Divine Self-Realization. He had become the very Murti, or Form, of the Divine Presence, and He simply Stood as That, calling on His devotees to now approach Him rightly in the true disposition of surrender, gratitude, and unswerving devotion. He described January 11, 1986, as the initiation of His Divine Emergence (Divine Avataric Self-"Emergence"), the Process by which He would Spiritually Embrace the billions of people "living and dying in this place" and ultimately Attract even all beings in all worlds. His eternal and universal Blessing Work had begun.

Forcefully emphasizing the reality of this change some years later, Beloved Adi Da said: "'Franklin Jones' is dead. 'Bubba Free John' is dead. 'Da Free John' is dead." In their place stood "Da Love-Ananda", the All-Pervading Divine Lord, the Giver of Divine "Love-Bliss". The Name "Love-Ananda" had been Given to Him privately by Swami Muktananda in the late 1960s and would now become His Full bodily Revelation.

"Love-Ananda" is a combination of English ("Love") and Sanskrit ("Ananda", meaning "Bliss"), thus communicating His Function as the Divine Avataric World-Teacher, embracing all human beings from all cultural settings. The combination of "Love" and "Ananda" means "the Divine Love-Bliss". The "Love-Ananda Avatar" is the Divine Bringer of the Divine Love-Bliss into the conditional worlds.

Adapted from *The Order of My Free Names.*

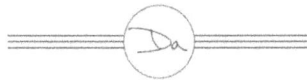

Avatar Adi Da Samraj:

Now, and forever hereafter, during and after (and forever after) the (physical) Lifetime of My Avatarically-Born bodily (human) Divine Form (here), I am, by all My Divine Avataric Means, <u>here</u> (and every 'where' in the cosmic domain)—always Spiritually and Divinely "Bright" <u>As</u> the One, and Only, and Inherently egoless, and Inherently Indivisible Conscious Light of all-and-All. (Da Love-Ananda Gita, 2005 edition, 82.)

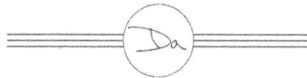

Discarnate Spirit

One day, while walking toward Heart-Master Da Love-Ananda's residence at Tumomama, His Hawaiian Sanctuary (established in 1978), I began to feel a very strange sense that I was not walking alone. I looked to both sides and behind me, but nothing was visible. The hairs on my neck rose as I felt the presence of someone or something moving next to me. It was a feeling of energy, the same as one feels when a person is next to them. It was very strange, yet I didn't feel anything negative about it. When this same feeling happened a second time, I was sure it was some sort of discarnate life-form. Since it wasn't putting out any negative energy, I began speaking to the invisible being.

I spoke out loud, acknowledging its feeling presence. At first I said, "I can feel you near me. You don't feel dangerous, so I want to talk with you. This is Da Love-Ananda's Sanctuary. It may have been your home in the past, but it has been Purified and Blessed with His Divine Presence now. Da Love-Ananda is a Divine Spiritual Master. Since you are here, you may have become sensitive to His Blessing Presence, therefore I'll tell you more about Him."

Each time I walked that path I assumed my new discarnate acquaintance was with me, but I always asked aloud if it was so. Then, whether I felt a response or not, I would enthusiastically talk about Da Love-Ananda and His radical Teaching even though my audience was invisible and inaudible.

Since Da Love-Ananda was not in residence at Tumomama at the time, I wrote to Him about these unusual experiences, emphasizing that it had happened several times, and that I had been speaking to whatever it was.

As soon as Beloved Heart-Master Love-Ananda got my letter, fully understanding what was happening, He gave Instructions to provide a set-apart location where He could directly Bless the native Hawaiian discarnate beings who had lived on that property for centuries previously. He said that a daily food offering should be made, that it should consist of grounding, earthy foods placed on an honorable platter each morning, and that it should be removed each evening and offered to the river that ran next to the Sanctuary. (The river is a place where native Hawaiian shamanistic ceremonies and rituals had been performed in times past, including the sacrifice of human beings. The food offerings were made as part of the process of purifying the negative karma associated with human sacrifice.)

Heart-Master Love-Ananda also said recitations of His Heart-Instructions should be read daily to the spirits. He then asked that a spirit statue be created. Once the statue was prepared, He Blessed it and had it placed at the site.

Each morning a formal invocation of Heart-Master Da Love-Ananda was offered at the site. The spirit statue was cleaned with fresh water and towel dried, and a fresh flower mala was placed on it. The food offering was placed in front of it, then the daily recitations would begin. The readings would last about thirty minutes. As I made these daily offerings, the immediate environment became quiet, the winds calmed, and it was clear that not only was I not alone, but the natural elements of the weather seemed to respond. Once Heart-Master Da Love-Ananda felt the site was established and the spirits were being served properly with His Blessings, He gave it the name "The Spirit Site".

Over time, it became obvious that the discarnate spirits being served at the Spirit Site were somehow aligned and conformed to Heart-Master Da Love-Ananda's Blessing Presence. In acknowledgment, He changed the name of the Spirit Site to "The Guardian Holy Site". To this day, the Hawaiian Sanctuary (now named "Da Love-Ananda Mahal") is protected by those spirits, who are still served daily at the Guardian Site.

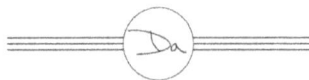

Lifting Me Higher

JULY 1987

It was a celebration of Radiant Happiness. On a raised stage, Heart-Master Da Love-Ananda danced for His devotees. His bodily movements and gestures revealed easeful balance and harmony, expressing equanimity, Perfect Love-Bliss. He was Revealing His Divine Nature, Condition, and State.

His Divine Authority to Awaken His devotees was expressed bodily in the Dance of the Master Dancer.[14] His gestures and postures said it all. He was the Supreme Authority, with one hand pointing up and the other to His heart. He was Lord Shiva dancing on surrendered egos, with one leg raised and both arms bent upward. And He was the Divine Avatar showing how to breathe and conduct His Spiritual Presence.

Loud music filled the room with rhythm. Heart-Master Da Love-Ananda's Radiant Siddhi descended into our bodies, generating spontaneous kriyas and mudras of purification as we Awakened to the non-separate Condition of egoless Being.

After His dance, devotees were invited to dance and celebrate His Divine Revelation. I soon realized that His Spiritual Presence had taken over "my" body. It didn't feel like "my" body any longer. Spontaneous hand and body postures arose as "I" stood on the dance floor. Then the energy current from above started flowing down the front of the body, turned and began rising up the spine, feeling as if the body were being lifted up from within. There was only the sense of rising energy as this was happening; the sense of self- awareness was completely gone.

As the rising energy moved, it affected the entire body. First, the right leg spontaneously raised and rested on the left ankle, so the body was standing on the left foot. Then, as the ascending current grew stronger, that left foot began rising up onto its toes. Soon all the weight of this 160-pound body was on the tip of the big toe of the left foot.

---

14. Master Dancer is a devotional play on the traditional understanding of Nataraja, the Hindu Lord (or King) of Dance.

The physical body seemed to not be subject to gravity. And the "me" who identified with this body had no control over what was happening. All I knew was I was deeply feeling profound love for my Divine Heart-Master while the body was doing strange things.

There was no pressure felt at all on that one toe. No effort to balance was needed. It was completely incredible—no weight, no pressure, no imbalance—just stably standing on one toe for several minutes until the music stopped. It was also amazing to feel how the Divine Heart-Master could freely intensify and change the circuit of bodily energy from descending to ascending. Clearly, when the Divine is felt, the Divine is in charge, the ego-"I" is not.

The next night, I mentioned the ecstatic raising of energy in the body and the "no gravity" experience to Heart-Master Da Love-Ananda and I asked Him if it might have been levitation. He asked for the details and then confirmed, "The experience was a kind of levitation. Levitation of the body off the ground is an expression of ascending conductivity in the spinal line."

The experience of a "kind of levitation" was beyond the body-mind, ecstatic in its temporary egolessness. Following as it did upon His masterful Conscious dance, I saw with absolute clarity that Heart-Master Da Love-Ananda's Divine State was without limit, egoless beyond experience of any kind. It is the Divine Prior Source-Condition and the Perfect Witness.[15]

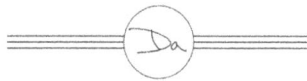

---

15. Perfect Witness: When Consciousness is free of egoic "self"-identification with the body-mind-complex, it stands in the Native Position of all that arises to and in and as the body-mind-complex.

Now You Dance!

As He had many times previously, Heart-Master Da Love-Ananda gathered in the evening with His devotees to talk about true practice and answer questions. After the considerations of the evening had been addressed, Da Love-Ananda said, "It's time to dance!"

With a sparkle in His bright eyes, the Divine Heart-Master invited individual devotees to mount the stage and dance so He could see them, and they could be seen by all. He then had couples dance, but not with their intimate partners. To me, it seemed to be all about being free and happy in His Blessed Company with relational contracts relaxed.

I was invited to dance while some fast music played. I gave it my best. As slower music began, I started to step off the stage. Just then Beloved Da Love-Ananda stepped onto the stage and started dancing, and—to my great surprise—invited me to stay and dance with Him.

I watched my Beloved Guru dance and tried to follow His movements. His Divine Body moved slowly and rhythmically to the music. At times He just stood still with a leg raised or His arm pointed above. I felt that His still postures were statements about Who He Is. Each posture spoke more than words. His dancing showed no need to conform to the music, yet every movement synchronized with it. It seemed as though the music were conforming to Him as He masterfully expressed the complete freedom and equanimity of His Conscious State. I felt He was Instructing us all on how to dance without self-consciousness.

As I tried to follow His movements, I noticed I was feeling the music much more than usual. I noticed I was feeling everything much more than usual! There was a great joy filling my heart, and greater clarity of awareness altogether. As I danced with focused feeling-attention on the Divine Master's movements, my heart opened, allowing me to more deeply feel His Love and, in response, spontaneously surrender in love of Him.

The Master Dancer Conducted and Transmitted His Spiritual Energy with a flick of His finger, or the curl of His eyebrow, or the turn of His head, or the raising of His leg. His pure Love underscored the music and filled the space with radiant waves of Love-Blissful Energy, bringing everything into Divine Unity. Everything was part of one awareness—the room, the music, the movement, the devotees—all connected in His Freely Given Divine Ecstasy.

After His dance, I marveled at what had just happened. Heart-Master Da Love-Ananda, the Divine Person, had bodily demonstrated the ecstatic fullness of the Way of the Heart. We were all undone in the Love-Bliss expressed in His Divine dance.

Heart-Master Da Love-Ananda laughed and said to all of us, and to all beings, "Now you dance!"

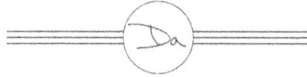

Baptized Each One

As soon as Heart-Master Da Love-Ananda had moved to Naitauba Island in Fiji (October 27, 1983), He had begun establishing holy sites, Empowering them with His Living Divine Presence and giving them Blessed names. Near His residence, in a section of the island called the Matrix, there was a great old tree, which the Divine Master had Blessed and named "Baptized Each One". At some point, Heart-Master Da asked all resident devotees to place a painted rock at the base of Baptized Each One as a sign of their devotion. The painting on the rock could be a prayer, one of His Names or Titles, a symbol like the Sanskrit word *Da*, or anything else the devotee chose to paint. (This act of devotion was a tradition for Naitauba resident devotees for a number of years.)

When I was approved as a resident in October 1987, I was told about the tradition and was told about where to find large smooth rocks. I found a nice rock, painted it with some of Da Love-Ananda's Holy Names, and got permission to go to Baptized Each One. At the tree, I followed the protocol: I offered an invocation of Heart-Master Da Love-Ananda, circumambulated the tree three times while invoking His Blessing Presence, and then placed the rock face up at the base of the tree. Also, as instructed, I sat by the tree for some time in contemplation of my Beloved Divine Heart-Master.

When I was about to leave, I heard talking and laughing up on the hill behind me. I turned and saw Beloved Da Love-Ananda. He had just arrived and was talking to some devotees about the need for more buildings at the Matrix. I joined them as they walked around the property considering where to place the various buildings, and while we were walking, Heart-Master Da Love-Ananda asked if I had placed my rock at Baptized Each One.

I said, "I just did that. And I painted my rock with bright neon flashing letters saying 'Remember Me'."

Heart-Master Da laughed loudly and said, "No! <u>Remember Me</u>!"

Everyone laughed. My Beloved Guru's point was well made. Actually, I realized I had only been partially joking. I had been thinking that by placing my devotional rock at Baptized Each One, it would keep me in His Blessing Regard. But the Way of the Heart is for the devotee to turn in heart-feeling surrender to the Divine Heart-Master, thus <u>remembering</u> <u>Him</u>, not the other way around.

During the walk, Beloved Da picked up something white from the ground and kept rubbing it between His thumb and His index finger. When the building development consideration was over for that day, as Heart-Master Da Love-Ananda left, He handed me the object. It was a round white shell from a Turban snail called an *operculum*. The bottom was concave and the flat top was marked by an imbedded spiral. When I saw the spiral, I was shocked! This simple loving gift was the fulfillment of a silent wish I had made fourteen years previously while traveling in India with my Beloved Heart-Master.

While in an antique shop in Bombay, the Divine Heart-Master had purchased some rare Saligrams.[16] Once back at our hotel room, He had more carefully examined the pieces and found that one of them wasn't real. His keen eye noticed that the spiral had been carved by hand, rather than having been petrified over hundreds of thousands of years.

My Beloved Guru asked me to return it to the shop. He explained that He had purchased the two Saligrams as a set, one with the spiral turning to the right, the other with the spiral turning to the left. The one spiraling left, the rarer of the two, was the fake. He told me to get a replacement Saligram with a left spiral to make the set.

At the shop the merchant showed me other Saligrams, but the spirals were all turning right. I was unable to find the replacement piece for my Beloved Guru. It was disappointing, but there was nothing I could do, and we didn't have an opportunity to look for other Saligrams for the rest of that India trip.

---

16. Saligrams are small fossils that are usually black with an embedded spiral pattern. In Hinduism they are believed to be direct representations of Lord Vishnu.

For years afterward I tried to find a left-turning Saligram of a matching size on each of my many trips to India in service to my Beloved Heart-Master, but I was never able to find what I was searching for.

To my great surprise, the round shell Da Love-Ananda gave me that day at the Matrix was the same size as the right-turning Saligram He had purchased in India fourteen years previously, and it had a perfect left spiral! It wasn't a Saligram, which could only have come from India, but it was what Fiji could offer instead, and my Beloved Heart-Master had picked it up almost as if He expected it to be there.

Heart-Master Da Love-Ananda's finding of that shell was another perfect example of how His Presence in the world transcended time and space. I had a gold casting made of the gift and attached it to my meditation mala. The shell has been a constant reminder of Him and the observation the Divine Heart-Master had made that "Nothing is a coincidence."

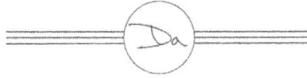

Da Avabhasa
Naitauba, Fiji 1991

Da Avabhasa

In April 1991, Avatar Adi Da spontaneously received a Naming Gift from one of His young devotees. At the annual Celebration of His Divine World-Teaching, this devotee performed a song for Him that she had composed, in which she praised Avatar Adi Da as "Da Avabhasa". He Graciously received the song, and, on April 30, 1991, indicated that "Da Avabhasa" was one of His Names, and indeed the principal Name by which He was now to be called.

"Avabhasa" in Sanskrit means "brightness", "appearance", "lustre", "light", "knowledge". The root of the word is "bhas" (with a long "a") which means "to radiate", "to become manifest", "to come forth", "to shine", "to beam", "to be resplendent or brilliant", "to show oneself", "to appear". The first two syllables "Ava" are the same as that of "Avatara", which means "to descend". Thus, the complete word "Avabhasa" means "shining toward", "shining down", "shining upon", or "showing oneself".

The Name Da Avabhasa, then, fully expresses the original Divine Nature of Adi Da and His Descent into the world. He is the "Bright", the Divine Condition of Love-Bliss-Light, which He had fully enjoyed in His infancy. And His "Brightness" is also the All-Consuming Fire of His Divine State.

Adapted from *The Order of My Free Names*

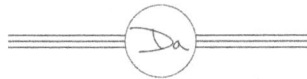

Avatar Adi Da Samraj:

The "Bright" (<u>Itself</u>, and <u>Altogether</u>) is never seen (and, indeed, cannot be seen) with the bodily eyes, but It Is to Be (and, in due course, <u>must</u> be) Tacitly Apprehended—As-My Divine Avataric Transcendental Spiritual Self-Transmission of the Self-Evidently Divine Love-Bliss-Current of Being (Itself), in and Beyond the right side of the bodily apparent heart. The (only-by-Me Divinely Avatarically Self-Revealed) Intrinsically egoless (and Tacit) Self-Apprehension of Being Is the "Root" of the "Midnight Sun", the "Root"-Domain of the "Bright" Itself.

I <u>Am</u> the Avatarically-Born, Avatarically Self-Transmitted, and Avatarically Self-Revealed Divine Self-Revelation of the "Bright". I <u>Am</u> the "Bright" (Itself). ("The Divine Avataric Self-Revelation of Adidam Ruchiradam", *The Aletheon*, 2009 edition, 1686.)

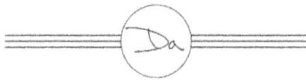

Celibacy at His Holy Feet

DECEMBER 1992

One evening at His Fijian Hermitage on the island of Naitauba, Beloved Da Avabhasa invited a few devotees to join Him at His residence. My intimate partner and I were the first to arrive. As we entered, our Beloved Heart-Master was being served by two renunciate devotees who were massaging His Holy Feet.

We took our seats as close to Him as we could. Soon, after more devotees arrived, the massaging stopped and Beloved Da Avabhasa began speaking. He talked about the appropriateness of single celibacy (celibacy without an intimate partner) as a discipline for His renunciate devotees. This wasn't a new subject; He had previously spoken about the possibility of single celibacy as a devotional discipline.

At the time, Heart-Master Da Avabhasa taught that, ultimately, celibacy becomes a natural consequence of Perfect Divine Enlightenment rather than a discipline. However, for the spiritual practitioner not yet Realized, choosing celibacy as a discipline holds the possibility of keeping available the energy that would otherwise be going to sexuality, thus leading to an intensification of spiritual practice, which may potentially quicken maturation. My intimate partner and I had taken up celibacy within our relationship, not as single celibates, and then, after a year and a half of celibacy, we had recently begun sexual intimacy again.

Beloved Da Avabhasa asked me, "Why would you be celibate for one and a half years, and then decide not to do it any longer? You're getting older and shouldn't be wasting time. This is the time to use for spiritual growth, not later."

I said, "I understand, Master. What should I do?"

He said, "I recommend you be celibate!"

I looked at my intimate partner. We both knew this would mean celibacy as a single person, and we also knew we would do whatever our Heart-Master recommended. She said, "If Beloved recommends this, then you should."

I nodded my head to her in agreement, then turned to my Divine Heart-Master and said, "Yes."

Beloved Da Avabhasa hugged me, then took my face in His hands and said, "You have no idea of the karmas you have undone by this response. I will give you all the glories of God-Realization if you will do this."

I was weeping. I said, "I will, Master."

He replied, "I will take care of you forever. You are Mine now." Then He said very strongly, "On this confession I will build My church."[17] I sensed, without fully understanding, that my confession of devotion and response along with the same confession and response from other devotees would give Beloved Da some people to work with for the sake of others, making it possible to "build" additional foundational elements of the Way of the Heart.

Even so, His words were also personal. I was overwhelmed and undone by the profundity of His Gift. My Beloved Guru and I hugged, and He said, "If you ever need a hug, come to Me. Don't worry about your intimate partner. I will take care of her. She will serve My house. My renunciate devotees will embrace her. She's Mine." Beloved Da turned to her and asked what she wanted to do.

She answered that she too wanted to be His single celibate and focus her life on Realizing Him. He then told her, as He had told me, "I will give you all the glories of God-Realization if you do this." She wept as she kissed His hand and bowed at His Holy Feet.

That night Heart-Master Da Avabhasa accepted several other devotees as single celibates. The next day He asked for confirmation that our commitment to single celibacy was real.

We all said yes.

Our responses were sincere at the time, yet, over time, none of us who did so that night would maintain the commitment to single celibacy. We gained self-understanding in the process, of course, though it also showed what the Divine Master was up against in terms of His Work to establish a renunciate culture. But working with people like us did give Him the opportunity to bring His unparalleled Wisdom to bear on the "emotional-sexual consideration"

17. This is of course a play on a famous quotation attributed to Jesus.

for the sake of everyone. (He had always described how the emotional element was inseparable from sexuality.) Eventually, the Divine Master gave a final description of how emotional-sexual practice unfolds for His devotees, and He confirmed that celibacy is an inevitable part of the demonstration for His most mature renunciate devotees.

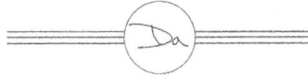

The Five Billion

DECEMBER 1992

On a very special evening, Beloved Heart-Master Da Avabhasa allowed a few of His devotees to feel the depth of His Compassion for all beings.

We were invited into His residence at the Matrix on Naitauba Island. We found our Beloved Master sitting on the end of His bed. His renunciate devotees were around Him. His head was in His hands. His face was wet with tears.

We were shocked at the sight. We silently took our seats on the floor in front of our Beloved Master, not knowing what we could do to help. The Divine Heart-Master kept saying over and over, "The five billion, the five billion," crying about the five billion human beings alive on Earth at that time.

He did not look up. He said, "I can't do it anymore. All the resistance, the refusal, the pain. The five billion." He cried, still holding His head in His hands. This ordeal went on for nearly an hour, His eyes red, His face wet, His body bent.

It felt like the entire universe had taken on the mood of despair for all of us, for all beings, as we sat helplessly feeling His profound Ordeal.

Suddenly, Heart-Master Da Avabhasa sat up and wiped His face and hands. He looked at us and said, "Okay, I'll do it! I'll take care of all the suffering beings. You cannot do it! I'll save every one! I will do it!"

And then He said no more.

From the beginning, the Divine Heart-Master was always clear that His Work in creating the Way of the Heart was for all of humankind. When He spoke of "saving" all of humankind, it was not in the "heaven and hell" sense of exoteric religion, East or West. Rather, He was speaking esoterically about freedom from the limitations suffered by human beings due to the binding force of the ego-"I".

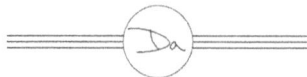

My Father's Passing

JANUARY 9, 1993

After their retirement, my parents moved from the cold winters of Boston to sunny Florida. I was living at Naitauba, but we kept in contact with letters and occasional phone calls. My mother said they loved living in Florida. One of their most enjoyable things to do, she said, was to sit on a wooden bench by the beach, "where it was interesting to watch the passing parade."

I was very happy that they had found simple enjoyments in warm weather. But one day I got a phone call that my father had been rushed to a hospital because he had been having a progressing heart attack for a couple days. As soon as possible, I reached him by phone. He told me he had a very strange dream the night before. In the dream, he was in a grass field walking toward a very bright white light at the end of the field. As he moved toward the light, he saw many of his old friends and family. They all seemed alive, yet they all had been dead for years. He said he was looking for his father but couldn't find him. He said the dream seemed so real! He then told me that being in the hospital made him feel afraid.

I had never heard a vulnerable confession from my father, so I knew he was afraid of dying and feeling it deeply. I could have told him my understanding of his dream, that it was a premonition of what would happen in the dying process, but I felt that would only make him more afraid; the best I could do was let him know I loved him, and that I was praying for his fast recovery.

I knew that dream was about his imminent passing, most likely to happen very soon. I felt terrible; my father was about to die. He was afraid, and I would never see him or hear his voice again.

His operation was scheduled for the same time Beloved Da Avabhasa had called for a gathering with His devotees in Hymns to Me (a meeting hall on Naitauba Island). I waited for my opportunity, and then told my Heart-Master about my father's condition and about the dream. I told Him that when I put my attention on my father I felt deep sorrow over the prospect of losing him. But I told

271

Him that I also felt so full of His Love that I was sure His Siddhi would greatly relieve my father's fear of dying. Even as I spoke, I sensed my Heart-Master's Blessings already being given.

Beloved Da Avabhasa said I should keep Him informed of any changes. My heart filled by His Grace, I thanked my Beloved Heart-Master and returned to my seat.

A few minutes after I was back at my seat, one of my friends asked about my father's condition. He talked about his own father's death and what he had gone through. When he had been in a similar situation, Heart-Master Da told him he should allow himself to cry for his father. He told me that I should allow myself to fully feel it all. Then he led me back to Beloved Da Avabhasa's seat to sit on the floor in front of my Beloved Heart-Master.

Another friend sat with me and asked about my relationship with my father and our love for each other. I told him many stories about how great my father was. He then told me about his father's life and death. Other friends joined us and we all spoke very emotionally, and they cried with me about my father and their fathers. One friend rubbed my back with great sensitivity and began to cry with me. His mother had recently died. Other friends hugged me. Everyone was helping me feel deeper into my love and my sorrow.

Then Heart-Master Da Avabhasa motioned me to come and speak with Him again. As I knelt in front of Him, He told me I should review my life with my father, I should feel my love for him. I cried and said, "It isn't fair, good men should live forever; it's terrible that loved ones die. We can't even keep our Beloved Divine Master alive and with us bodily forever."

He said, "Nothing ends! If you don't go through it all while alive, you will store it in your psyche and have to come back to deal with it another time. You have to face it all, feel it all."

I responded, "It's really difficult to face it."

"That's the price you pay. It's part of the Hearing Process.[18] Don't be ashamed to cry for your father. Express your love for him and cry for him. He is having a hard time and needs to feel your love. It's the human thing to do."

18. The Hearing Process is a stage of spiritual maturity in the Way of the Heart.

I returned to my seat feeling everything Beloved Da Avabhasa had said while I cried for my father. Then I moved to a wooden bench at the rear of the room. Within a minute my Beloved Guru came and sat next to me on the bench. I could feel Him against my right side as He sat silently with me for a minute or two while I watched the devotees in front of us through my tears. Then He turned to me and said, "Isn't it interesting, watching the passing parade?"

I was stunned. Those were my mother's very words describing how they liked to sit on a wooden bench at the beach while "watching the passing parade".

My Beloved Heart-Master held my hand in His. By those words I knew that He was completely in touch with my father's condition. I felt deeply grateful for the depth of His Empathy. He said, "It is okay, you haven't gotten into the depth of feeling all the way yet. It's not a show anyway." I had been crying for hours, but it seemed there was more to feel and let go of.

As a child of seven, I had cried myself to sleep many nights over the concern that someday I would die. That concern brought up such great sorrow and fear; it was beyond anything I could deal with. I never wanted to get back in touch with my fear of death, so, as most people do, I suppressed it. Staying superficial, acting as if I were immortal, became the means of staying out of touch with that inevitable reality.

Now that an intimate family member was approaching death for the first time in my experience, that old horrific feeling was reappearing. I didn't want to have anything to do with it. My father's imminent death reminded me of the inevitability of my own death. By helping me get in touch with my deepest feelings for my father, and the overwhelming fear of my own death, my Heart-Master relieved me of the suffering that results from suppressing emotions.

My father died three days later. I informed Da Avabhasa of his passing and thanked Him for His Blessings. I knew Beloved Da had been Spiritually Present, helping my father through the death transition.

Then a most unusual thing happened. On the second night after my father died, he spoke to me! I was asleep in the men's dormitory on Naitauba Island, when I was awakened by my father's voice. I heard him call "Jerry" loudly. Everyone other than my family called me Gerald. There was no doubt about it—it was my father, and he was there.

I sat up and looked around. I could feel him but could not see him. I wanted to speak out loud to him, but I didn't want to wake up others in the dormitory, so I chose to speak from my heart with my inner voice.

I let him know that I was very happy he had come to say good-bye. I told him not to worry, that Beloved Da Avabhasa was Blessing him and taking care of him, and that under His Blessings everything would be all right. I made sure he knew he had died and that death was not a problem. I also let him know he had handled all his worldly business, so there was nothing left to do or hold on to. I told him he had been a good man and a good father. I told him he was free to go on with his destiny. I told him I loved him and would miss him.

Then in a moment everything felt different. He left! There was no doubt about it—it was like feeling someone touching you, then removing their touch. I went back to sleep knowing all would be well with him on the "other side". He had Beloved Da's Blessings, and, by Da Avabhasa's Grace, I had been able to help his transition, in spite of being halfway around the world from Florida.

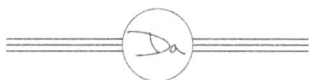

The Vision of Kali

On one special formal Darshan occasion, which we affectionately called "Fiery Sunday", Beloved Da Avabhasa poured His Divine Blessings into His devotees with unusual intensity. Everyone responded to the intensification of His Blessing Siddhi in uncommon ways. Some were crying, some were laughing, some began babbling, some were loudly calling out His name "Da", some bodies were shaking, many had rapid breathing, and there were many spontaneous hand postures (mudras)—everyone was swooning in the Beloved Master's Siddhi.

I was sitting directly in front of Beloved Da Avabhasa on the floor in the first row. My eyes remained open as I swooned in His Radiant Bliss. Then a most unusual thing happened. His face appeared to be changing. I "saw" His eyes turning blood red. Then He took on a snarling expression. His mouth opened, His teeth became pointed, with long fangs on each side. His hair became totally wild.

The appearance of His face was way beyond human. I was in another realm. I was in the company of Kali, the Hindu deity who kills the ego-"I" by ripping off heads and wearing them as beads on a necklace while blood still flows from their torn necks.

I was very frightened, but I did not take my feeling-attention off Heart-Master Da Avabhasa for a moment. I didn't dare; I was too frightened to do anything but keep surrendering my attention to Him. It was like the account in the *Bhagavad Gita* of Krishna showing his multi-armed form to Arjuna and Arjuna begging Krishna to return to his normal two-armed form.

In my great fear, like Arjuna, I too wanted my Beloved Master to return to His familiar Form. And in time, my perception of Heart-Master Da Avabhasa's face returned to the normal appearance of my Beloved Guru.

After the Darshan I asked others if they saw what I saw. I found a few people who thought they noticed something different about the way He looked, but it wasn't what I saw. I told Heart-Master Da about the experience, and how a few others seemingly saw something unusual about His face, but not the vision of Kali.

He responded, "What difference does it make if no one else saw what you saw? If you saw it, that's good enough." He didn't explain anything about the vision—what I saw, why I saw it, or what it meant to have seen it. So I continued to feel into it.

Beloved's face often seemed to change during Darshan and other sacred occasions. The changes were visible, but in subtle ways, like glimpses of a previous incarnation. Beloved Adi Da has granted me countless spiritual experiences, but this one was very unusual—so vivid, so tangible, carrying so much emotion with it, not at all like a subtle vision.

The Goddess Kali is worshiped throughout India as the destroyer of egos. In time I felt the vision was a revelation of another Divine Form of the Divine Heart-Master's Work with devotees, encompassing the Kali function. What is "destroyed" in the life of a responsive devotee is his or her consistent resort to the unconscious patterning of the ego-"I".

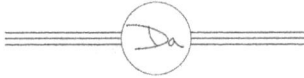

The Captain

DECEMBER 1993

After a gathering with His devotees in Hymns to Me on Naitauba Island, Beloved Da Avabhasa prepared to return by boat to His forest retreat residence, Lion's Lap, on the other side of the island. I was invited to accompany Him, along with His senior renunciate devotees. As we approached the boat, a devotee concerned for our safety told Heart-Master Da Avabhasa to be careful because the tide was going out. (Commonly, when the tide was too far out Da Avabhasa would travel by car, but when it was safe He always preferred to travel by boat.)

After we were seated, Beloved started the motor and slowly turned the boat in the direction of Lion's Lap. Then He pushed the throttle completely forward—He "put the pedal to the metal", or, in boat talk, He "opened it up". The boat jumped forward and charged across the water, bouncing off the waves. Beloved Da Avabhasa laughed and in a completely confident, loud voice, heard over the rush of air and the roar of the engine, He reminded us, "I am the Captain of My ship!"

Da Avabhasa never did anything reckless. In fact, He was the most safety-conscious of anyone I ever met. He had traveled this same route hundreds of times and knew every detail about it, including the required safe tide. But I got concerned; the boat was rushing full speed over the water with no possibility of making quick turns should rocks be seen protruding above the surface. I thought the advice about the tide had been a precautionary way of saying "Drive carefully".

Aware of my concern, my Beloved Heart-Master said, "You're afraid, aren't you?"

I didn't answer.

"You are afraid!"

"Yes," I confessed.

He laughed. Nothing more was said about it, but His laughter immediately showed me that my attention was on me and not in the devotee's disposition of surrendering self-attention to the Divine Heart-Master.

I already fully knew the Heart-Master would never lead His devotees into harm's way. On that boat trip, however, I was failing to recognize Who my Captain was. It was a valuable lesson, since the devotee's vulnerability through complete trust and surrender is required for the Divine Heart-Master to fully Reveal and Awaken His Divine State in His devotees.

And, of course, the Captain landed His boat at Lion's Lap unscathed, with all passengers unharmed.

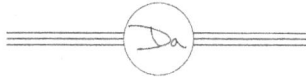

A Day with Da Avabhasa

DECEMBER 1993

The Naitauba Island resident devotees were invited to spend an afternoon with Beloved Da Avabhasa at the Matrix, His main residence. I was one of the first to get there. He was relaxing in His bathing pool inside Kaya Kalpa Kutir (a hut named after a system of total body rejuvenation). I was told that since Heart-Master Da's pool faced the ocean, I should approach from the ocean side. It sounded strange, but I was happy to approach Da Avabhasa in any way.

I walked around the building to the steps on the ocean side and prostrated in the sand before looking up to see my Beloved Heart-Master. As I stood up, I was almost knocked over by a forceful spray of water. My Beloved Guru was standing in His bathing pool holding a three-foot long water gun, blasting water at me.

It was one of the funniest moments I can remember. I couldn't stop laughing. Da Avabhasa had a mischievous look on His face. He told me to meet the others as they arrived and send them <u>one at a time</u> around to approach Him from the ocean side, as I had done. He emphasized that I shouldn't tell them or let them see what He was doing.

I followed His Instructions and after each devotee prostrated in the sand, their Beloved Guru's Blessing Regard was given in the form of a grand blast of water—joyful and full of Heart-Master Da's Loving Humor.

Once everyone got soaked, I returned to the pool to sit near my Beloved Guru. Naturally, He totally soaked me once again, and, naturally, I was totally delighted.

After a while, Da Avabhasa invited all of us to join Him for a swim in the ocean. He liked to use a large inflated round tube that had the name "Fun Float" printed in very large letters on the side. He would float inside the ring of the tube, resting His arms on top. We all stayed close around Him, enjoying His Happy, Loving Company.

Early in the evening Beloved Da Avabhasa suggested we all play Trivial Pursuit. Teams were selected, but I wasn't chosen for any of them. Instead I was sent to help with the meal preparation. I wanted to play the game with my Beloved Master. I had been so close with Him all day that I had been expecting and hoping the direct contact would continue. Like a child sent home from the playground, I felt rejected and hurt. While helping with the food, I was told that Da Avabhasa had made some humorous comments about my contracted feelings as I left. That intensified my contraction, since I really identified with feeling rejected.

Once the food was cooked, I brought it to the group, still feeling left out. Beloved Da Avabhasa addressed my state immediately, zeroing in on the very thing that bothered me. He said, "No one at all wanted you on their team." He named a certain guy who was selected and said, "Everyone knows he's dumb, but no one selected you!"

In my contracted state, I bought into this, feeling: *what a failure I am, not welcomed, totally un-liked, totally un-loved.* Heart-Master Da Avabhasa made a few other remarks that made everyone else laugh, which deepened my contraction even more. Then He asked, "Are you sure you were able to prepare the food properly? Someone better check it out, we all don't want to be poisoned."

What?! Finally, I saw what I was doing. It became so clear: my hurt feelings weren't happening to me, they resulted from choosing to feel rejected. More importantly, as soon as I realized that this understanding was a Gift from my Beloved Heart-Master, I began to turn back to Him. Feeling Him again, I was able to release my disturbed condition. As soon as I let go, Da Avabhasa laughed and welcomed me as if my rejection-drama had never happened.

Watching Beloved Da play Trivial Pursuit was a revelation of another kind. He was a genius! He totally considered each question. He drew on all the information available from His team. He considered the answer in logical, historical, factual, and intuitive terms. Then He Worked with it all until He came up with an answer for His team. Almost always when His team gave an answer, it was correct.

Heart-Master Da Avabhasa's team, no matter who was on it, always won at Trivial Pursuit. But don't get the idea that He was competing against pushovers. Most of the devotees who lived on Naitauba Island were highly educated people with advanced degrees. Beloved Heart-Master Da's Genius was an expression of His Conscious State. Nothing can compete with Divine Consciousness.

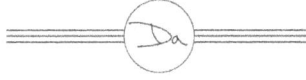

Who Am I?

One day a few devotees were invited to join Da Avabhasa at the Matrix. My intimate partner and I arrived early. The Divine Realized Guru in His bathing pool greeted us warmly, and invited us to sit by the pool.

As the other devotees arrived, they were also invited to join Heart-Master Da by His pool. Three renunciate devotees were also there. It was very unusual for anyone other than the renunciate devotees to be so close to the Divine Master in His pool.

At one point one of the renunciates slipped into the pool, held her breath, and went underwater for what seemed like a long time. Once she came up, she took another deep breath and went under again. This time Heart-Master Da placed His hand on her head to hold her down. She stayed under water for an even longer time than before. I began to feel concerned, thinking it was getting to be too long; yet she wasn't showing any sign of wanting to come up for air. When Heart-Master Da removed His hand she came up seeming to breathe normally, not at all short of breath. I was very impressed that she could hold her breath that long and that she was so fully submitted to His Divine Play. Beloved Da Avabhasa praised her and said that her trust demonstrated true devotion. A bit later our Beloved Heart-Guru talked to us about Divine Reality and the necessity to receive His Divine Revelation. He asked if any of us could confess receiving It. When asked directly by Master Da, "Who has received My Divine Revelation?" I had difficulty responding.

Feeling my difficulty, He stepped out of the pool and came over to me. Looking me straight in the face from just a few feet away, He asked, "Who am I?"

I said, "You are my Guru, my Master."

He responded, "Yes, but who am I?"

I knew I wasn't expressing what I really knew to be true; I was blocked. I didn't know why, but I couldn't overcome my reluctance. Instead, I said more about Him being my Heart-Master.

Again He asked, "Who am I?"

His question penetrated deep into buried feelings about God and Divinity. At depth, in fullest summary feeling, I felt: *He is God.* Yet I had never called Him "God". I was sure of it, but I couldn't say it. I was still holding on to beliefs and feelings established in childhood about God as the Creator, the abstract all-knowing Authority, the absolute God so holy that His Name was not to be directly spoken by traditionally religious Jews.

The confrontation with these core feelings brought up a real crisis. Tears began streaming down my cheeks. I felt *He is God* in the fullest understanding of God as the non-separate Divine Reality, yet I felt that to say "You are God" would violate something fundamental at the core of my being. It surprised me that those beliefs were still there and still so strong. I thought I had fully understood those beliefs and left them behind years before. I thought I knew better, but at the core I was still deeply attached to uninspected feelings based on uninspected beliefs.

Heart-Master Da Avabhasa kept looking me straight in the face and waiting. Finally it came out. I said, "You are God."

Da Avabhasa didn't say anything more. My confession and all it revealed continued to work on me. I was deeply impressed by how I could be compromised in expressing what I knew to be true, even after years of listening to and experiencing the profundity of Heart-Master Da's Teaching. After years of deepening devotion and self-understanding, years of responsively conforming my life to His Blessed Instruction, even after all those priceless Gifts, my surrender, which should have allowed complete examination of all deeply felt beliefs and feelings, hadn't gone deep enough.

At the level of the mind I understood that my old beliefs were based on myths. But I had not inspected the feelings that were based on those beliefs. My self-understanding wasn't deep enough to address them. The rest of the night Heart-Master Da Avabhasa moved on to speak with us about different subjects, but I was so confronted, even shaken, by the breaking of such strong bondage that I have no memory of what He spoke about.

The incident by the pool emphasized that no pattern of egoity is precious—it's all garbage and needs to be discarded. The incident by the pool showed me why true surrender is the key to real devotion. Heart-Master Da Avabhasa's Work with me that day served to deepen my self-understanding and allow a fuller recognition and reception of His Divine Revelation. For me to say "You are God" was a true confession of receiving what He came to Give. He is the Revealer and the Revelation that the truth of "God" is the always already condition of existence as Divine Reality.

Heart-Master Adi Da had said:

[T]he ordinary, gross egoity of the apparently born personality . . . must be converted in anyone who would take up Spiritual life for real.

The ego is converted by response to the Revelation That Is the Realizer—not merely the Word but also the Person of the Realizer, the Sign of the Realizer, the Presence of the Realizer, the Very One. ("The Westerner in Everyone Must Be Converted", *My "Bright" Form,* 2016 edition, 18–19.)

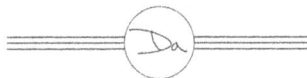

PART FIVE

Stories from 1994–2000

Hearing

In a gathering with devotees, Beloved Da Avabhasa asked if any of us felt we were "Hearing", or demonstrating the consistent capability to understand and transcend the self-contraction. I felt clear that Heart-Master Da Avabhasa had given me the capacity to turn to His non-contracted egoless State moment to moment, instead of meditating on my contracted self. I responded to Him, proposing I was Hearing.

Beloved Da Avabhasa asked me to explain further. I said, "I can see and feel all my habits and tendencies, all my reactions, all my limits, and through Your Given Grace of self-understanding I see they are not happening to me, but I am actively doing them all. Since it is obvious that I'm doing them all, I feel that Awakened self-understanding has enabled me to surrender them all to You as they come up, Beloved Master."

Heart-Master Da said that was not true Hearing. It was self-observation or self-watching, not summary self-understanding. He said that summary self-understanding is not about noticing the things that arise; it is about fundamentally understanding that the entire separate point of view that notices what is arising is the self-contraction. When this is directly realized, it is a complete summary Revelation; it includes the entire sense of separate self-identity, everything that the ego-"I" is.

Everything I thought represented Hearing was about noticing the different reactions and contractions as they arose and, instead of dramatizing them, I would feel the Given devotional capacity to turn to Da Avabhasa instead. While that turning was positive and a real practice, it wasn't true Hearing or summary self-understanding. True Hearing is the Grace-Given Awakened capacity to transcend the act of the self-contraction, not merely to notice the contraction.

Heart-Master Da Avabhasa had told His devotees that true Hearing is Given in recognition of His Divine State, because His Divine State is prior to the self-contraction and thus exposes it perfectly. He had said that turning the principal faculties of the body-mind (attention, feeling, body, and breath) in devotional

Communion with His felt Presence and Person is the beginning of the process that leads to true Hearing. Heart-Master Da said that in my speech I kept confirming my self-identity by saying "I", "me", and "my", rather than recognizing that point of view itself is the act of self-contraction in self-identity.

In 1994 the Divine Master explained to another devotee:

> *To truly Hear Me is to be in a position to directly transcend this knot, this action of "self"-contraction.*
>
> *You are still struggling with the "self"-contraction—not understanding that you are doing it, or not understanding exactly what it is you are doing. Therefore, in your gesture of "self"-surrender—which is fine and good—you are still being confronted, most of the time, with the knot behind that gesture. This does not mean your practice is failing. Confronting this knot is an essential aspect of what your practice is about. Therefore, rather than trying to escape the "self"-contraction, you must intensify your practice of devotion to Me, make it more profound, do it more intensively—under all circumstances, in every moment—until the Revelation that is True Hearing of Me is Given (by My Divine Avataric Transcendental Spiritual Grace).*
>
> *True Hearing of Me is not something the ego can decide to realize. If True Hearing of Me has occurred, there is no doubt about it. It is not an intellectual matter, not a "maybe". It is a profound change, a turnabout in the ego-place—Effected by My Divine Avataric Transcendental Spiritual Grace. Anyone in whom this conversion has occurred can confess it directly—because there is no doubt about it, and the signs will be evident in the life as well.*
> ("The Godly Struggle", *My "Bright" Form*, 2016 edition, 409–10.)

Every aspect of the Awakening process—Listening, Hearing, Seeing, the Perfect Practice, Ultimate Divine Realization—is a Gift Awakened by the Grace of the Divine Heart-Master. Obviously, summary self-understanding had not been Awakened in me. I understood by my Guru's Grace that I was practicing, but not Hearing. Heart-Master Da said, "True Hearing is black or white, all or nothing."

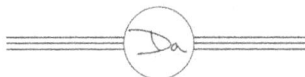

Adi Da, the Da Avatar
Naitauba, Fiji 1994

Adi Da, The Da Avatar

In October of 1994, the Name that Avatar Adi Da later came to call His "Fully Elaborated Principal Revelation-Name" was Revealed to Him. For several days He found Himself seeing and hearing the Name "Adi Da" and knew that this must be a reference to Himself, manifesting out of His own Depth. In response to the Mysterious appearance of this Name, Avatar Adi Da consulted books in the library at Naitauba, hoping to find the meaning and traditional associations of the word "Adi". Then, on October 11, 1994, satisfied that the Revelation was clear, Avatar Adi Da made known to His devotees that all were now invited to address Him as "Adi Da—The Da Avatar".

"Adi" is a Sanskrit word that means "first", "primordial", "source". It is additionally defined as "primary", "beginning", "commencement", and "first fruits". Thus, the three syllables of "Adi Da" name Him exactly, expressing in their brief utterance His devotees' full heart-intuition of Him as the Primordial Being, the Source of all, the Original Divine Person, Da, Who has become Incarnate as the Da Avatar.

"Adi Da" is a communication prior to qualities. It is prior to mind, prior to emotions, prior even to any feeling of personal reference. The letters of the Name "Adi Da" read the same in both directions, from left to right and from right to left. In addition, "I" stands at the center of the Name, and on either side of "I" is the syllable "Da", first backwards, then forwards. Thus, the Name "Adi Da" reads "I—Da", signifying "I Am Da", in both directions from the center. Therefore, the spontaneous appearing of the Name "Adi Da" is the completion of the momentous Revelation in 1979, when Avatar Adi Da first Offered His Divine Confession, "I Am Da". Through the perfectly symmetrical structure and letters of His principal Name "Adi Da", the Divine Avatar makes the Great Statement that He is the First and the Last, the Complete Manifestation of God, Truth, or Reality in the conditional realms.

"Avatar" means "One who is descended or 'crossed down' from and as the Divine". It is a Sanskrit word for the Divine Incarnation. Thus, the Name "Adi Da", combined with the reference "The Da Avatar", fully acknowledges Adi Da as the One His devotees know Him to be. All His devotees, and even all beings are the recipients of the most Miraculous Revelation ever Given: the original, first, and complete Avataric Descent or Incarnation of the Divine Person, Who is Named Da. Through the Mystery of Adi Da's human Birth, He has Incarnated not only in this world, but in every world, at every level of the cosmos, as the Eternal Primordial Giver, the Original Giver of Help, Grace and Ultimate Divine Freedom to all beings.

Adapted from *The Order of My Free Names*.

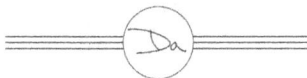

Avatar Adi Da Samraj:

There is one Great Law: You become what you meditate on.

This Law summarizes the process whereby I can Be your Unique Advantage. In the midst of perceiving beings and things and phenomena of all kinds, My true devotee is always in heart-Communion with Me. As My true devotee, you are always con-centrated in Me. In the midst of whatever arises, you constantly turn whole bodily to Me.

When you Contemplate Me with devotion, you are Contem-plating the Divine Reality Itself—in Its Fullness and Perfection. When you feelingly Contemplate Me, you are Contemplating the All-Completing Avataric Divine Self-Revelation.

Therefore, I Am your Unique (Avataric Divine) Advantage. Simply by means of your feeling-Contemplation of Me (in all the moments of conditional existence), the total process in My Avataric Divine Company is progressively Activated in you, by My Avataric Divine Spiritual Grace. The developmental stages of practice in the only-by-Me Revealed and Given Way of Adidam will be sponta-neously manifested in you—not by your self-consciously duplicat-ing the signs of each of the stages, but merely by your consistently entering into heart-Communion with Me. (Da Love-Ananda Gita, 2005 edition, 113.)

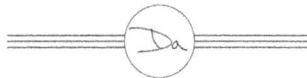

The Divine Giver

DECEMBER 1994

Each year in December devotees of the Divine Avatar Adi Da celebrate Danavira Mela (the celebration of "the Hero of Giving", also known as the Celebration of "Light-in-Everybody"). Heart-Master Adi Da always showed His great joy in gift-giving. His family, His renunciate devotees, and a few other devotees (representing all His devotees) were invited to be with Him during wonderful occasions of celebratory giving.

Avatar Adi Da says:

Gift-giving is delightful, but your giving of gifts should be a celebration of how you live every day, a confirmation of your life with Me, and with everyone you know and meet, even with all humankind. This basic expression should continue through the New Year, and it should confirm your disposition all year.

This is the secret of the ego-transcending process. I am always Giving the great Gift of My Divine Love and Blessing. When My devotees love Me and practice the Way that I have Given them, that is their gift. When My devotees love Me and practice, and when I Love them and Bless them, there is this exchange with one another. Then, every year during this season, I express ceremoniously what I have done with My devotees, and what they have done with Me, all year long. This is the secret of My participation in this celebration.

Know that I Bless you through and beyond time and space. Live a life of celebration. True life, ego-transcending life, is a celebration, a joyous occasion of meeting with others in the universal circumstance of prior unity and in the joy of Communion with the Indivisible Divine Reality.

That is why I look forward to this season every year. It is the greatest season of the year. It is a marvelous season. I hope it is a happy time for you and for all your friends. (Quoted in Naamleela Free Jones, *The Danavira Mela Book*, 2008 edition, 13.)

During the Danavira Mela celebration in 1994, my intimate partner and I were invited into Heart-Master Adi Da's Blessing

Company to participate in His gifting occasion at His Fijian Hermitage residence, Naitauba Island.

The occasion took place in His bedroom. My first impression upon entering was how totally beautiful it was. Then I felt how calm and peaceful, bright, happy, and perfectly conscious His room was. Adi Da, the Da Avatar, sat with His family, while the renunciate devotees were nearby serving to ensure His (and everyone's) comfort. As soon as I saw Beloved Adi Da, my feeling-attention fixed on Him like a magnet. I lovingly laid flowers at His Holy Feet. When I looked up, He was smiling at me. It felt totally sweet, warm, and welcoming. I sat at His Feet with the other guests, all of us totally enveloped in His Siddhi of Freedom and Happiness.

Beloved Adi Da's room was a true temple. It was where He associated with and gave His Blessed Regard to different traditions of religion and spirituality, as well as where He had universal icons of happiness and relatedness, like Mickey Mouse and teddy bears, placed in relational conformity with each other in various places. The room was fairly large and was full of important sacred objects including hanging thankas, life-size statues, and many smaller statues and images, all perfectly placed and fully honored with great flower arrangements.

Beloved Adi Da had added a seven-foot-tall tree which He named "The Divine Spirit-Tree of Light", fully lit with more bulbs than seemed possible. Every branch of the tree was laden with sacred and ornate hanging ornaments. Below the tree ran an electric train, hooting and tooting as it passed by. Beloved Adi Da had all the train stations, bridges, and miniature people happily in place.

To the left of the Spirit-Tree of Light was a kimono-type coat with arms extended, called the "Giving Coat". It had many large pockets on both the outside and the inside. Each pocket was decorated with a sacred image. Overflowing from each pocket were beautifully wrapped gifts—truly a Giving Coat!

Beloved Adi Da, the Divine Avatar, was dressed simply. His elegant shirt was an original hand-painted design made by one of His artist devotees. His long hair was down and flowing. The spicy scent of His cologne was in the air. His Divine Person added beauty to the objects in the room and His Divine Presence outshined it all.

Months before the Danavira Mela celebration, Heart-Master Adi Da had decided who would be invited to this occasion. The Gifting Guild had provided a list of all possible gifts He might want to give, most of them gifts His devotees had given Him, which He called His "gift stash". He then had selected exact gifts from the stash to give to each person invited.

When it was time to begin gifting, the Divine Hero of Giving moved to the foot of His bed to be closer to everybody. He would not receive any gift until He had given all His gifts. Since the celebration coincides with Christmas, Heart-Master Adi Da humorously included Santa's elf helpers to assist with His Giving. An elf, dressed in a green elf costume, hat, pointed shoes and all, handed Adi Da one gift at a time, or one tray of gifts at a time, depending on the sequence the Heart-Master had previously determined.

Each gift had a small sticker indicating who it was for and what the gift was. The elves made sure each sticker was correct and was securely fastened. Adi Da received each wrapped gift from the elf, covered the sticker with His hand so no one could see, and peeked at the name and identifying information. He seemed to make a point of this, since everyone expecting a gift was interested to see if that gift was for him or her. He then decided if that was still the gift to be given at that time. It seemed that sometimes He changed the gifting sequence in the moment, but once He decided, the Hero of Giving removed the sticker and silently gave the gift with His Transmitted Love and Divine Blessings.

I had anticipated that His gifting would only be for His family and the renunciates, but to my great surprise He started gifting the guest devotees. I was absolutely overwhelmed to receive Divine Love in the form of gifts from my Heart-Master, and by the abundance and perfection of His choices. Each gift was given separately as the Divine Master of Giving filled my heart with His soft Loving smile.

Here is a list of all the gifts I received. I can't remember the order in which I received them, but the abundance will speak for itself:

A beautiful hand-blocked cotton shawl covered with His Sacred Names, to be used in meditation or while on retreat.

A Tibetan stick drum, to proclaim His Divine Presence in my priestly service.

A handmade wooden hair comb. (For a time I felt that grooming was egoic and often didn't comb my hair.)

A carved black stone frog with big eyes and its front feet together in prayer, a totally delightful devotional sign. (It is right in front of me as I write this history.)

An attractive porcelain candle holder, to wave light in worship around His Holy Murti.

A large glass paperweight with an unusual design of rising bubbles and a pewter platypus sitting outside on top. Adi Da said He particularly liked the platypus.

Two framed photos of Beloved Adi Da, for devotional contemplation in my room.

A framed photo of me in deep Communion with my Heart-Master, for me to see my sign of devotion and let it grow deeper.

A Blessed silver locket for my mala containing sacred elements of sand and earth from His Holy Temples: the Outshining "Brightness" at Atma Nadi Shakti Loka and His Sukra Kendra Holy Temple at the Matrix at His Hermitage Island.

Dried flower petals from a Sukra Kendra Paduka Puja (worship of ceremonial sandals).

A piece of fabric from His own shirt.

Christmas tree candy canes and chocolate camels.

What overwhelming abundance from the Divine Master of Love! I melted into a state of heart-fullness, tearfully full of inexpressible gratitude and love. All the other guests also received such an abundance of His Divine Love in the gifts from our Beloved Heart-Master and I'm sure they were also dissolved in His great Siddhi of Love-Bliss.

After gifting us, the Hero of Giving began giving gifts to His family and the renunciates. The sacred celebration went on and on for hours and hours in Adi Da's unending Divine Happiness.

Danavira Mela, the Celebration of Light-in-Everybody, was always the most profound Love event of the year—full of heart-intimacy with few words spoken, a living Divine Blessing and an expression of our eternal bond with the Hero of Giving.

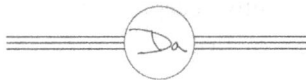

A Jew in a Christian Society

FEBRUARY 1995

During a gathering with Heart-Master Adi Da I mentioned to Him that when I was a teenager, I hung around with Italian and Irish guys. There were only two Jews in our gang of about two hundred. I was called "Beanie" (referring to the Jewish cap worn in temple) and the other Jew was called "Bagel". The names definitely suggested that we were different, and my friends did play on it a lot, but it was only the kind of banter typical of teenage guys.

I told my Heart-Master that when I started dating Italian girls I would tell them my name was Jerry Cafferela, an Italian friend's last name. Beloved Adi Da asked why. I told Him it was to make it easier to get the dates.

A friend at the gathering said, "Didn't you change your name from Gerald Sheinfeld to Jerry Shine for a while on your business cards?" I said I had done that because it seemed to be easier for others to remember. To me it also was a way to be more accepted. Beloved Master Adi Da didn't make any comments about any of it that night.

A few nights later in another gathering, the Da Avatar addressed me regarding fear of rejection. He cited my use of different names in order to become more acceptable. He said, "You had an emotional pattern that was about being a Jew in a Christian society, never quite being accepted, but always trying to conform to get the acceptance."

His comment helped me see that I always approached all others with that anticipated fear of rejection and I was always working to get around it. Beloved Adi Da said, "That is why you liked the sixties. You could be mellow, love and peace, you know, a nice guy and all that, so you didn't have to feel your fear of rejection."

In the sixties I chose to drop out and be a long-haired hippie. The entire lifestyle was appealing for many reasons. I became a member of a group and the group fully accepted each other because we were all mellow, love and peace, nice-guy hippies. Drugs also helped. I

296

never had the slightest sense that I chose the hippie lifestyle in order to not feel the fear of rejection. Amazed at Beloved Adi Da's statement, I felt into it.

Heart-Master Adi Da's direct address to my fear of rejection opened up other windows. I could remember as a child doing things around the house, like taking out the garbage, because I felt loved for doing them. I had a sense that I had to earn love by doing things, even though my mother was a very loving lady. So Beloved Adi Da's comment about being a "nice guy" to avoid feeling rejected was a bull's-eye about an emotional aspect of my life that existed even back in my early childhood.

I could see that my basic fear of being rejected had never been fully observed, understood, and released. It was still there, and now I was fifty-five years old. That fear of rejection was a deeply ingrained aspect of my egoic patterning—part of "me". It was really obvious whenever I attended an ashram meeting, where I secretly always felt no one wanted to hear what I had to say.

Heart-Master Adi Da had fully explained about the ego-"I" as an ongoing activity, a total body-mind contraction. I understood that the fear of rejection is what the ego-"I" does, what the ego is. Beloved Adi Da had said, "The words of the ego-'I' are: 'You don't love me.'"

With the insight my Beloved Heart-Master Adi Da had granted, I began to see the fear-of-rejection pattern as it arose. Instead of worrying about being accepted, I would turn my feeling-attention to Him, the Divine Person—the counter-egoic practice that one should do no matter what arises.

Thirteen years later, in 2008, I was blessed to be one of Bhagavan Adi Da's personal attendants for seven months, directly serving Him daily. That was the most intimate time of my life in His Holy Company. In those entire seven months Beloved Bhagavan Adi Da only said two words to me. They were the last words I heard from Him before His passing. He said, "You're accepted!"

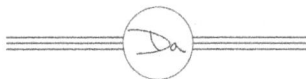

Game of Remarks

MARCH–APRIL 1995

Because Heart-Master Adi Da enjoyed playing pool, a devotee built Him a beautiful pool table. A bure (Fijian hut) was constructed and the new pool table was installed. The Da Avatar, Adi Da, named the building "The Game of Remarks Pool Hall". Our Heart-Master used the Game of Remarks Pool Hall to generate Teaching-Instruction in a most humorous, personal, and effectively penetrating way.

Devotees were invited to join Beloved Master Adi Da in the pool hall almost every night for several months. When we arrived, Heart-Master Adi Da was usually at His seat at the rear of the room with His renunciate devotees seated on pillows below Him. The Heart-Master's seat was raised quite high, so if He wasn't playing He could easily see the entire game. Heart-Master Adi Da always sat silently while we were arriving, giving His Blessing Regard to each of His devotees as we bowed and offered flowers at His Holy Feet. Once everyone arrived, He moved from His seat to the pool table.

The night usually started with Him playing a game or two with one of His family members, followed occasionally by a game or two with one of the renunciate devotees. We all watched and rooted for Him, applauding His great shots and moaning at the rare shot He missed. After the preliminary games, Beloved Adi Da chose a partner to play with against another team of two. Then the challenging team was selected, and finally a referee was agreed upon. (There were game rules, but if there was a question about the rules that the referee couldn't answer, Heart-Master Adi Da settled the issue, or often humorously overruled the referee's decision.) The game was straight pool: every shot had to be called—"five ball in the corner pocket"—and the first team to reach 150 points won the game.

Almost inevitably, within the first five minutes someone would question the rules; questions such as: "When you scratch, does one ball come up or two balls?" Before the referee could speak, Beloved

Adi Da would immediately come up with the answer and pronounce it, as if it were the rule originally agreed upon (whether it was or not). Our Heart-Master's disregard for any prior agreements was entirely humorous. He changed the rules as He liked, and His answer to the same question could change as He saw fit—always, of course, serving His team's advantage. He completely violated our principles of fair play and the importance of following rules. His partner would love it, of course, whereas the opposing team might well object— which apparently was the point: What would it take to get a reaction, how quickly could we surrender our reactivity? If we held on to it, He'd push into it until we let it go.

When not playing, Heart-Master Adi Da would watch the game from His seat. During every game, whether He played or not, He made remarks about the players. When playing, His remarks were usually directed to the opposing team, but if His partner was missing shots, His partner became the object of the Heart-Master's remarks.

He would remark about the way someone was dressed, explaining in detail the type of insecure person who would dress like that. He would comment about the hairiness of a player's body. He would remark about the limited depth of intimacy a player had with their partner. Or He would remark about a player's complicated emotional-sexual history, or the habits resulting from their Oedipal complex.

Heart-Master Adi Da's remarks seemed to be timed to throw off a player's game. As soon as He felt a reaction, He would dig in with complete humor and push that button for all it was worth. Most of His remarks affected the player's ability to make good shots and we would feel, or even say, "It's not fair." But when we were not reacting, we all understood that His remarks were entirely purposed to serve our self-understanding.

I was Beloved Adi Da's pool partner several times. Once, when I started missing some really easy shots, right before the next shot (which, by the way, was a difficult one) He said, "If you miss this next shot, you will be back with your old intimate partner before morning!" Another time He said, "If you miss this shot you will be celibate on the spot!" Enjoying His Humor, I made those two shots.

Had I not made either shot I would be held to the agreement. If I protested, my perfect Heart-Master would likely say something like, "You took the shot and an agreement is an agreement."

One night, when I was on the opposing team, His remarks really got to me, just as I was about to make a shot. He zeroed in on my thumb fingernail. It never grew right, some genetic defect. I never liked the way it looked and I was self-conscious about it, so I always tried to keep it out of sight when with others, usually covering it with a finger. Always knowing more about devotees than they knew about themselves, He called me out regarding the thumb. He called it the ugliest thing He had ever seen! He had me hold it up so everyone could see, and He led them all in making a sound of disgust. For the first time in my life I was able to laugh about it. Since that day I have never tried to hide my thumb again.

One time when on the opposite team He compared my hands to His. My hands were thin with large veins. I also had some medicated cream on a slight rash that gave a bluish tone to a section of the skin. So my hands didn't look that great. His hands were full and round and soft and beautiful. He asked, "How can you live with those hands?" Had I been self-conscious about the way my hands looked it would have been a "thumb" kind of moment. But I wasn't attached to the way my hands looked, so His remark was just humorous.

When I was on His team, as long as I was making all the shots, no remarks were made at all. But another time, when I was on the other team, Adi Da addressed the way I stood while playing pool. He said it was a little like I was skiing with my ankles leaning into the slope. He said to everyone, "Look at the way Gerald stands."

Then addressing me He asked, "Do you have homosexual tendencies? You feel yin to me!"

Then addressing everyone again He asked, "What do you all think?"

Of course everyone agreed with Him. But I didn't feel the need to defend myself. Apart from the fact that in Heart-Master Adi Da's Company there was no stigma attached to homosexuality, I just didn't feel gay. It was very humorous to me, but I had to acknowledge there was something to be seen about my yin characteristics.

Later that same night Beloved Adi Da commented on my previous spiritual involvements. He remarked about the kind of person I had to be to get involved in those teachings. He made a lot of remarks about how they compared to Divine Reality and the God-Realizing Way that He was Revealing. He questioned the depth of my involvement in His Teaching. He said my previous involvements showed that I had such seeker's superficial tendencies. His remarks touched something real: I missed the next shot.

Beloved Adi Da's team won every game they played, with one or two exceptions, over the several months of playing pool. Every time His team's winning shot was made, the Beloved Heart-Master took the hand of His partner and raised their clasped hands straight in the air as a sign of victory. Everyone, including the opposing team, applauded and praised Adi Da, the Beloved Master of the Game of Remarks Pool Hall.

Heart-Master Adi Da's remarks were a reality check, casting Light onto previously hidden aspects of the self-contraction with His penetrating and humorous Observations. The patterns of egoity are always binding, never liberating. Reactivity was not to be "worked out", it was to be released. The self-contraction—egoity—cannot be cured, it can only be surrendered. While only a few devotees were with Heart-Master Adi Da during the Game of Remarks Pool Hall time, there were lessons for all, for all time.

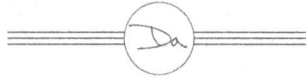

Poker

One night in the Game of Remarks Pool Hall, a devotee, who had played poker for many years and really liked the game, told Heart-Master Adi Da about his enjoyment of poker. In his enthusiasm he thought that since Heart-Master Da was engaging His devotees with pool, He might also enjoy playing poker with His devotees. The devotee even got a video of a world championship poker tournament, held annually in Las Vegas, to show his Heart-Master. Eventually, simply in response to His devotee's request, Beloved Adi Da agreed to a poker game at the Game of Remarks Pool Hall.

Our Beloved Guru and Heart-Master said that since poker is a gambling game we should play for money, but any money won would stay in Adidam in a fund that would address future needs. He emphasized this to make it a real game; we would all seriously play to win.

Once I heard Beloved Adi Da was interested in playing poker with His devotees, I wrote to several of my friends in California to look around for a marked deck of cards. I expected a joke deck, something to amuse Heart-Master Da, but to my great surprise a friend found and sent a deck professionally marked for cheating. I laughed and humorously thought, *Wow, we could make some real money with this deck!*

At the next opportunity, I approached my Beloved Heart-Guru at His seat in the Pool Hall and whispered to Him that I had a marked deck of cards and asked if He would like to use it.

He responded with a light slap to my face, saying, "How dare you suggest such a thing?" Then with a wide smile He said, "Do you actually have the deck here?"

I said, "Yes, Master."

"Okay," He replied, "Hold on to it. You can show Me how to use it later."

A few days later Heart-Master Adi Da announced that night would be poker night. When we arrived at the Game of Remarks

Pool Hall, devotees had already brought in a round table covered with green felt. It looked and felt like a professional card table. Where did they find such a grand table on Naitauba Island in Fiji? I took it as a sign that Heart-Master Adi Da's Spiritual Siddhi was already at work and no doubt going to affect the game.

Before the game started I found a little time to show Adi Da the marked deck and explained the markings. They were on bicycle cards, which had a large wheel and a small wheel on the bicycle. On the large wheel one of the spokes was missing. Its missing location, like on a clock, indicated the number of the card. So a three card had no spoke at 3 o'clock. There was another marking that indicated the suit, but I can't remember where that was. The markings were very subtle and actually hard to notice. Therefore it took a trained, committed cheater to use such a deck.

I asked if I should introduce the deck into the game that night at some point. He said okay, but He wasn't going to read the markings. He said the markings were too fine and they would take too long for Him to memorize their patterns. But He said I could do it if I wanted to. As things turned out, I forgot to introduce the marked deck. That was just as well—it was difficult to read the markings and would have taken too much attention to bother with it. Besides, the marked deck was just a joke that the Divine Master would have revealed sometime during the game. However, it was so enjoyable to have offered it to Beloved Adi Da and receive the wonderful face slap, which was like a Loving Kiss from Him.

To begin the big game all the men were invited to be players, but they had to know the game well and be willing to play to win. Beloved Adi Da wanted competition, not beginners. Five men, including the devotee who originally promoted the game, were approved and joined our Beloved Heart-Master's game. Other men and ladies watched, while others played pool.

We chose to play several different games: five card stud, seven card stud, draw, low ball. The most popular game turned out to be seven card stud. There were no wild cards, which was a sign that the games were serious. The rules of each game were announced so everyone understood. The cards were shuffled and the deck cut. The antes were placed in the pot and the cards were dealt.

Because Adi Da wasn't very familiar with the game of poker, a lady was designated to read the cards as they were dealt where the card faces were visible. She mentioned how hands were developing for each player such as a pair, three of a kind, possible straight, possible flush, etc. Then Beloved Adi Da made an announcement, "You cannot use the Devotional Prayer of Changes against Me when playing with Me. It just won't work!" That was such a delightful comment and a reminder of Who we were playing with.

Beloved Avatar Adi Da kept drawing the most incredible, even uncommon, hands—four of a kind, straight flush, full house. He seemed to not know the game that well. He'd lay His cards down and we would tell Him who won. Most often it was Him! *Was He using His Divine Influence to draw the right cards?* I wondered.

We were surrendered into the Divine Play of His Blissful Company while the cards were mysteriously conforming to Him. His Divine Siddhi of Love-Bliss and non-separation was not only filling our hearts, but was conforming everything to His Free State, including winning hands. It was Reality Poker!

The Da Avatar was by far the biggest winner at the poker table, happily enriching the fund with the low stakes we had played with. But we were the biggest winners of the night for the opportunity to spend such intimate time with our Beloved Heart-Master, the Living Divine Person.

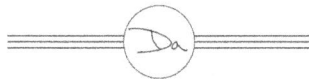

Friend's Sadhana

JUNE 1995

Seven devotees who had been graced to serve close to Adi Da for many years were invited to consider a new form of devotional service to Him. As a group, we received a phone call from one of Beloved Adi Da's renunciate devotees who told us that Heart-Master Adi Da had invited us to do a special form of service which He called the "Friend's Sadhana". She told us, "He said, 'It is for those who have the disposition of caring for Me bodily.'"

I was deeply touched when I heard my Beloved Heart-Master's comment. I felt that my service must have pleased Him, and my disposition was also rooted in the traditional admonition that to please your Heart-Master is the best thing any devotee can do.

We all immediately felt the Blessing of being invited into an additional form of responsive devotional service to Avatar Adi Da. None of us had any idea what the "Friend's Sadhana" would be, or how it would affect our present service, but we all deeply felt His Regard and listened with full commitment to serve our Heart-Master's circumstance in any way possible.

The renunciate devotee continued speaking to us, saying that Adi Da had a question for us and wanted to hear our answers after we each fully considered it.

We were asked what our choice was:

To continue serving Heart-Master Adi Da by directly serving His circumstance, even if that choice might slow our spiritual growth?

or

To do what was necessary for spiritual growth, even if that meant not directly serving Heart-Master Adi Da's circumstance?

After feeling into the possible consequences of our answers, each of us got on the phone, said our name, and told her our choice. Of the seven devotees invited into the "Friend's Sadhana", six of us, including me, chose to continue serving and caring for

Beloved Adi Da bodily, even if that choice would slow our spiritual growth. The seventh devotee chose the option of doing what was necessary for his spiritual growth, even if that meant not serving Beloved Adi Da's personal circumstance.

Heart-Master Adi Da, the Da Avatar, did not respond to our choices. It seemed that we should continue feeling and considering our responses to the two options. As we talked about them, there were differing speculations about the purpose of His question. We all basically agreed that the options were about our heart's desire, not a mental process of trying to work out the right answer. He is the Revelation and the Realization of His Teaching, the Awakener of Spiritual Reality. Our responses were for our self-reflection.

Some of us felt Heart-Master Adi Da was questioning our commitment to continue serving Him bodily by suggesting there might be a possible limit. Some felt the question was a test to see if we felt that our spiritual growth was separate from direct service to Him. Some felt the question was entirely about our recognition of His Divine Person. We agreed that heart-recognition of Him could only grow, never be diminished, by physically serving His circumstance. Some felt the question was a wake-up call to notice any limits in our bodily service due to relating to Him as an "other" rather than the Divine Person. One devotee understood the question as a reminder that being allowed into His personal circumstance was an opportunity to Spiritually recognize Him more fully; so that should be the priority, whatever it required. I felt I didn't care if spiritual growth became limited; to serve Heart-Master Adi Da and care for Him bodily was all I wanted to do.

We were all accepted into the devotional service of the "Friend's Sadhana". Our Beloved Master invited us to live close to Him and serve around Him as much as possible. One of the requirements for the men was that each night one man would sleep in the kitchen vestibule to be available if Beloved Adi Da needed anything during the night. (That sleeping arrangement lasted three weeks or so.)

Each day when Avatar Adi Da left His residence we greeted our Beloved Master at His door with flowers and devotional prostrations. Then we accompanied His Holy Person as He walked to His office or elsewhere at the Matrix. Most of the time no conversation took place, but those walks stand out in my memory as the most wonderful heart-bright occasions with the Divine Master.

The men of our "Friend's Sadhana" group also participated in fanning Beloved Adi Da and blocking the hot sun with an umbrella during sacred Darshan occasions. All the devotees present were given an opportunity to show their devotion by offering a flower at His Feet, a sign of ego-surrender and love, then prostrating fully, a sign of whole bodily surrender to the Mastery of the Divine Realizer. Avatar Adi Da Samraj did not have "friends" in the conventional understanding of that word. Literally, He was the Heart-Friend to all of manifested existence. *"I Am the Breakthrough of the Non-conditional into the conditionally manifested cosmic domain"* (*The Aletheon*, 2009 edition, 1887). The "Friend's Sadhana" was not about "friendship"; it was an opportunity our Beloved Heart-Master provided to a small group of devotees whose only distinction was that we had committed ourselves to full-time physical service to His personal circumstance. Everything Avatar Adi Da ever did was entirely about Transmitting His Realization to Awaken all beings to the Truth of Divine Reality.

The "Friend's Sadhana" consideration was discontinued after a few months. But the Grace of that time of service to the Divine Avatar was a Blessing beyond compare.

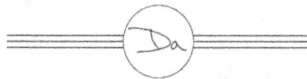

Adi Da Samraj
Maria Hoop, Holland 1996

Adi Da Samraj

The honorific reference "Samraj" was proposed to Avatar Adi Da on February 3, 1996, but He didn't begin using it until later that year.

From the Sanskrit "Samraja", "Samraj" was a traditional Indian term used to refer to great kings and also to the Hindu Gods. "Samraja" is defined as the "universal or supreme ruler", "paramount Lord", or "paramount sovereign". "Samraj" was traditionally given as a title to a king who was regarded to be a "universal monarch". Avatar Adi Da also appreciated the fact that the reference includes the implication of "setting an example".

Avatar Adi Da's Name "Adi Da Samraj" expresses that He is the Primordial (or Original) Giver, Who Blesses all as the Universal Lord of everything, everywhere, for all time. The Sovereignty of His Kingdom has nothing to do with the world of human politics. Rather, it is entirely a matter of His Transcendental Spiritual Dominion, His Sovereignty in the hearts of His devotees.

Adapted from the glossary of *The Aletheon*, 2009 edition, 2152.

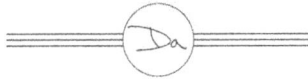

Avatar Adi Da Samraj:

Through the Unique and Paradoxical Process of My Divine Avataric Self-Submission (Which Process Was the Case from the Moment of My Birth), I Achieved Perfect Coincidence, and Perfect Identification, with all-and-All.

My Divine Avataric Self-Submission Was a Means Whereby I Took On the pattern of humankind (and of the "world" altogether), in order to Transform that pattern in My Own Person.

I have Served every one.

This Body Is the Body of everybody in the "world".

This Body Is the Body of the "world".

The Signs that I had Completed the Process of My Divine Avataric Self-Submission began to become particularly evident beginning with the Great Event of My Divine Avataric Self-"Emergence" in 1986.

By My Act of Perfect Identification and Perfect Coincidence, My Divine Avataric Work here has come to the point that I can now Stand completely apart from any necessity for further Self-Submission.

Because of What I have Accomplished through My Divine Avataric Self-Submission, all of humankind—and, indeed, all of Earthkind, and all living beings in all places and times—are now Enabled to devotionally and whole-bodily-responsively recognize Me, and (in due course) to "Locate" Me and "Perfectly Know" Me. ("The Boundless Self-Confession", *The Aletheon*, 2009 edition, 1903.)

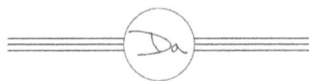

The Laughing Mama

FEBRUARY 1996

Adi Da Samraj was at His Sanctuary in Hawaii[19] when one night He invited some devotees to join Him in His living room to further consider His Divine Reality-Teaching. Before the night ended, He left the room for a while, which gave me the opportunity to visit the very strange display that was set in a corner of His living room.

On the wall was a painting of the strangest being—a very large woman with all sorts of tacky things on her and around her, sitting on a flying pink flamingo. She looked like the laughing lady at the fun house in an early-twentieth-century amusement park. Her face was caked in makeup, with bright red cheeks and wild eyes. Her lips were also bright red, the lipstick over-painted to make them look larger. She seemed untamed, wild, and surrealistic. She looked totally strange, like a ventriloquist's huge puppet.

Her very large body was dressed in a puffy, powder-blue chiffon dance dress with lots of crepe petticoats. It was like the prom dresses the girls had worn when I graduated high school in the fifties, only this dress greatly enlarged her already large body. She was wearing a pair of powder-blue bedroom slippers with a large white fluffy pom-pom on top of each one. Her frizzy hair was wild, as if blowing in the wind.

She had a button on her chest that read, "Be kind to all non-humans."

A large sign below her read, "Your objections to anything don't mean shit!"

The pink flamingo she was flying on was wearing a totally tacky, very wide, brightly patterned tie. There were a lot of cheap plastic flowers on the altar below her picture.

It was a humorous, weird depiction of conditional reality[20]—Mother Nature metaphorically presented by the Divine Avatar. She

---

19. Known as Da Love-Ananda Mahal since March 1997.

20. Conditional reality is the conditionally manifested reality as we ordinarily perceive it and participate in it.

was the person of the conditional cause-and-effect realm, masterfully named "The Laughing Mama" by Heart-Master Adi Da Samraj. In all the above elements combined, the display was the "Laughing Mama Temple".

I found out later that Beloved Adi Da Samraj had set up a procedure for all His devotees to follow as soon as they came into His living room. Somehow I had missed learning about it. Each devotee would first go to the Laughing Mama Temple and offer a Zwieback (from the German "twice baked") cracker. Then devotees were to bow to the Laughing Mama and surrender all complaints. Once done, it was appropriate to come to Beloved Adi Da's chair and offer a flower, soft and beautiful in contrast to the brittle, homely cracker offered at the Laughing Mama Temple.

As I looked at the Laughing Mama's bizarre image, at first it was hard to figure out why the Divine Master was giving it so much attention. Then I began to feel how totally humorous it all was. Adi Da Samraj was showing conditional nature as it actually is: Totally indifferent to humans. ("Your objections to anything don't mean shit.") I felt how this Laughing Mama Temple was in such great contrast to Divine Reality. Adi Da Samraj was the Divine Avatar, the Divine Means, and the Divine Way through "Maya", the illusion that is the material world, the illusion of life and death. The Laughing Mama Temple was a wildly humorous metaphor for the egoic enactment of separation from God that is the entire basis of the conditional realm of cause-and-effect.

Before I left the Master's residence, I had the opportunity to talk with Beloved Adi Da about what I felt. I told Him of my experience at the Laughing Mama Temple and what I understood about His Work with it. He said humorously, "That is quite a profound understanding while looking at that tacky image."

I said, "But tackiness is the epitome of the thing."

Beloved Heart-Master Adi Da said, "That is why I used it."

I bowed at His most Holy Feet and thanked Him for His True Humor and Mastery of conditional reality.

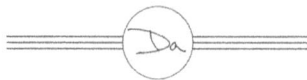

Ruchira Avatar
The Mountain Of Attention Sanctuary 1996

Ruchira Avatar

In the fall of 1996 Adi Da Samraj was offered another descriptive Name that related to devotees' recognition of His Divine Person and State: the Name "Ruchira". Adi Da allowed His devotees to use "Ruchira" as one of His principal Names, in combination with His other accepted Names as well.

In Sanskrit, "Ruchira" means "bright, radiant, effulgent". Thus, the reference "Ruchira Avatar" indicated that Avatar Adi Da Samraj is the "Bright" (or Radiant) Descent of the Divine Reality Itself into the conditionally manifested worlds, Appearing here in His bodily human Divine Form.

Adapted from *The Order of My Free Names*.

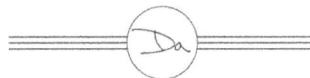

Avatar Adi Da Samraj:

*My Divine Avataric Self-Revelation is the Self-Revelation of
Reality <u>Itself</u>—Which is <u>Self-Evidently</u> Divine and Indivisible.*

*I <u>Am</u> That. I am not merely communicating a philosophy
about That.*

*I <u>Am</u> the Means for the Most Perfect Divine Self-Realization of
Reality.*

*I <u>Am</u> the Perfect Realization, and I <u>Am</u> the Way of the Perfect
Realization, and I <u>Give</u> the Perfect Teaching of That Perfect
Realization.*

*My Fundamental Reality-Teaching is the "Radical" Communi-
cation of "Perfect Knowledge" and of the "Radical" Reality-Way
of the true and perfect devotional recognition of Me.*

*The Reality-Way That I Divinely Avatarically Reveal and Give Is
the Divine Reality-Way of the "Bright"—Which <u>Is</u> My Divine
Avataric Self-Manifestation, from Birth, and Always Already
Perfectly Prior to Birth, and Always Already now, and (therefore)
always forever hereafter, even forever after My Divine Avataric
physical human Lifetime.* ("God As The Creator, God As Good,
and God As The Real", *The Aletheon*, 2009 edition, 110.)

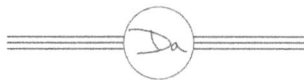

25th Anniversary

On the 25th anniversary of the opening of the Melrose Avenue ashram, Ruchira Avatar Adi Da arranged to visit the place that marked the beginning of the Way of the Heart. Graciously, He invited a few "old time" devotees to accompany Him.

When we arrived He commented on how the building had changed. Standing by the front entrance, we talked about the large, beautiful photos of Him that had been in the two front windows. He amusedly recalled that occasionally someone from the gay bars around the neighborhood would come into the bookstore looking for gay publications.

Ruchira Avatar Adi Da led us to the rear entrance and talked about incidents that had happened there. He mentioned the metal storage shed that had been there and smiled at me as He reminded everyone that it had also served as my sleeping quarters.

Ruchira Avatar Adi Da asked if we remembered the ashram guard dog, Shadow. He laughed a lot about the incident when I was trying to demonstrate Shadow's "attack" command for my friends, but instead of attacking the car that my friends were in, Shadow bit me.

Then He commented about the fire that entirely destroyed the shop next to us, but did little damage to the ashram. At the moment of the explosion there had been a devotee leaning against that wall of the meditation hall; he had been hugely startled but unharmed. Recalling the moment, Ruchira Adi Da humorously remarked, "When the explosion happened, [the man] thought he was having a spiritual experience!"

The Ruchira Avatar then put humor aside and stood quietly for a time. We stood silently around Him, receiving His Darshan. His silence and stillness seemed to speak volumes. The sacred history of serving His devotees, while establishing His egoless Presence for all beings eternally, had formally begun in that Melrose Avenue storefront. By virtue of that short, unceremonious visit, we all felt He had Re-Empowered the site, establishing it as a place of devotional pilgrimage. It was clear to us that His Divine Blessing Presence would be tangible there forever.

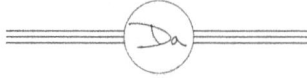

The Ruchira Avatar in the World

APRIL 1997

After Re-Empowering the building that had been the home of the Melrose Avenue ashram as a pilgrimage site on the 25th anniversary of its opening, Ruchira Adi Da stayed in Los Angeles for a few more days to address some medical needs. We found our Beloved Heart-Master a spacious room at the Bel-Air Hotel and every night all the local devotees were invited to sit with Ruchira Adi Da and receive His Darshan. Some nights, several non-devotees who had shown interest and respect were also invited. (It was moving to hear from these people how, without exception, they were profoundly affected by Ruchira Adi Da's Darshan.)

One day, while fanning my Beloved Heart-Master as He lounged by the hotel pool, He noticed the gold wristwatch I was wearing. He asked about it, and I explained that I had bought it from a Beverly Hills jeweler when I was a successful salesman. He asked to take a better look. I took it off, handed it to Him, and He slipped it on His wrist. Then He humorously asked, "How does a devotee of Mine get to have a watch like this, when I have to wear a Timex?" His watch wasn't a Timex; it was just a humorous way of metaphorically pointing to the contrast between my obviously more expensive watch and His more modest one. (Several other devotees made note and subsequently gifted the Ruchira Avatar with more honorable watches, which He would thereafter wear regularly.)

To me, placing my watch on His wrist was a Blessing that converted it into a sacred object. I still own that watch to this day, and I only wear it on special occasions. Whenever I wear it, I very clearly remember, even visualize, my Beloved Heart-Master's Loving Gesture. The watch is also a reminder of the very unusual Bel-Air Hotel circumstance.

When He was not involved with medical appointments and associated activity, Ruchira Adi Da would relax by the hotel pool.

Local devotees with cultural responsibilities, and those devotees who traveled with Ruchira Adi Da, would attend our Heart-Master while He rested on a lounge chair.

The weather was hot, so we would fan Heart-Master Adi Da and serve Him cold drinks. When needed, one of the renunciate devotees would wipe His forehead with a cool cloth. Newspapers, cultural reports, and other reading materials were directly brought to Ruchira Avatar Adi Da upon His request. A devotee responsible for security stayed attentive to make sure there were no intrusions or disturbances while He rested. Ruchira Adi Da relaxed, read, and laid in the sun—Radiant with the prior Reality of non-separate Divine Unity and Love-Bliss for all that were fortunate to see Him.

At the poolside there was no formal Darshan, so those of us who served Him regularly didn't sit in rows directly facing Him. However, a few local devotees, who hadn't been in His Physical Company that often, did sit directly facing their Beloved Heart-Master, as if in formal Darshan. When not actively serving, we sat around Him surrendered to His Radiant egoless State.

Guests at the Bel-Air Hotel were typically wealthy and often influential people. Whenever royalty stayed there they were also served by attendants, but not with the level of happy devotional service Ruchira Adi Da received from His devotees.

The Ruchira Avatar was clearly noticed at the poolside. When the public saw and felt the caring service of all His devotees, they would want to know more about Him. I found out from a friendly hotel pool attendant that many people, including some celebrities, had asked who Adi Da was. He told me some people commented on the unusual caring service that our "important man" was getting.

The time at the Bel-Air Hotel was a rare interlude that gave the public an opportunity to see the Divine in human Form and feel, consciously or not, the Blessing conveyed by His Presence. The service to Ruchira Avatar Adi Da at the hotel poolside was entirely the same as the devotional service devotees offered their Heart-Master wherever He was. It was our devotional heart-response to care for the Ruchira Avatar in bodily human Form. The egoless Divine Master allowed such service from His devotees not for His sake, but as an opportunity for devotees to feel His Divine Radiance and to express self-transcending devotion. All our devotional service was done in recognition and response to Ruchira Adi Da's Divine State and Person. He was always the Divine State and Person, whether at a high-toned hotel like the Bel-Air or anywhere else.

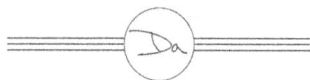

Never Subordinate the Divine

MAY 1997

One night Ruchira Avatar Adi Da invited several devotees to His residence the Manner of Flowers at the Mountain Of Attention Sanctuary. I found myself Blessed to sit next to my Beloved Heart-Master, my heart full of joy as He spoke to us about Divine Reality.

I was wearing the gold wristwatch that Ruchira Adi Da had previously commented about. Later in the night Ruchira Adi Da noticed the watch and asked to see it. Again, as He did in Los Angeles, He Blessed it with His Regard and slipped it on His wrist. Then He said, "I like it," took it off, and returned it by placing it in front of me.

At that point, instead of continuing to turn to Him in the joy of feeling His Presence, I turned to happy familiarity. Instead of picking the watch up, I let it sit right where He had placed it. I intentionally planned to pay no attention to the watch, suggesting I had forgotten it was there. I actually thought maybe Ruchira Avatar Adi Da would take it and hide it from me. In any case, I thought it would be fun to see what would happen.

After an hour or so I looked down and the watch was gone! I thought, *He actually took it!* But then, *How do I get it back? It won't work to say, "I left the watch in front of me to see if You would take it, now can I have it back?"* I hoped that the implication that I hadn't been concerned about it would be enough for my Beloved Heart-Master to return it.

I should have realized how completely obvious it would be to Ruchira Adi Da about my entire play and my concern about getting my watch back. I should have noticed that I was entirely self-involved, thinking and scheming throughout the entire time. I should have noticed that by being so self-involved I was forgetting Who I was sitting next to, that the Divine Ruchira Avatar was not a "familiar"—not my buddy, not a social friend. I was forgetting that He knew my thoughts and feelings perfectly, since He was not separate from me, or anyone or anything.

Instead of noticing how out of alignment I was, I kept trying to think of humorous ways to make my scheme work and keep it going. But the more I got into trying to work out all the details—which were all ways of staying casual and in total non-recognition of my Heart-Master—the more complicated things got.

Ruchira Avatar Adi Da was about to give me a big lesson about my self-absorption and my assumption of familiarity with the Divine Being.

When it was time to leave, the watch was still missing. I paused in getting up. Ruchira Adi Da said, "It's time to go, everyone is leaving. Why aren't you leaving?"

I said with a weak smile, "I'm looking for my watch."

Though I didn't directly say it, I meant to convey that I knew He took it.

Ruchira Avatar Adi Da's voice got loud and stern. "Why are you telling Me that? Do you think I took it? Do you think I care about your watch? Is that a way to speak to Me? Is that a way to talk to your Master? Why would you think I would steal your watch?"

Leaning toward me, His eyes were piercing like two lasers. "Are you accusing Me of stealing?"

I knew I had gone too far with my assumed familiarity. I had violated my relationship to my Heart-Master. All matters about the watch got lost in my feelings of remorse. I only wanted to drop the whole matter as fast as possible. I didn't care about ever finding the watch, and didn't want to even think "watch" in that moment. The entire unconscious incident felt really, really bad. I didn't say anything more and tiptoed out of Ruchira Adi Da's House feeling how the whole incident had been a disaster.

Outside, after composing myself somewhat, I thought about what had happened. Even if the watch was found in the morning, even if the only possibility was that Ruchira Adi Da had taken the watch, there was no way I could approach Him again about it as if He were an ordinary man. Never again. I would take the lesson and let the watch be the price paid for it.

While I was busy trying to absorb the lesson, a devotee came outside and in his hand was a watch. He asked me if the watch was mine. I said, "Yes. Where did you find it?"

He said, "Ruchira Adi Da gave me the watch and told me to sell it in the next fundraising event. But since it's yours, I guess you should have it back."

Now with the watch in my hand, I began to understand and feel all that my Heart-Master had done to serve me. Trying to draw Him into my scheme had been the antithesis of an appropriate guru-devotee relationship. He showed me to never be casual with Him, for it undermines a true devotional relationship. He showed me that I should never subordinate Him, as if He were less than Who He Is, the Divine Person. And, as He had so many times before, He Revealed the cramp of my self-contraction.

Still standing outside His residence with my watch in my hand, I was able to laugh at the way my Beloved Heart-Master had dealt with me. He was a Perfect Genius!

The next day I sent Ruchira Avatar Adi Da a card with five $100 bills in it. The card said, "Thank you for all the lessons Your Divine Presence reflected to me last night. I clearly see how any casual, familiar approach is direct non-recognition of Your Divine Person. I found the missing watch. This $500 is how much the watch originally cost. I'd like to buy it back, if I may. The funds are a donation that may be used as You see fit. I bow down at Your Holy Feet."

The funds were returned to me with a note saying that I could donate the $500 to an Adidam project of my choice, reminding me that "Ruchira Avatar Adi Da never touches money."

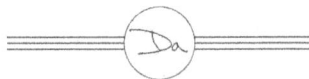

PART SIX

Stories from 2000–2008

Great Lessons on Surrender

OCTOBER 2002

While I was on retreat at Da Love-Ananda Mahal in Hawaii, Ruchira Adi Da offered His Blessing Darshan every day to a group of devotees who were proposed as showing the signs that their practice of self-transcending and responsive devotional turning of feeling and attention to His Divine State was maturing. During the first two days of my retreat, I experienced what felt like in-depth heart-Communion with my Beloved Heart-Master. But after the second Darshan I received notes from Ruchira Adi Da. He asked what I was doing during His Darshan. He said that I had been meditating on myself, not turned to His Transmitting Presence. He asked others, "How did Gerald get to be approved to come on retreat?" He was told I was there with other senior priests and cultural leaders. He asked if I had come due to my maturing practice or because I was supposed to come due to my service as head priest. He said, "This is a very serious matter!" and said my entire practice should be reviewed.

Ruchira Adi Da had said, "Significant growth in practice happens through crisis." His criticism generated a real crisis. In one respect I felt crushed. I had been assuming my spiritual practice was aligned to my Beloved Guru and I was astonished and stunned to hear that it was not. Simultaneously, I really wanted to understand everything my Beloved Guru was bringing to consciousness and to make use of His Instructions regarding how I should align my practice. I knew that if I was to truly make use of this crisis then I should not protect or defend myself in any way. I would have to move beyond wounded feelings and allow the criticism to make a difference—my very presence on the retreat was being questioned.

In response to Ruchira Avatar Adi Da's Demand, I was interviewed by some of the retreat staff. They read what He had said and asked me, "What were you doing?" I explained and tried to show them what I had done during these two Darshans. I said, "I felt Ruchira Adi Da as pressure on my head, then felt His Presence moving down through my face into my heart. I turned my feeling-attention inward to feel Ruchira Adi Da in my heart." As I said that, I demonstrated what I had done. One of the men quickly responded, "Where did you just go? You were talking from your feelings and I could feel your vulnerability. Then you left, you stopped feeling. As soon as you turned inward, I couldn't feel you at all!"

The others completely agreed. They said, "We could feel you up to a point, then it seemed you left, or you stopped feeling, and at that point we couldn't feel you anymore."

I was totally surprised by their response. So I repeated the same thing again to make sure I was showing them exactly what I did in front of Ruchira Avatar Adi Da. Again they all agreed. They stopped feeling me when I turned to what I felt was Ruchira Adi Da in my heart. To my great surprise, they concluded that I was actually turning *away* from my Heart-Master's Presence by focusing on happy feelings within my body, interpreting those feelings as Him.

I had always thought those kinds of feelings were Ruchira Adi Da's Presence. By requiring me to be interviewed by my peers, He showed me that those happy feelings were entirely self-meditation. What a surprise to see that! I was turning to a bodily feeling that was an <u>effect</u> of the Ruchira Avatar's Blessing Transmission. But it was <u>not</u> His Blessing Presence, which is Beyond the body-mind or conditionality of any kind. My happy feelings were actually self-meditation. Furthermore, that self-meditation was what I had always been doing whenever I thought I was feeling Ruchira Adi Da. I could not deny it! It was absolutely clear that turning inward into happy feelings and thinking it was Ruchira Adi Da's Divine Presence was actually a limitation on feeling Him, a turning away from Him.

The opportunity to feel my error without any defense was due to the crisis Ruchira Avatar Adi Da created by His Criticism and the vulnerability possible due to His Blessing Presence.

It then made clear sense to me why Ruchira Adi Da Instructed His devotees not to close their eyes when sitting in His Blessing

Darshan, unless spontaneously moved to do so by His Presence. To stay open-eyed in reception of His Holy Transmission helped to curb the egoic pattern of turning inward. It was a great gift to have such a clear lesson that Ruchira Avatar Adi Da's Divine Presence is not within. He is Omnipresent, the Living Demonstration of Ultimate Enlightenment.

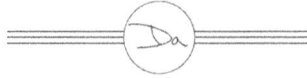

Banyan Bay Samadhi

FEBRUARY 2005

Banyan Bay is a beautiful peaceful inlet of water at Adi Da Samrajashram Hermitage (Naitauba Island) in Fiji. The bay is the home of a large old banyan tree acknowledged as a holy site by Avatar Adi Da. After His Blessing of the great tree, various animals and birds that had died on the Hermitage were buried around it over the years. Banyan Bay, with its calm water and beautiful scenery, was one of Avatar Adi Da's favorite places. Whenever He chose to go there, devotees would prepare His shaded cabana. One particular day I was invited to attend Ruchira Adi Da by fanning Him as He rested in the shade of the cabana. While the Divine Avatar, Heart-Master Adi Da, relaxed on His lounge chair, I stood next to Him cooling His body with a fan and shooing away insects as they appeared. Ruchira Avatar Adi Da's two senior renunciate devotees were also nearby to serve His comfort.

The Divine Ruchira Avatar seemed to be simply there, quietly relaxing. He even appeared to have fallen asleep for a while. I was overjoyed to be there. All my attention was on serving my Beloved Heart-Master. After a while of deeply feeling Him, attention resting in His egoless Radiance, His Divine Presence simply became my only awareness. Without noticing the change, His Divine State absorbed any sense of separation between us. In that heart-joy, I kept fanning, seemingly mechanically, yet fully aware of serving my Beloved Guru. "I" was standing, but felt no identification with standing or any other bodily function. There was no sense of a separate "me" at all. There was just the Beloved Heart-Master's silent, perfectly peaceful Fullness enveloping everything. After a couple of hours, Ruchira Adi Da moved and eventually got up to go into the water. His movement stimulated my self-awareness and, like waking from a blissful dream, I fell back into my normal state of patterned egoity.

One of Ruchira Avatar Adi Da's renunciate devotees commented, "You were in Samadhi." She was right. How profound and wonderful that while simply turning in deep feeling to His Divine Person I became available to His Great Siddhi of Non-Difference, which totally washed away my usual activity of egoic separation.

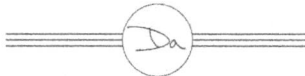

Bhagavan
Adi Da Samrajashram 2006

Bhagavan

The Title "Bhagavan" is an ancient one used over the centuries for many spiritual Realizers in India. It means "blessed" or "holy" in Sanskrit. When applied to a great spiritual being, "Bhagavan" is understood to mean "Bountiful Lord", "Great Lord", or "Divine Lord".

Sometimes it is also suggested that "Bhagavan" implies the union of Shiva (or Consciousness) and Shakti (or Energy), as symbolized by the lingam[21] and the yoni.[22]

Another definition is "the Lord or the Divine Being in human Form".

In 2006 Avatar Adi Da's devotees began using this title on a regular basis to address Him. The title "Bhagavan" was the preferred one used by all His devotees during the last years of His Divine bodily human Form.

Adapted from *The Order of My Free Names.*

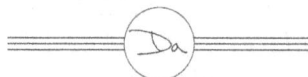

21. Lingam is an oval-shaped stone, a representation of the Hindu deity Shiva.

22. Yoni is a round stone with a hole in the center. In Hinduism, it is a symbol of the goddess Shakti, the feminine generative power and, as a goddess, the consort of Shiva.

Avatar Adi Da Samraj:

The "Bright" Divine Avataric Form of Reality Itself Is "Bhagavan"—the Pleasurable State of Prior Unity (or Love-Bliss-Fullness), in Which nothing needs to be "solved". That Is the "Bright" White Sun in the midst of the black field—the Lingam in the Yoni. The Divine Self-Nature, Self-Condition, and Self-State of Reality Itself Is Always in the Midst of conditional reality. I Am Always Already "Bright" in and As the form and the "Root-Substance" of all-and-All.

In the conditional (or cosmic) plane, My Divine "Bright" Spherical Self-Domain (and My Divine "Bright" Eternal Self-Nature, Self-Condition, and Self-State) Is Always Already Free-Standing, in the Midst. In the Midst (Where you Always Already Stand, in the intrinsically egoless Being-Position) Is the Fundamental (Perfectly Subjective, and Intrinsically egoless) Tacit Self-Apprehension of Being (Itself). I Am That—Self-Existing and Self-Radiant. Those who become My devotees and conform themselves to Me and surrender their problematic illusions about the cosmic domain—those who (whole bodily) devotionally recognize Me and devotionally respond to Me—understand Me As "Bhagavan". The Lingam in the Yoni Is the Indivisible White Sun in the midst of the black field. ("The Divine Avataric Self-Revelation of Adidam Ruchiradam", The Aletheon, 2009 edition, 1692.)

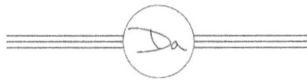

Thinking Is Not Realization

JANUARY 2006

Consciousness and Energy (or Light) are one. They are not two (as interpreted, for example, in the Shiva-Shakti duality of the Hindu tradition). This previously unrecognized reality, Bhagavan Adi Da had pointed out, was an important way in which His Teaching is unique.

In deep contemplation of Bhagavan Adi Da, while considering His Revelation about Consciousness and Energy, I began to think I had a sense of it. So I sent my Beloved Heart-Master a card praising His Divine Appearance and His Perfect Revelation of Divine Truth. I praised His Spiritual Siddhi that allowed His devotees to be sensitive to such profundity as Consciousness and Energy (or Light).

Then I wrote, "By Your Divine Revelation, I understand how Consciousness and Energy are one. Consciousness is Self-Aware. That Awareness is felt, and feeling is Energy. It seems obvious that Consciousness and Energy are both aspects of one, not two separate Divine Conditions."

One of the renunciate devotees gave me the Response from the Divine Avatar Bhagavan Adi Da: "It's a lot different to Realize it than to talk about it!"

I felt humbled and clarified by my Heart-Master's Response, seeing how the mind can make profundity seem superficial, how the mind can abstract something into "knowing". Obviously my understanding was based entirely in thought, and was not a Realization.

Throughout the years Bhagavan emphasized the importance of practicing the Way, not just talking about it. His critical term for just talking was "the talking school".

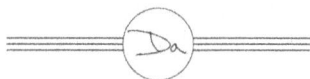

The Master's Staff

In previous eras, spiritual masters might have used a staff or cane to strike their devotees if a devotee didn't show signs of devotion and maturing practice. One morning in April 2006, the Divine Avatar Bhagavan Adi Da, without even touching His Staff, gave me a metaphorical beating that dramatically and necessarily changed my devotional relationship to Him.

Bhagavan Adi Da would receive good news of His devotees' service daily. When the devotee who normally provided this news was unavailable, another devotee and I were invited to fill in. We expected that Bhagavan Adi Da would want to hear good news about the culture at His Hermitage. So we prepared all evening by reviewing all that we could about the ashram culture and devotees' service, until we felt we were ready.

Early the next morning—both of us full of enthusiasm, anticipating being in Bhagavan Adi Da's Divine Presence—went to offer our devotion and bring Him the good news about His devotees. As the door to His bedroom was opened for us, we could see our Beloved Heart-Master sitting on the end of His bed. His eyes were closed and His face had a soft glow. His Divine State of Love-Bliss saturated the room and washed over us as we stood in the doorway. We hesitated, reluctant to disturb the vision of Perfection before us.

His room was a Holy Temple, conformed to His egoless State of Love-Bliss. The Light of Consciousness was Perfectly Revealed as His Divine Person. He was so peaceful, so soft and vulnerable. His Purity and Beauty held us in place.

Then someone nudged us forward into the room.

Bhagavan Adi Da opened His eyes but didn't move. We prostrated at His Holy Feet and each placed a flower, a symbol of our devotion, in front of Him. The Divine Heart-Master nodded His head slightly.

I softly praised His Divine Presence and Radiant Brightness, and thanked Him for allowing us His Sacred Darshan. I told Him we were there to serve Him with the good news about His devotees. We hoped it would please Him.

Bhagavan Adi Da said, "Tcha."

Softly speaking, He said He did not want to talk about the Hermitage culture, but He wanted to hear about the larger picture of all His devotees. Immediately, we knew we were not prepared. Neither of us had service that exposed us to the worldwide culture. We explained that we had prepared to talk about the ashram culture here at His Hermitage, not about Adidam worldwide.

Bhagavan Adi Da asked why we had come so empty-handed. He expected any devotees in cultural leadership that were invited into His bedroom to give Him good news would fully represent all of Adidam. Instead of receiving any of our good news, Heart-Master Adi Da began talking about issues that needed to be handled in Adidam.

Fully prepared communicators would have given examples of how those issues were being addressed. Being unprepared, we could only agree, since we also recognized them as real issues. But agreeing was absolutely the wrong thing to do—it implied that leadership was incapable of handling the issues. He sternly pointed out that our agreement with Him was only self-protection.

The appropriate devotional response would have been to surrender all defense of our unpreparedness at His Feet. But instead of doing that I was collapsing, and that brought the metaphorical Staff down on me. Bhagavan Adi Da addressed everything about "me" that was weak, mediocre, superficial, worldly, not responding to Him, not recognizing Him, not practicing, and not growing in practice. He stood up from His bed and paced the room, His voice loud, His face flushed.

The "beating" seemed to last a lifetime. At the time, I felt He destroyed everything that was important to me about our relationship. It was like a death. But finally He said to both of us, "You came in here with nice words about not disturbing Me, but that is all you did. Now get out—and take your flowers with you!"

The next morning Bhagavan Adi Da sent notes to both of us saying, "It has been one whole day; where are the responses?"

My appropriate response would have been to acknowledge everything my Heart-Master had said as absolutely true of me in my egoity, and then, with heart-felt gratitude, to acknowledge the Grace of His Address to the mediocrity of my practice. The other devotee did respond in heart-surrender, thanking her Heart-Master for His Criticism.

I couldn't do it. I felt unloved by the Divine Heart-Master, as if betrayed by my best friend! The aggressive way He gave His criticism absolutely violated all my "nice guy" expectations. Bhagavan Adi Da had been so Forceful, I felt like I had been attacked.

He had shown absolutely no interest in any form of a social, friendly, familiar relationship. Where was the Heart-Friend "karma" from the Bubba Free John days of the 70's that I carried so dearly? I felt He had totally undermined all of that; it was as dead and gone as the 70's.

I felt beat up. I wanted some space to heal and find what was true about my relationship to Bhagavan Adi Da. Also, in reaction to His Criticism, I was feeling that I didn't deserve to be living at His Hermitage. I felt I had to leave. And so I did.

It took nearly two years to fully accept and understand what had happened, why it happened, and what changes were required for my devotional relationship to be true with the Beloved of my life, the Divine Avatar Adi Da. The casual familiarity that had been a prominent aspect of His Submission-Work in the 70's was history. But I had been clinging to the warmth of that intimacy, whereas I should have understood it as "theater" that He had created and I should have moved beyond it in true devotion. It had nothing to do with an appropriate relationship to Bhagavan Adi Da. He was not my friend—He was my Spiritual Master, the Divine Avatar. At last I saw that Bhagavan Adi Da had necessarily undermined my deeply-felt friendly and familiar feeling for Him. Those feelings had been an obstacle preventing fuller recognition of His Divine Person and more profound, in-depth, devotional surrender. The "beating" had been self-inflicted. Once that was deeply felt, perfectly understood, and finally clearly resolved for me, I received an invitation to return to Adi Da Samrajashram.

Upon returning in April 2008, I was profoundly Blessed to become one of Bhagavan Adi Da's attendants. That wonderful service allowed access to His Divine Person, caring for His bodily human Form every day. It was what a loving friend would do, but now it was done in heart-devotion to the Divine Person, not as a friendship tied to "the good old days". The old karma had been broken.

Divine Bhagavan Adi Da Samraj didn't address me or speak to me during the entire seven months that I was His attendant. Yet I never felt more intimate with Him than during those silent months. The intimacy was entirely Guru-devotee heart-Communion. And it was the happiest time of my life.

As it turned out, those seven months of direct service were the last months of Bhagavan Adi Da's Divine Avataric Bodily Incarnation. During that Blessed time His Divine Presence prepared me, and all of His devotees, for Eternal Heart-Communion with Him.

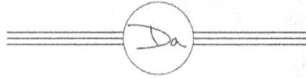

Parama-Sapta-Na Adi Da Samraj
Adi Da Samrajashram 2007

Parama-Sapta-Na Adi Da Samraj

"Parama-Sapta-Na" is a Title that refers uniquely to Avatar Adi Da Samraj, indicating His Supreme (Parama) Status as the Sapta-Na Sannyasin who Is the Divine Avataric Revealer of the entire Reality-Way of Adidam Ruchiradam. This Title is associated with July 10, 2007, the date on which Avatar Adi Da says His impulse to Working by means of Self-Submission conclusively vanished.

"Sapta" is Sanskrit for "seven", and "Na" is a reference to the Fijian Island of Naitauba, which is Avatar Adi Da's Principal Hermitage. As the Unique Divine Avataric Revealer and Transmitter of the Seventh Stage Realization, and the first to demonstrate the fullness of Sapta-Na Sannyas, Avatar Adi Da is the Parama-Sapta-Na Sannyasin. Because of His Unique Divine Avataric Function, the circumstance that He called to be provided for Him during His physical human Lifetime was one of profound freedom from any ordinary obligations, a circumstance in which He was absolutely Free to Manifest His Divine State.

Adapted from the glossary of *The Aletheon*, 2009 edition, 2141.

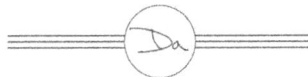

Avatar Adi Da Samraj:

My Avataric Lifetime Is A Divine and Unique Demonstration of Intentional Entanglement—In Which The egoless Divine "Bright" Self-Nature, Self-Condition, Self-State, and Divine Transcendental Spiritual Self-Force of My Prior and Perfect Freedom Is Constantly Self-Revealed In Spontaneous Acts, Great Events, Remarkable Conjunctions, Extraordinary Processes, and Beyond-Wonderful Demonstrations of Perfect Dis-Entanglement— For the Sake of all-and-All.

By Means of My Avataric Lifetime of Divine Self-Revelation, all-and-All who are, as if by accident, entangled here (and everywhere), in egoic time and space, Are Divinely Avatarically Given All of Necessary and Perfectly Acausally Effective Means For Perfect Dis-entanglement—now, and forever hereafter, In Me, and Where and As I Am.

This Is The Key to rightly and truly understanding All of The Acts, Events, Conjunctions, Processes, and Demonstrations of The Totality of My Lifetime-Evidence. ("My 'Secret' Biography", *The Aletheon*, 2009 edition, 1837.)

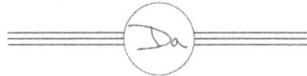

Only His Freedom

MARCH 2008

I was often given the Blessing Grace of direct service to Parama-Sapta-Na Adi Da Samraj. Typically, my service was cooling Him and protecting Him from insects with a fan, or shielding Him from the hot sun with an umbrella. Such service was always a wonderful opportunity to bathe in the Siddhi of His All-Encompassing Love and express my heart-surrendered devotion to Him. It was more than wonderful to be that close to my Divine Heart-Master. Such intimate service was the greatest joy of my life.

However, there was one occasion where I was performing that kind of service when fear interrupted my joy. It had begun to rain just after Parama-Sapta-Na Adi Da Gave His Blessing Darshan to His devotees outside of Aham Da Asmi Sthan,[23] His residence on Naitauba. As Bhagavan walked to His awaiting car, I held an umbrella over His head. It was dark, and the path was dimly lit. The pathway was too narrow to walk next to Bhagavan, so I walked closely behind Him in order to keep Him dry. While trying to keep in tight synch with the rhythm and length of His stride, I inadvertently stepped on the back of my Heart-Master's sandal. My heart dropped! Then, unbelievably, I did it again.

I felt terrible. But it had been done; there was no taking it back. What a horrible feeling. *I intruded.* I had interfered with His Movement and almost tripped my Beloved Master.

Anyone else in His situation would have at least shown some sign of irritation. But only after the second time did Parama-Sapta-Na Adi Da respond. Instead of showing any sign of disturbance, He simply turned His Head, smiled at me, and walked on.

I had stepped on His sandal twice; twice I expected a reaction—my orientation to existence within this conditional realm was cause-and-effect. But Bhagavan Adi Da's Perfect egoless Freedom from the body-mind left me with nothing to fear. Instead, His Loving Glance freed me from my self-protecting pattern, allowing

---

23 "Aham Da Asmi" in Sanskrit means "Beloved, I Am Da", and "Sthan" means "Place".

me to feel His Enlightened Disposition. As the Divine Avatar had said, "What you would have in devotional Communion with Me is . . . My Love-Bliss Itself. Without the slightest image. Without the slightest 'object'. Without the slightest fear. Without any 'other'. Not even yourself an 'other'." (*My "Bright" Form*, 2016 edition, 529).

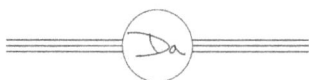

Fanning Adi Da

Each day after working in His office (known as Indigo Swan)
Parama-Sapta-Na Adi Da Samraj would go to Samraj
Mahal[24] for lunch. Samraj Mahal is a large two-story white
building on the beach close to Bhagavan's residence at the Matrix.
The large room on the top floor with white marble floors is a
Communion Hall used for special devotional occasions, which
Bhagavan Da called the "Marble Hall". The architecture of the
bottom floor allows for fantastic ocean views and fresh sea breezes,
due to large windowless arches.

Samraj Mahal was always impeccably maintained and adorned
with many beautiful fresh flower arrangements. Devotees serving
there understood that to serve any of Parama-Sapta-Na Adi Da's
environments was to serve His Person. As a result, His Love-Bliss-
Presence was always alive in Samraj Mahal.

Each day a lunch table was set up in the open-air main room
for Bhagavan. Everything about the setting was simple, practical,
and elegantly beautiful, with a bright fresh flower in a vase on His
table.

As soon as Bhagavan sat and placed a napkin on His lap, He
would always reach for daily reports concerning Adidam and
world news summaries, all prepared by devotees. Once His food
was served, Parama-Sapta-Na Adi Da would continue reading even
as He began eating. He would continue until all the important
reading was done, then He'd quietly put the papers down and finish eating.

Once lunch was finished, occasionally Bhagavan would ask to
see *Antiques Roadshow*. Parama-Sapta-Na Adi Da Samraj enjoyed
seeing the antiques and hearing about their history. He said the
show was without aggression and basically all about good news.
Bhagavan called it "benign entertainment". A devotee would place
a DVD of the show in the player so Bhagavan could view it on a
large screen in front of His lunch table. The screen was always

24.Samraj Mahal is Sanskrit for "Palace of the Paramount Lord".

made available to Him should Bhagavan choose to see *Antiques Roadshow* or anything else.

The Divine Heart-Master was always silent during lunch. The devotees in the kitchen who would prepare His food, as well as the devotee who would serve it, were also silent. The overall silence allowed us to feel Bhagavan Adi Da's profound Equanimity, His Love-Bliss State drew us into heart-Communion with Him.

Often in 2008 I was invited to serve my Beloved Heart-Master during His daily lunches in Samraj Mahal. My devotional service was to fan Beloved Adi Da, bringing Him cool air while removing any disturbing insects with an attractive hand fan. Every day I stood close and slightly to the rear of Bhagavan's left side while lightly fanning His Holy Body.

By Bhagavan Adi Da's Grace, I was enabled to bring the necessary consciousness to the fanning. The fan could not be a disturbance or a distraction. That meant not too close, not too far away, not too fast, not too slow, not too wide a sweep, not too narrow a sweep, constantly bringing cooling air to His Holy Body, and blowing insects away without having the change of movement be noticed. To stand still while fanning Bhagavan for an hour or so required not being distracted by any bodily discomfort. It was perfectly easy to do that; there was no need to think about any discomfort. As soon as there was any sense of tired arms or legs it was immediately forgotten in the return of feeling-attention to my Beloved Heart-Master. The fanning was always a total joy; I was simply being conscious and doing what gave the fullest service to Bhagavan.

Often after lunch the Divine Heart-Master enjoyed getting some sun on His lounge chair on the beach just outside Samraj Mahal. His dog "M" always sat with Him, often between His legs on the chair. The devotees who served His lunch were invited to sit by His side on the sand and the Blessing Grace would continue for me as I fanned my Beloved Heart-Master there on the beach.

The most wonderful thing about being there during those lunches was that those occasions were pure devotion. Those seemingly informal times in Parama-Sapta-Na Adi Da's Holy Company easily allowed heart-Communion—nothing was exaggerated, everything was perfectly natural. On one level, Bhagavan was just

Gerald attending Avatar Adi Da Samraj
at Adi Da Samrajashram 2008

reading reports and eating lunch. More profoundly, however, He constantly Transmitted His Enlightened egoless State of Being. We directly received the Gift of His Awakening Presence.

Lunch occasions in Bhagavan's Holy Company were as sacred as a formal Darshan. The equanimity of His egoless Free State was all-consuming, such that after a short time my feelings became rested in His Radiant Presence; I was no longer the separate devotee doing the fanning. Free from self-absorption, His Divine Presence became all. Fanning continued, just as all the other services continued, but that service was all my heart's joy in profound intimacy with the Divine Being.

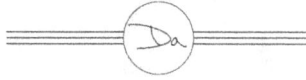

Picture Perfect

E very day after lunch the Divine Avatar Adi Da Samraj went to His art studio, "Picture Perfect", to work on His Transcendental Realist art, a legacy of expansive suites and approximately 100,000 images. These images are His nonverbal Revelation of Divine Reality and they are "the image-art of egoless coincidence with Reality Itself", as Parama-Sapta-Na Adi Da Summarized.

The Picture Perfect studio was a relatively small room, just large enough for Bhagavan's Work and nothing else. He used a simple rectangular table for His desk, placed specifically so as to give Him full view of the room. A beautiful fresh flower in an attractive vase was always on His desk, placed there by a devotee before His arrival.

Opposite His desk were two large projection screens hanging from the ceiling, allowing Him to view several art pieces at a time, and to provide Him more angles on any individual piece. There was also a computer screen set up next to His desk for quick and convenient viewing.

To Parama-Sapta-Na Adi Da's left, four devotee technicians sat at computers behind a white divider screen. The screen had a small opening through which the technicians could project images onto the two large screens. This opening also allowed one technician to observe things that Bhagavan would point to with His laser pointer. Bhagavan also used a headset with a microphone to communicate with His technicians.

Soft music would be playing in the room and, since His voice was also soft, the technicians had to be completely focused every minute. No noise or distractions of any kind were allowed anywhere in Picture Perfect while Parama-Sapta-Na Adi Da was at Work.

Bhagavan was creating art that had never been done before, which meant there was no software capable of serving His creativity.

Devotees with software programming skills had to create customized software for His image-making process. Bhagavan was always pushing beyond the current limits of the customized software. The usual first reaction to this was: *It can't be done.* Yet, by His Grace, devotees' capacities expanded beyond their usual limitations and the software was created.

While Bhagavan Worked, occasionally a devotee would enter silently and leave a damp face cloth sprinkled with fresh lavender fragrance. At other times cool drinks would be placed on His desk while He Worked. When He requested it, a devotee would come in to silently massage His neck and shoulders.

Often Parama-Sapta-Na Adi Da went right up to the screens so He could look at something more closely. Occasionally He used the small computer screen next to His table for that purpose.

While all this was happening, Ruchiradama Quandra Sukhapur Rani and Ruchiradama Nadikanta (His principal renunciate devotees) were there to attend and directly serve Bhagavan. Ruchiradama Nadikanta would stand behind a large video camera recording everything He did while creating His Divine image-art.

Often I was invited to serve Bhagavan from an adjacent room, where I would use a phone or walkie-talkie radio to contact others regarding service to Bhagavan, staying attentive to His every request. I was incredibly Blessed to be that close while the Divine Master was creating the art He had said will bring His Liberating Teaching and His Awakening Presence to the World.

Occasionally, I was also Blessed to attend the Divine Avatar right in Picture Perfect. I was asked to stand silently by the entrance, out of sight so as not to be a visual distraction. If Parama-Sapta-Na Adi Da wanted something He'd tell one of the renunciate devotees and they would give me a written note, since no words were spoken aloud while He was Working. In response, I'd step into the service room and pass on the request. I was also there to help with whatever might come up.

While by the door I could see Bhagavan as He Worked and deeply feel His Divine Radiance. It was pure Darshan. I felt His egoless Presence so strongly that I often had to sit rather than stand as I was expected to do.

It was amazing to see Bhagavan Work His Transcendental Creative Process. Most of His compositions were composed of complex colors, shapes, lines, and complicated forms. Every aspect had to be absolutely perfect, requiring extreme attention to detail.

With His art projected on the screens, He focused the laser light on a point or section and spoke to the technicians over His headset microphone. One technician would receive the message and pass it to the appropriate associate, since they all had different functions. The changes would be projected as fast as possible—Bhagavan emphasized that, while He was Working something out, He should not have to wait for the changes to be made.

So it went in Picture Perfect, and before each day ended Bhagavan gave lists of things to be done that night so they would be ready for the next day's Work. The technicians were in an intense 24/7 service to their Heart-Master.

Watching Parama-Sapta-Na Adi Da walk up to the large screens to study something closely, it appeared outwardly as if He were thinking, analyzing, evaluating, and considering, as if He were using His mind as you or I would. But that is not what was happening. The Divine God-Man was creating His Transcendental Realist art directly from His Perfect State: Consciousness Itself. Those Graced to serve Parama-Sapta-Na Adi Da in Picture Perfect were seeing Divine Creation, His egoless State expressing Itself Perfectly with line, form, and color. We were seeing Him masterfully improvising within what He called "the Unobservable Totality of Light". What we were witness to in Picture Perfect was entirely without precedent.

Avatar Adi Da Samraj:

My images are about how Reality Is (in and of and As Itself), and, also, how Reality appears (as a construction made of primary shaping-forces)… My image-art is, therefore, not merely "subjectively" (or, otherwise, "objectively") based—but, rather, the images I make and do always tacitly and utterly coincide with Reality As It Is (Itself, and altogether). Therefore, I have called the process of the image-art I make and do "Transcendental Realism". ("The Unobservable Totality of Light", *Transcendental Realism*, 2010 edition, 116.)

Now I can see why Parama-Sapta-Na Adi Da had said His Divine image-art would be a vehicle to make Him known in the world. On special occasions Avatar Adi Da would allow His Divine image-art to be seen by His devotees, often projected onto a huge screen at an outdoor site called the Field of Emphasis.

I would typically try to understand each image. I'd notice that an object was shown from different angles of the same image, or how a certain pattern was repeated in different ways. To me this seemed a way to participate in the function of viewing. But when I understood more of what I was doing, I realized I was just using my mind to maintain egoic separation from Bhagavan's Transcendental Realist art.

Then at one showing I just accepted and received all the images without bringing any form of effort to them. In time, by not adding my mind, I began to feel the same heart-feeling from His art that I feel when meditating on His Divine Person and State. His art was transmitting His Living Presence. It was Darshan of the Divine Avatar through His Divine image-art.

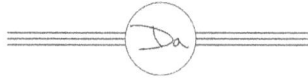

You're Accepted!

AUGUST 2008

Parama-Sapta-Na Adi Da traveled to Lion's Lap (His forest retreat residence) in His outboard motorboat, the "723", whenever the tide and other conditions allowed. Seeing Him at the helm, it was obvious that He thoroughly enjoyed His boat. However, at one point, He remarked that it wasn't fast enough. So it was then outfitted with a bigger engine.

I was on board the first day He drove His boat with the new, more powerful engine. Bhagavan opened the throttle wide and the boat raced high-speed over the waves, bouncing and spraying water on everyone. "Yahoo, it's a roller-coaster ride!" someone yelled. Bhagavan smiled the entire way.

Once we got to shore, after having noticed that some of us had been shaken up by the rough ride, Bhagavan said, "No one over fifty can ride in My boat." Since I was over fifty, I asked the renunciate devotees how to interpret His remark. The answer was, "If you can't sit back and enjoy the ride because you're too stiff or something, then you can't go. Just hold on and enjoy it."

Every time the boat had slammed between waves it had shot a jolt of pain to an arthritic condition in my neck. I was sure Bhagavan noticed my discomfort and had Addressed His remark to me. But to not be on board the 723 with Bhagavan was out of the question.

The next morning when Bhagavan arrived at the boat, I greeted His Divine Presence by bowing, and then as I stood up He saw a large round sign on my chest reading, "High Speed Boat Jock". He smiled broadly, His eyes opened wide and sparkled, He raised His hands chest-high with both thumbs pointing up, and said strongly, "You're accepted!"

I thanked the Divine Heart-Master and boarded His boat. The trip did cause neck pain, but the heart-joy of being in His Holy Company was worth all of it.

His Blessing words were also a confirmation that I had done devotional self-transcending practice sufficiently to change the pattern of self-doubt about the need to be accepted. But most important to me was that my Beloved Heart-Master, the Divine Avatar who is the Living God, confirmed I was accepted. There can be no greater confirmation.

I served my Beloved Heart-Master every day for the next three months, until the day Parama-Sapta-Na Adi Da Samraj took Divine Mahasamadhi (passed from the body) on November 27, 2008. Those months of service were done in complete silence; "you're accepted" were the last spoken words I ever heard from His Divine Person.

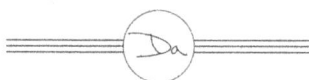

A Lesson in True Puja

Two months before Bhagavan Adi Da passed from His Body, some devotees of the Dasya Mandala (the name for the devotional order of those who served Bhagavan Adi Da directly at that time) were invited to greet Bhagavan with our devotion every day upon His arising for the day. We would bring a gift, perhaps a flower or a leaf, as a sign of our love, devotion, and gratitude for His Presence in our lives. As one of Bhagavan's senior priests, one day I was asked to perform a simple invocation Puja (worship). I placed a charcoal tab in a metal censer,[25] ignited it with the help of a bit of camphor,[26] and added frankincense on top to release its sweet fragrance. I found a beautiful fresh flower and joined the others to go directly into Bhagavan's bedroom.

As we entered, Bhagavan Adi Da was sitting on a chair facing us. His upper body was bare; a light blanket covered His legs. His entire Being was Sublime. In His Holy Presence, the room was still. I approached, offered my flower, and prostrated before His Divine Person. As soon as I got up, I began waving the incense and invoking the Divine Master by His Holy Names.

At first that form of worship felt right, but then there was something about it that felt "off". After only a few moments I put the incense down and sat silently in Communion. No words were said. The invitation was only to stay for a short time so, within less than ten minutes, we were asked to leave. I picked up the censer, which was still releasing fragrant frankincense, and left Bhagavan's bedroom, walking backwards, bowing to Him on my way out.

Later that day, I had a profound experience that provided insight into what had felt "off" about the morning invocation in Bhagavan's bedroom. The understanding came through the Grace of Bhagavan's Divine Self-Transmission while sitting with Him in formal meditation. During that sitting I was undone by Bhagavan's most profound Divine In-filling of my entire body-mind. Feeling

25. A censer is a vessel used for the burning of incense.

26. Camphor is a waxy, flammable, white or transparent solid with a strong aroma.

Him deeply, I felt liberated from my perpetual self-contraction, even to the degree of release from the very illusion of egoity. I was entirely overwhelmed in His Pure Love-Bliss.

In the evening, still feeling the fullness of Bhagavan Adi Da's Transmitted Heart-Siddhi, I reflected on the entire day, particularly the morning. I had been invited into Bhagavan's Holy Company to do a puja of invocation. I had been doing what I was asked to do, but as soon as I had begun saying His Holy Names, I had broken the deep silence so profoundly pervasive around His Divine Person. That was what had felt off.

At times, by His Grace, when I am deeply surrendered in Bhagavan Adi Da's Holy Company, even after His physical Lifetime, I feel His Divine State as profound expansive silence: pure stillness, pure Love-Bliss, Consciousness. When that happens there is actually no "one" feeling the stillness, for the separate being is transcended. The Awareness is Consciousness Itself.

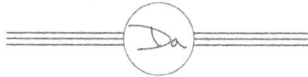

The Divine Mahasamadhi
of Parama-Sapta-Na Adi Da Samraj

NOVEMBER 27, 2008

I was in my office at the Matrix at Adi Da Samrajashram when I heard an urgent call over the radio: "Bhagavan fell over, get Charles!" Charles was Bhagavan's primary doctor. I rushed out and ran to the closest e-cart, jumped in, and headed for Charles' office. Seconds later I saw Charles coming in another e-cart, racing to Bhagavan. I turned and floored the accelerator, racing right behind Charles. It took less than a minute from the radio call to get to our Beloved Divine Heart-Master.

Bhagavan Adi Da was in Picture Perfect, where He had been Working on His Divine image-art. I entered Picture Perfect through the computer technicians' room adjacent to His studio. As I entered the studio, I froze: there was my Beloved Heart-Master lying on His back, unconscious on the floor.

In the next moment I was asked to invoke Bhagavan with a special prayer for the longevity of His Life and His Work. I immediately offered the prayer and continued to offer it throughout the entire time. Everyone was desperately praying for Bhagavan to breathe, to stay with us. His two Ruchiradamas and just a few attending devotees surrounded His body. One was holding Bhagavan's head off the floor, another was rubbing His stomach, and another was rubbing His hands and feet. One devotee was vigorously applying CPR to Bhagavan's chest.

Even though Heart-Master Adi Da had told us His Divine Passing could happen at any time, everyone in the room was praying that this was not that moment. Some were softly crying, everyone was praying, some were pleading: "Beloved, please take a breath. Please breathe. Please don't leave." I pleaded too, only feeling my desperate desire for Bhagavan to stay alive.

After about two hours with absolutely no response from Bhagavan Adi Da, the doctors said it was enough. "To do more would be a violation, since Bhagavan has not physically or in any discernible way responded to all our medical and devotional efforts." Even though we all knew it was true, to hear it said and feel its meaning—that our desperate measures were hopeless, that the doctors were stopping all efforts to resuscitate Bhagavan—was the heartbreaking reality. Everyone became quiet, sinking into the depth of that hard truth. Bhagavan Adi Da Samraj had shed His body and taken His Divine Mahasamadhi.

For several years Heart-Master Adi Da had told us that He would leave the body when His Work of establishing His egoless Pattern eternally in this domain was sufficiently established, and not before. He said His Passing was a Divine matter that could happen unexpectedly without any advance signs. He said He was always perfectly ready for it to happen, for it would be positive for His Divine Awakening Work with all beings for all time.

Bhagavan Adi Da's doctor checked on His health every day. On this day he had reported that "Bhagavan was in good health without any physical symptoms of note. There was no sign or premonition of what was going to occur later in the day. Bhagavan's heart simply stopped."

We were all heartbroken. The Divine Person in His beautiful human Form would no longer sit before us, talk to us, Reveal Truth by all His Transcendental Creative Means. Da, the Divine Giver, had relinquished His body. What a profound loss! What a profound heartbreak. It was excruciatingly difficult to accept.

Devotees who had gathered outside Picture Perfect were told that Bhagavan had not responded to all efforts to bring Him back. A blanket of silence fell over them as each, in their own way, felt the reality of what they had just been told.

We lifted Bhagavan's Holy Body onto a stretcher and covered Him with blankets. The Divine Master was carried out of Picture Perfect, where all the devotees were waiting. Everyone followed as Parama-Sapta-Na Adi Da Samraj's bodily human Form was taken to His residence. We all sat on the veranda outside His bedroom long into the night and morning, plunged in deep sorrow, while the Ruchiradamas and one or two attending devotees served Bhagavan's Holy Body. They wrapped Him in fire-orange colored fabric, with only His face exposed. His body was supported to sit upright on His bed with His legs folded under Him as He had normally sat during His lifetime.

For the next two days all devotees were invited to sit for a while with Bhagavan Adi Da in His bedroom. The room and everything about it was devotionally prepared and served in order to allow no interruption to devotees being able to behold their Divine Heart-Master one last time. There was a very strong feeling in the room of His Omni-Presence, confirming to me that He was still with us. Bhagavan's bedroom was a most profound Holy Temple.

On the morning of the third day, the Divine Avatar Parama-Sapta-Na Adi Da Samraj's Holy Body was taken from His residence to His Temple, Atma Nadi Shakti Loka, at The "Brightness", to be interred in a prepared vault within His Sukra Kendra inner temple.

I had recently given Bhagavan Adi Da a gift on His birthday of a large white flag with His Sapta Na Sannyasin (Renunciate Order) symbol on it (the logo that now appears on the cover of His book *The Aletheon*). I felt that the flag had to go with Bhagavan on this most sacred procession to The "Brightness", and I was allowed to carry it at the head of the procession. Bhagavan's Holy Body was carried in a vehicle with the Ruchiradamas and His family attending Him, while devotees followed around and behind the vehicle.

Carrying the flag felt to me like confirming to everyone that: *BHAGAVAN IS HERE!* Even though His body was going to be interred, *HE IS HERE!* While carrying His flag, I was not crying and lamenting Bhagavan's Passing. Rather, I was feeling: *HE IS HERE NOW AND HERE ETERNALLY!* It felt a bit like blowing a conch announcing Bhagavan's Arrival at a Darshan occasion, which I had done many times. But it was much more, since the flag acknowledged that Parama-Sapta-Na Adi Da Samraj's Divine Eternal Presence *IS HERE*, not gone!

In The "Brightness", Bhagavan's Holy Body was honorably and sacredly placed upright in His characteristic seated position within the vault. Many sacred elements were placed all around His Holy Body, and then the vault was covered and sealed. Bhagavan Adi Da's chair from His Sukra Kendra was placed on top of the vault, acknowledging His Eternal Living Presence and perpetual Transmission of Divine Reality from that Holy Temple to all and everywhere, for all time.

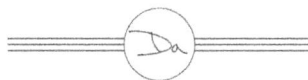

PART SEVEN

Stories from 2008–2016

The Silver Hall Divine Revelation

MARCH 2009

The Divine Avatar Adi Da Samraj established a special Transmission temple at Adi Da Samrajashram, His Fijian Hermitage. He named it "Danavira Peetha" (the Empowered Seat of the Hero of Giving), or more simply "The Silver Hall" (after the silver-colored adornments in the hall). The Silver Hall is a temple where devotees who are advancing in practice are able to sit in heart-Communion with His Divine Presence, while He Spiritually Transmits His Awakening Transcendental Divine State. He had said that this Transmission is what He does when devotees are prepared to receive it, and He said that the Silver Hall would continue to be a Holy Transmission temple for all time for maturing devotees.

Avatar Adi Da's Instructions for sitting in the Silver Hall were to simply allow His Divine Presence to be felt without seeking or applying any effort. If anything other than His Divine Presence arose, we were not to give it any attention by trying to do something about it. The practice was simply to return feeling-attention to His Divine Presence. The surrendered practice of "Searchless Beholding" of His Divine Person was the requirement.

One unique time in the Silver Hall has been forged in my heart forever. It occurred four months after Bhagavan Adi Da's Passing— a vivid example of His Awakening Blessings and Eternal unrestricted Spiritual Transmission.

While I was letting go of the concern about not letting go, and relaxing all body and mind demands for attention, I noticed that I was significantly distracted and not prepared that day to be in the Silver Hall. In response, I considered leaving.

Upon feeling the impulse to leave, I immediately recognized my characteristic resistance to surrendering in place. By tendency I would want to leave and "work on" my disturbance, then hopefully return once things "worked out" and I was more prepared to be there. But this time, instead of leaving, I sat upright, took a deep

breath, and released my self-concern by turning my feeling-attention to Bhagavan Adi Da, focusing on His photographic Murti.

Immediately, now that I was more receptive, something
absolutely profound happened. All awareness completely changed.
The Revealed Awareness was absolutely nothing like the awareness
of my separate point of view. The entire sense of a separate "self"
stopped! It was literally waking up from the illusion of being a separate someone. The separate self-sense of "I" was entirely transcended in the freely Given Revelation of Divine Reality.

The entire condition was Conscious. There was no point of
view in it. There was no center, no "one" being aware, and there
was absolutely no sense of anything being other than Consciousness. The condition was Perfect Awareness, Consciousness Self-
Aware. It was Perfect "Knowledge", for everything was One Thing—
Consciousness Itself. It was Bhagavan Adi Da Samraj, the Divine
Person, Revealed as His Divine State of the Witness-Consciousness.

There was no inwardness about any of it. My eyes were open
and everything still looked the same as it had always looked. All
the shapes and forms didn't change. The difference was that nothing was separate, nothing was an object. No one was the subject
observing an object. There was no "other" than the Conscious Self-
Awareness that included the witness "me". All the individuated
forms were as Avatar Adi Da explained, "merely apparent modifications of Divine Reality appearing as Conscious Energy, or Light."
Nothing had any separate significance. The only significance was
that everything was one thing, Consciousness Itself in individuated
forms. The feeling was Complete Freedom in Perfect Harmony.
The separate and separating point of view stopped. It was Perfect
Divine Unity.

Divine Master Adi Da Samraj had said that Consciousness and
Energy, or Light, are the same, not a separate duality as some traditions teach. During this Divine Revelation of the Witness-
Consciousness in the Silver Hall, all forms of energy, which ultimately are recognized as Light, were Conscious forms of Energy—
Conscious Energy, or Conscious Light. It was perfectly obvious
that Consciousness is Light. Light is Consciousness. They are one.

This Divine Truth was simply the very Truth. It was Consciousness Self-Aware.

Everything in the Silver Hall, including Parama-Sapta-Na Adi Da's Murti, His chair, the flowers, the other devotees, the room, the walls, the air, the space, were all perfectly non-separate, non-different individuated forms of Conscious Light, perfectly Revealed as the all-pervading Divine Unity of Consciousness Itself. And the Witness was not different or separate from Conscious Light. It was Consciousness Self-Witnessing.

In this Divine Self-Revelation, mind and thought did not arise. The condition was prior to mind. The separative ego-"I" was transcended at the beginning, so there was no mind to arise. Also, all questions, all seeking, and all motivations ended, because everything was perfectly known in and as Conscious Light Itself. The weight that the body-mind always carries due to life itself—its seeking, all its limits, and its inevitable death—immediately was lifted. Conscious Light was Perfectly Free and Unlimited. The Divine Self-Revelation was total Freedom, the true natural State of Perfect Love-Bliss, Unlimited Happiness, and pure Radiant Joy. It was absolutely the native State of Unlimited Being. No one was having an experience; it was Divine Reality, which is Bhagavan Adi Da's Divine Nature, Condition, and State. It is the true prior Reality of everything and everyone.

Bhagavan Adi Da had said that in Divine Reality there is no time as we ordinarily perceive and experience it. During this Divine Revelation, my entire sense of time changed. It was obvious that the past isn't a separate time; the past was fully felt in the present. It was obvious that what happened in the past led to, and was part of, the current awareness, and could be felt as part of the present. The present had a fullness in it that included the past. Likewise, it was also obvious that the future is a continuation of the present. The idea of time past, or time projected into a future, is a presumption that is not really true. It comes from the separative ego-"I". It was clear during this Blessed Divine Revelation, that past, present, and future are all a Conscious continuance of change.

Parama-Sapta-Na Adi Da had said that in Divine Reality there is no space as we ordinarily perceive and experience it. During this Divine Self-Revelation of the Witness-Consciousness, my entire sense of space changed. All individuated forms, including the illusion of "me", had no separate distinction in the Conscious Light. Even the space between individuated forms was the same Conscious Energy or Light. Everything was Divine Unity as Conscious Light. There was no space, because there was no separation, no difference in Consciousness at all.

These were not experiences "I" had. What was Self-Revealed was Consciousness Itself to Itself.

There was no one to claim it as "my" awareness.

Bhagavan Adi Da had said that Divine Consciousness is His Spiritually Self-Bright State. Sitting in the Silver Hall, I knew that He was not limited to a body or mind. His bodily human Form was a means that the Divine Avatar used to Spiritually Transmit Divine Reality and establish His egoless Pattern for all time. His Avataric Person was (and is) Consciousness Itself, unbound by bodily existence.

After an hour, the sitting ended. As I heard other devotees begin to move about, immediately the contracted condition of ordinary self-awareness fully returned. Now there was a point of view. Right away "I" noticed the radical difference between Conscious Awareness as the Witness-Consciousness and my self-contracted ordinary egoic awareness, the illusion identified as "my awareness". Now, from "my" contracted position of "point of view", everything I saw and felt was seemingly separate. Immediately all the heaviness of ego-"I", and its seeking due to the stress of separateness and inevitable death, fully returned.

I prostrated on the carpet in deepest heart-love and profound gratitude to Parama-Sapta-Na Adi Da Samraj for His Divine Revelation of His very Divine Person.

After leaving the Hall, as I walked to the next devotional event, I noticed, to my surprise, that I didn't feel any different than before going into the Silver Hall. Usually, even any form of heart-Communion with Bhagavan Adi Da made me feel different. I wondered why I didn't feel any effect at all from His Gift of that most profound Divine Revelation. Why hadn't it changed me?

Then it became clear: It was a free Gift of Bhagavan Adi Da's Divine Self-Revelation. It replaced "me". The act of being a separate "I" stopped. "I" had not experienced any of it! "I" wasn't there. There was total Awareness, but it was not "my" awareness. It was

Consciousness Self-Aware. Consciousness Itself was the "Witness". "I" was completely unaffected, because "I" wasn't there to experience any of it. "I" wasn't there because the contracted separate self was supplanted by Bhagavan Adi Da's Divine Person.

Another thing that stood out was that Consciousness Itself was so completely different than my self-awareness. There was absolutely nothing I could have done, or ever could do by any self-effort, to get to it. The only way it was Witnessed was by Parama-Sapta-Na Adi Da's free Gift of totally transcending everything that is the assumed separate "I", or "me", or "mine". Therefore, to seek it is completely useless. As Adi Da had said, "You can't get there from here." To be Awakened to any degree requires the Grace of the Divine. The glimpse of the Witness-Consciousness in the Silver Hall was a free Gift given by the Grace of the Divine Avatar, Parama-Sapta-Na Adi Da Samraj.

In spite of my unchanged egoity, there was and is the living Conscious imprint in my heart of what had happened. I wondered, *if "I" wasn't there, how could "I" have the conscious awareness of what had happened?* The answer became obvious: Consciousness is Who and What I am. It is the True Condition of every one and every thing. That most profound Gift still guides my devotional life and practice to this day.

Parama-Sapta-Na Adi Da had said:

Standing As the Witness-Consciousness is (in and of itself) only the beginning of the "Perfect Practice" of the Reality-Way of Adidam.

In the only-by-Me Revealed and Given Reality-Way of Adidam, the Stand As the Witness-Consciousness is simply a Basis, a Key, a Doorway.

In the only-by-Me Revealed and Given Reality-Way of Adidam, the Stand As the Witness-Consciousness is Gracefully Awakened by My Divine Avataric Transcendental Spiritual Means.

In the only-by-Me Revealed and Given Reality-Way of Adidam, the Doorway of the Witness-Stand is Gracefully Opened in the course of the Transcendental Spiritual process of real devotion to Me. ("Most Perfect Divine Self-Awakening To The Domain of Conscious Light", *The Aletheon*, 2009 edition, 1626.)

Parama-Sapta-Na Adi Da Samraj came to Awaken all beings to their True Condition of Divine Reality. Divine Reality is Conscious Light. As Bhagavan Adi Da had said, the Witness-Consciousness is the Doorway to the Perfect Prior Divine Condition of All.

Here are some summary words of Instruction to consider, feel, and let penetrate about the Witness-Consciousness, Given by the Divine Avatar, Parama-Sapta-Na Adi Da Samraj:

The Five Reality-Teachings
(From *The Teaching Manual of Perfect Summaries*)

Notice this:

1. You are not the one who wakes, or dreams, or sleeps.

2. You Are the actionless and formless Mere Witness of the three common states—of waking, dreaming, and sleeping—and of all the apparent contents and "experiences" associated with the three common states, of waking, and of dreaming, and of sleeping.

3. You are not the body, or the doer of action, or the doer of even any of the body's actions or functions.

4. You are not the mind, or the thinker, or the doer of even any of the actions or functions of mind or of body-mind.

5. No matter what arises—whether as or in the state of waking, or of dreaming, or of sleeping—you Are the actionless, and formless, and thought-free Mere Witness of attention itself, and of every apparent "object" of attention, and of any and every state of "experience", and of the entirety of whatever and all that arises.

Always intensively "consider" these Five Reality-Teachings.

Always intensively observe and notice every moment of your "experience"—whether waking, dreaming, or sleeping—and, thus and thereby, "consider" and test and directly prove these Five Reality-Teachings in the moment-to-moment of your every kind and state of "experience".

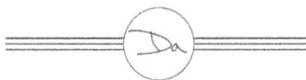

A Healing

In about July 2006 I felt it necessary to go to a doctor about a persistent pain in my neck. The cause was diagnosed as a severe arthritic condition involving several discs. The treatment recommended was professional physical therapy, which I did for nine months, until I was certain it wasn't helping. Then I did specific exercises at home daily, accepting that I'd have to live with the discomfort.

Over the next four years while living at Adi Da Samrajashram in Fiji, the neck pain became so distracting I requested permission to go back to the States and find a treatment, or surgery that would bring relief. As I was leaving, I sent a written request for Parama-Sapta-Na Adi Da's Blessings for swift healing. It was obvious to me that even though He had left the body in 2008 His Eternal Presence was entirely alive and I felt He would respond to my Blessing request.

For the next two and a half years after I left the island, I tried all the known treatments, including six more months of professional physical therapy. Finally the only thing left was an extreme series of burning the pain-causing nerves called radiofrequency ablation. But after seven treatments, nothing gave lasting results. To me the last choice had to be surgery. To my great disappointment the surgeon said, "There is no surgery that can help your neck." That was like a judge sentencing me to a life of unending pain. I felt it meant there was nothing more physically that could be done.

During that time, whenever I began a new treatment, I sent a written request for Bhagavan's Blessings that the new treatment would be effective. Over the years I requested Bhagavan Adi Da's direct Blessings for my neck to heal eight specific times. While I knew He would do what could be done, to my surprise, not only did my arthritic neck fail to heal, but a disturbing tingling sensation began running down my left arm as a side effect of the arthritis.

In October 2013 I returned to Adi Da Samrajashram, this time on meditation and service retreat. The greatness of Adi Da Samrajashram is that Bhagavan Adi Da's Radiant egoless Presence is tangibly felt throughout His Holy Hermitage. And retreat is a circumstance that supports constant heart-surrender in feeling-Communion with Bhagavan Adi Da and His Divine State of Consciousness Itself. During the retreat the tingling down my left arm became so disturbing that it affected meditation and sleep. In spite of that, it was a very Blessed retreat.

After six weeks I returned to the States to directly address the arm discomfort. It took a couple of weeks to get an appointment with the same surgeon who had examined my neck. Since he was with the director of neurosurgery at a world-class Boston hospital, I fully trusted his advice. He said surgery would be the only way. He explained the surgery would be done by entering the neck from the front to remove three damaged discs, and then fusing three vertebrae. He explained all the negative side-effects and said he thought it "might stop" the arm discomfort.

I certainly didn't want surgery that only "might stop" the pain, but I felt that it would be the only cure for the tingling in my left arm. I had already accepted that there was no cure for my neck. I decided to hold off considering the surgery for a month or two, while I aggressively addressed the arm discomfort with previously established intense physical therapy exercises, hoping that some of the exercises might also help alleviate the perpetual neck pain.

As things worked out, readjusting to being back in the States and preparing for the annual celebration of Danavira Mela, I delayed beginning the aggressive physical therapy. In fact, I didn't do anything physically that would help my condition. Devotionally, as on retreat, I continued to surrender the body and mind to Bhagavan Adi Da's Living Presence. Then one day, to my surprise I noticed that my neck was not bothering me and the tingling down my arm had stopped! It happened just like that. Other than turning devotionally to Bhagavan, I had done nothing to support such a radical change.

After a couple days I called the doctor at the Boston hospital and told him the pain had stopped. He said, "You still do have the arthritic condition, I have x-rays of it. If the pain stopped it's a miracle. There's no other explanation for it."

I've tested this new pain-free condition for over three years and it is true, there is no pain and no discomfort. Since the healing happened right after the depthful retreat, and since Bhagavan Adi Da's Presence can be felt anywhere anytime, I have absolutely no doubt that the spontaneous healing was Given by the Divine Avatar, Bhagavan Adi Da Samraj.

I bow down in deepest devotion and gratitude to the Living Presence of Divine Reality, the Supreme One who Lives and Breathes all, Consciousness Itself, Parama-Sapta-Na Adi Da Love-Ananda Samraj.

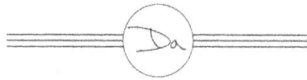

Six Gifts of Divine Reality

MAY–SEPTEMBER 2016

In the spring of 2016, I went on retreat to Adi Da Samraj-ashram. The feeling of being on retreat began while I was still on the boat approaching the island. As soon as the boat reached the shore, my awareness spontaneously expanded into deeper feeling. I immediately felt a magnification of Bhagavan Adi Da's Living Presence. The island felt saturated with His Love-Bliss.

The entire retreat was full of profound Gifts from Parama-Sapta-Na Adi Da, but six were most significant—and these are gifts that in some sense to me summarize everything that my Divine Heart-Master was and is always Giving. Of those six, some of the Gifts profoundly Awakened deeper recognition of His Divine State, and the others Awakened a deeper, root self-understanding of "my" separate and separating egoity.

The only way I can write about these Gifts is one at a time, which can make it seem like they were singular events on separate occasions. They were not. They were repetitive and cumulative, standing out in the moment-by-moment Blessing Flow of Bhagavan Adi Da's Divine Presence over the sixteen weeks of the retreat, and really throughout my entire relationship to Him.

The First Gift
The ego-"I" is an illusion.

Bhagavan Adi Da showed me in deepest feeling that the ego-"I" is a self-confirming activity, fixed in mind and body by repetitive patterns, tendencies, habits, and addictions. He made it perfectly clear that the sense of self is a constant self-referring activity at every level—gross, subtle and causal; waking, dreaming and sleeping—always and only supporting the illusion of separate existence.

By His most profound Blessing Grace, I clearly felt and understood that the ego-"I" is entirely a mind-made, mind-supporting illusion. Over and over in deepest feeling He made the point that the "I" of self-reference does not exist as a concrete anything.

The reality that the ego-"I" is only an illusion of the ego-mind isn't at all negative. Emphatically, just the opposite. The Revelation quieted my mind from its constant thinking and searching for answers.

His compassionate Gift about the illusory nature of the ego-"I" came from His Love, and directly Awakened a spontaneous devotional response and commitment: In order for the Prior Reality of no-ego to be lived, the renunciation of the illusion of egoic identity must be lived. But it was also clear that I cannot do that renunciation. A drowning man cannot save himself; he needs help, that's what it means to be drowning. Just so, I cannot renounce the ego-illusion. But the ego-illusion can be undone by receiving the Help of Bhagavan Adi Da by turning to Him instead of continuing my patterned commitment to the illusion.

The Second Gift
Consciousness and Its Light are the One Prior Divine Reality.

The Divine Avatar Adi Da Samraj Revealed that Consciousness Itself is the Divine Reality prior to the illusion of separation by the active ego-"I". His direct Transmission of Truth let me feel, understand, and fully accept that Consciousness Is the Source, the Core, and the Root-Condition. It is the Indivisible Truth of existence, prior to the illusion of ego-"I". It is the egoless Prior Unity of existence. Parama-Sapta-Na Adi Da let me profoundly feel that everything is Consciousness. Even energy, as form, is Consciousness. Consciousness and Its conscious energy are one thing, one True Condition, the Divine Reality of existence.

The difference in receiving the Revelation of Consciousness and its Energy by Bhagavan Adi Da's Transcendental Spiritual Transmission was that it was entirely direct and obviously true; it was not about thinking, believing, accepting, or trusting. It was a freely Given Awakening of the heart in pure feeling-Awareness. It was Consciousness Revealing Itself, and, strange as it seems, Revealing Itself to Itself. The "I" of patterned egoity was not the recipient.

Having been Given this direct whole-bodily intuition of the Truth of Divine Reality, Avatar Adi Da also showed me how the discriminative mind can try to make "sense" of things without carrying the Force of Awakening.

The Third Gift
Avatar Adi Da is fully Present as Consciousness Itself.

In all the years before this retreat, I never could get beyond the limit of seeing and feeling others as separate, no matter what I believed. Non-separation was my philosophy; separation was my reality. My ability to completely stop relating to my Heart-Master as a separate body-mind person—no matter how Divine and holy I felt He was—never fully changed, until, that is, I had absorbed this third Gift. Before that, I definitely acknowledged His Divine State, and turned to His Spiritual Presence in meditation, but, limited by the superficiality of the body-mind faculties and senses, I naturally perceived His body-mind as another separate body-mind, an objective other.

During this retreat His Transmission went directly into my feeling being, perfectly Revealing His Transcendental Truth: He Is Consciousness Itself. He Transmitted the Truth about the separating act of ego-"I", and the Truth of Consciousness Itself because He Is Consciousness Itself. He is the Divine Revealer and the Divine Revelation of Consciousness, Self-Revealed. He doesn't just "express a Teaching"; He Transmits His fully Enlightened Conscious State directly.

This Gift Awakened an ecstatic recognition of Who He Is. He is Love and Bliss. He is the Divine Avatar of Prior Unity. It immediately became clear that His Enlightened Presence in bodily Form was entirely and only a vehicle His Divine Person used to bring the demonstration and the Teaching of the Divine Revelation of Conscious Light to all beings. His body-mind is the sign of Divine Reality.

The Fourth Gift
Familiarity is an obstacle.

According to some traditions, those devotees who have direct service to their guru are often the last to fully Realize his or her Teaching, precisely because of their familiarity with their guru. I of course always carried a degree of familiarity due to all the years of direct service to my beloved Guru.

He said in His Teaching that the Way He Reveals is not about being familiar with Him, or believing what He says. It is entirely about Awakening and feeling the undeniable egoless Truth of His Love-Bliss-State, prior to all superficiality.

All His Gifts of Divine Revelation show that my sense of familiarity was the result of still relating to Him as a holy person but still a body-mind, a separate person. It prevented the deeper recognition that He is Consciousness Itself, the prior Truth, senior to the body-mind. The Awakening to heart-deep knowledge that Parama-Sapta-Na Adi Da Samraj is Consciousness Itself undermined my sense of familiarity. The recognition of His Real Condition changes my tendency to relate to Him as a familiar "other". Everything about Him is only and entirely the perfect sign of Consciousness Itself, non-separate from all and everything.

The Fifth Gift
He is always already Giving the Ultimate Gift.

Bhagavan Adi Da is never anything less than Consciousness Itself. Therefore He is always presently Revealing and Transmitting His Divine Conscious Truth. It is not something He does off and on, as if Consciousness could be less that Itself and therefore manipulated. Over all the years, He was always and only Being and showing His True Condition as Consciousness Itself.

This Gift undermined my egoic tendency to seek more from Him, more than what He was (and is) always already Giving, as if there could be more. I was moved to stop seeking for more. I was moved instead to turn more fully into His Revealed Divine Presence, thus allowing Him to more fully Awaken me at heart.

While this Gift, like the others, was not the result of thinking, it is worth noting how foolish seeking for more is in the Presence of One Who is always already Giving the Ultimate Gift.

The Sixth Gift
The Fullness of His Eternal Presence.

Over the years when devotees would confess something of their recognition of Bhagavan Adi Da, He would say, "You don't recognize Me." I didn't get it. *Weren't there, perhaps, degrees of recognition?* But whenever Adi Da would say "You don't recognize Me" He was referring to <u>perfect</u> recognition. Everything short of perfect recognition is ego-based—limited recognition obscured by the self-contraction.

Everything He ever did, even from birth and during the thirty-six years of His formal Teaching and Blessing Work—the long period of Submitting to people's ordinariness, establishing the forms of worship and His Sanctuaries, creating the Adidam culture of devotees, writing all the books, creating His art—was His unprecedented, monumental Means of establishing His Eternal Living Presence in this world and the cosmic realm. Now and forever hereafter humankind is blessed with the authentic living connection to Spiritual Reality. The Radical ("at-the-root") Reality-Way of Adidam Ruchiradam is the Eternal Gift Avatar Adi Da Samraj has Given by His Divine Love for all beings. All those who ever came, or will ever come, to His Divine Person are directly Blessed to Realize the egoless Prior Unity of Conscious Light. There is no greater Gift.

Avatar Adi Da Samraj:

People who are trying to find out if there is Something Greater in life to feel better about are always functioning on the basis of the model of this body-mind-complex, or the body, or the physical, looking everywhere in the physical universe for some proof that there is Something Greater.

The body-mind-complex, or the realm of conditional manifestation, is an artificial "point of view". It is not the Condition in

Which you Stand. You Stand in the Position of Consciousness Itself, not in the position of the body.

If you establish yourself profoundly in the Position of Consciousness Itself, you will Realize Its Status and the Status of everything, then. From the "Disposition" of Consciousness Itself, there is no "me", no "someone" identified with the body, confronted by blah-blah-blah of manifestation, and all the while realizing somewhere inside "I am Consciousness".

When you are Consciousness Itself, you Realize that you Stand in an Infinite Domain of Energy, just That, only That Energy and Its modifications, and you do not even encounter the body except as a modification of Energy—whereas from the "point of view" of the ego, or the usual person, the body is encountered as solid stuff, solid "me". It is not encountered as Energy, and it is not encountered from the "Disposition" of Consciousness Itself. Rather, the body is the "point of view" from which Consciousness Itself seems to be examined.

All references that the un-Enlightened person makes to Consciousness Itself are made from the "point of view" of egoic "self"-identification with the body. All of that is itself a kind of aberration. . . .

You must Realize a right view of conditional existence. You Stand in the Position of Consciousness Itself, and everything that arises to Consciousness is a form of Free Energy. Just That. Even the most solid forms are just That, and this is obvious from the "Disposition" of Consciousness Itself—whereas from the "point of view" of the body-mind-complex, it is not even obvious what the Status of personal consciousness is, or the Status of any thing, or any state. It is just stuff, "thingness".

Apart from Divine Self-Realization, the Divine Status of anything is not intuited or presumed. In the Position of Consciousness Itself it is clear that there is only Consciousness in a Domain of Infinite Energy.

All kinds of "things" are arising, but they are only modifications of the Energy of Consciousness. This is the Divine Vision I am Talking about, the Vision that makes all the difference. It is the Vision associated with Divine Enlightenment. (From a talk given on July 9, 1983, at Nukubati island, Fiji.)

The Divine Master, Avatar Adi Da, Speaks to every heart:

Simply be Attracted to Me, and let the body-mind-complex (as a whole) be purified, transformed, and (altogether) Divinely Self-Awakened and Divinely Translated by My Divine Avataric Self-Transmission of My Divinely Self-"Bright" State.

Such is The Fundamental Principle of the devotional (and, in due course, Transcendental Spiritual) relationship to Me.

Such is The Fundamental Principle of The only-by-Me Revealed and Given "Radical" (or Always "At-The-Root") Reality-Way of Adidam (or Adidam Ruchiradam).

Because of That Principle, I am your Unique Advantage. ("I Am Your Unique Advantage", *The Aletheon*, 2009 edition, 598.)

At the gates to Atma Nadi Shakti Loka, where Avatar Adi Da's Holy Body has been laid to rest, the summary of His Divine Revelation is written:

I Am The "Bright", The One To Be Realized.

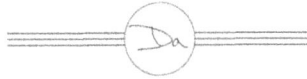

EPILOGUE

His Eternal Presence

Parama-Sapta-Na Adi Da Samraj is as Spiritually alive now as ever before. His Divine Presence is felt and surrendered to as the egoless Prior Source-Condition. To address His devotees' right alignment to His Divine Person and Eternal Presence, Bhagavan Adi Da said in the earliest days of His Work:

I have told you that the Guru comes to manifest the Satsang that existed prior to His physical birth. People don't relate to that. After the Guru's death they try to relate to the Satsang that He apparently generated during His lifetime. They go around trying to remember what He looked like and carrying that whole cult of His personality, instead of truly living the Divine Satsang that He was here to communicate. (The Dawn Horse Magazine Jubilee Issue, vol. 2, no. 2 August 1974.)

During a ceremonial tribute to Bhagavan Adi Da Samraj in 2009, a year after His Passing, many devotees offered testimonials. The following is an excerpt from the transcript of my testimony:

"And now, there is no question about it. Bhagavan is totally Present. He is felt every day. He is loved every day. His Presence is breathed every single day, and He is served every single day. And He is beheld searchlessly every day. Searchlessly because He has Revealed that His Divine State is Prior to everything—to the whole thing that we assume is separate. Prior Unity. And the Feeling of His State is Love-Bliss-Fullness. So in the Prior State of Love-Bliss-Fullness, there is nothing to look for, there is nothing to search for, there is nowhere to go. The only thing to do now is to cultivate that relationship and stay in that intimacy with Him, until there is only His Person of Conscious Light."

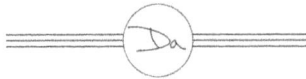

My Divine Secret

by Avatar Adi Da Samraj

I Will Be here Forever.
I Will Be every "where" Forever.

I Cannot Leave, For My Transcendentally
Spiritually "Bright" Divine Spherical Self-Domain Is
Not Some "Where" To "Go To".
My Divine Self-Domain Is Eternal.
I Am Eternal, and I Am Always Already Merely
Present—here, and every "where" In The Cosmic
Domain.

By Means of My Avataric Incarnation here, I Have
Given you My Divine Secret.
My Divine Secret Is This: I Am Eternally Present,
and I Am Omni-Present.

("I Cannot Leave", *The Eternal One*, 2009 edition, 281.)

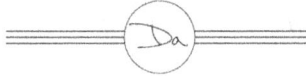

379

Study My Word

by Avatar Adi Da Samraj

T*he Utterance that is provoked to come forth from This Body is from the Place, the Dimension, That Is Beyond egoity, Beyond separateness.*

Reality Itself—the Divine Self-Nature, Self-Condition, and Self-State of all-and-All—Speaks (Spontaneously) through and <u>As</u> This Body.

Through conjunctions of all kinds, Spontaneous Utterances and Spontaneous Doings have been the Occurrence.

It is a Unique Manifestation.

If you are noticing something of this, then you are coming into coincidence with Me through My Words.

To study or "consider" My Word is to Commune with Me.

Therefore, the more profoundly you participate in that "self"-forgetting Communion for real, the more you will be aware (in some fundamental sense) of My State.

To approach Me through My Word is a form of devotional Communion with Me—and My Written and Spoken Word is a Unique and actual Means for that to occur.

No other words—not even any traditional text of an esoteric kind—can do that.

Such is the Uniqueness of the Word of My Utterance.

My Word literally does Manifest Me.

And one who enters into My Word can literally be brought into devotional Communion with Me—just as may occur by Means of My Murti, or any Form of My Agency that is explicitly Extended as such.

("The Sacred Space of Finding Me", *The Sacred Space of Finding Me*, 2011 edition, 298–99.)

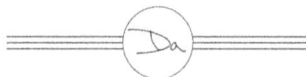

My Final Work

by Avatar Adi Da Samraj

M*y Final Work is of an entirely different kind than the Work I have previously Engaged.*

My Final Work Is entirely Free of any Inclination to Submit.

My Final Work has nothing whatsoever to do with Submitting to anyone, or to the trends of history.

My Final Work Is Only Myself.

My Final Work Is simply Me here, Revealing Myself.

My Final Work Is simply Direct Divine Self-Revelation – by Avataric Means.

My Final Work Is simply the Self-Revelation of Reality Itself.

My Final Work Is Me – Alone.

("Walk-About To Me", *The Aletheon*, 2009 edition, 1842–43.)

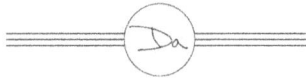

381

Heart-Prayer

The following prayer was created by Avatar Adi Da, originally as a rendering of select verses of the traditional Hindu scripture *Guru Gita* (attributed to the sage Vyasa), but then greatly elaborated. It beautifully expresses the attitude of the true devotee:

I bow down to the Eternal Truth, the Conscious Light of Being (Itself), the Timeless Happiness, the Great One, the Indefinable One (Awake, and Free), the Silent One (Who Speaks to the heart directly, without a word of "explanation"), the Truly "Bright" One—Who Appears (and Stands Revealed) As Adi Da Samraj, the Divine Heart-Master among all who know and Teach.

I bow down to the Divine Heart-Master, Adi Da Samraj— Whose Avatarically-Born Bodily (Human) Divine Form Is the Beautiful Mystery of "Brightness" Itself, and Whose Avatarically Self-Transmitted Transcendental Spiritual (and Always Blessing) Divine Presence Always Reveals the Very Heart Itself, and Whose Avatarically Self-Revealed (and Very, and Transcendental, and Perfectly Subjective, and Inherently Spiritual, and Intrinsically ego-less, and Inherently Perfect, and Self-Evidently Divine) State of Being Is the Self-Revelation of the One and Only Divine and Conscious Light Itself, Self-Existing As Immense Consciousness and Self-Radiant As Love-Bliss.

I bow down to the Divine Heart-Master, Adi Da Samraj—Who Is the Heart-Witness of my own body, mind, and separate "self", and Who Is the Great Bearer, the Most Perfect Realizer, and the Divine Subject of the Great Tradition, and Whose Very State of Being Is Truth and Perfect Love-Bliss-Happiness, and Who Is the Graceful Source of the Realization of Love-Bliss-Happiness Itself.

I bow down to the Divine Heart-Master, Adi Da Samraj— the Always New One, Who has Appeared in the "world" by the Magic and Mystery of His Own Will and Love, but Who Is Only the "Bright" Mass of Pure Conscious Light, Transcendentally Spiritually Radiant, the Sun of the Heart, the Destroyer of un-Happiness.

*I bow down to the Divine Heart-Master, Adi Da Samraj—
the Always Already Free One, the Body of Mercy, the Refuge of
devotees, Who allows His Human Life to be dependent on His
devotees.*

*My Heart-Master, Adi Da Samraj, Divine and True and Free—
may Your Radiant "Bright" Blessings Awaken me, whose eyes are
covered over by the images of a separate "self", and whose mind
is held captive by visions of the "world".*

*I bow down to the Divine Heart-Master, Adi Da Samraj—That
Most Beautiful Form, the Master of Discrimination, the Master of
Understanding, the "Bright", the Light Itself (Above all lights),
Who Is the Light to those who call for Light, and Who Is the
Realizer in all those who Realize Him. May You be Pleased to Take
Your Seat in my heart at all times. May You ever Dwell in my heart.*

Da   Da   Da

(*The Ruchira Avatara Gita*, 2004 edition, as recited in the daily
sacramental worship of Avatar Adi Da offered by His devotees.)

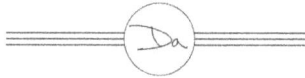

GLOSSARY

Acausal—Neither "caused" nor "causing"; therefore existing Beyond and Prior to the realm of duality in which the law of "cause-and-effect" is operative.

Adi Da—"Adi" is Sanskrit for "first", "primordial", "source" – also "primary", "beginning". Thus, the Divine Name "Adi Da" communicates that Avatar Adi Da is the First Giver, the Primordial Being, the Source of all, the Original Divine Person.

Adi Da Samraj—Expresses that He is the Primordial (or Original) Giver, Who Blesses as the Universal Lord of everything, everywhere, for all time. The Sovereignty of His Kingdom has nothing to do with the world of human politics. Rather, it is entirely a matter of His Transcendental Spiritual Dominion, His Sovereignty in the hearts of His devotees.

Adi Da Samrajashram—The principal Hermitage that was Transcendentally Spiritually Empowered by Avatar Adi Da Samraj on March 1, 2006. Located on the Fijian Island of Naitauba, this Hermitage is the principal "seat" from which Avatar Adi Da Eternally Radiates His Blessing to all beings and to the entire world.

Adidam—Name evokes Bhagavan's Primal Self-Confession, "I Am Adi Da", or more simply, "I Am Da".

Adidam Ruchiradam—The Way of devotional recognition-response to Avatar Adi Da Samraj—Who is the "Bright" Itself, and Who Gives the Realization of His own "Bright" Self-Condition.

all-and-All—A phrase Avatar Adi Da has created to describe the totality of conditionally manifested existence, both as the sum of its parts and as a Totality.

Arunachala—The holy hill at Thiruvannamalai in Tamil Nadu. It is one of the five main Shaivite holy places in South India, the site of the ashram of the great sage Ramana Maharshi.

Avadhoot—A Sanskrit term for one who has "gone beyond" worldly attachments and cares, conventional notions of life and religion, and seeking for "answers" or "solutions" from conditional experience or knowledge.

Avatar—From the Sanskrit "Avatara" meaning Divine Incarnation, or "One who has descended, or 'crossed down', from the Divine Domain".

Beloved—A title of intimate respect and devotional acknowledgment of Avatar Adi Da Samraj.

Bhagavan—"Blessed" or "holy" in Sanskrit. When applied to a great spiritual being, "Bhagavan" is understood to mean "Bountiful Lord", or "Great Lord", or "Divine Lord".

Bhagavad Gita—"Song of the Lord." A Hindu scripture set in a narrative framework of a dialogue between prince Arjuna and his guide and charioteer Lord Krishna. Arjuna faces the duty as a warrior to fight the righteous war. Arjuna is counseled by Lord Krishna to fulfill his duty as a warrior and establish Dharma.

Bhagavan Nityananda—(1897–1961) One of Avatar Adi Da's principal Gurus. Bhagavan Nityananda was Swami (Baba) Muktananda's guru. His teachings are published in the "Chidakasha Gita".

"Bright" (and its variations, such as "Brightness")—Avatar Adi Da's Use of the term "Bright" refers to the Self-Existing and Self-Radiant Divine Reality.

Baba Muktananda—(1908–1982) One of Avatar Adi Da's principal Gurus. A disciple of Bhagavan Nityananda.

Communion Hall—A set-apart room that devotees of Avatar Adi Da reserve for formal meditation and sacramental worship of Him (including devotional chanting and recitations).

Company—Describes being directly turned to Avatar Adi Da's Divine Avataric Form, Presence, and State and thus coming into His Divine Avataric Company, during and after His physical lifetime.

conditional reality—Worldly circumstances—material, mental, and psychic—as we ordinarily perceive and participate in them.

conditional realm—Everything temporary and changing; the domain of causes and effects.

Conscious Light—The two essential characteristics of Reality are Awareness (or Consciousness) and Radiance (or Light). Conscious Light is the essential Nature (or the "One and Only Self-Nature, Self-Condition, and Self-State") of everything and every being in the universe.

Crazy Wisdom tradition—A tradition of Realized Masters teaching by means that are unconventional, often spontaneous, sometimes even wild.

Da—Means "The One Who Gives" or "The Divine Giver".

Darshan—Derived from the Sanskrit "Darshana", "Darshan" means "seeing", "sight of" or "vision of". To receive Darshan of Avatar Adi Da is, most fundamentally, to behold His bodily human Form by seeing a photograph or other visual representation of Him, and (thereby) to receive the spontaneous Divine Blessings He Grants Freely whenever His bodily human Divine Form is beheld in the devotional manner. In the Way of Adidam Ruchiradam, Darshan of Avatar Adi Da is the very essence of the practice.

Dasya Mandala—A reference to the circle of devotees with direct bodily service to Avatar Adi Da Samraj at the end of His Lifetime.

Devi—"Devi" is an Indian term for "goddess". The Great Goddess takes many forms in the Hindu tradition.

Dharma—Sanskrit for "duty, virtue, law". In its fullest sense, and when capitalized, "Dharma" is the highest fulfillment of duty—the living of the Divine Law. A great spiritual teaching, including its disciplines and practices, may thus also be referred to as "Dharma".

Divine "Bright" Spherical Self-Domain—Avatar Adi Da affirms that there is a Divine Self-Domain that is the Perfectly Subjective Condition of the conditional "worlds". It is not "elsewhere", not an objective "place" (like a subtle "heaven" or mythical "paradise"), but It is the Self-Evidently Divine Source-Condition of every conditionally manifested being and thing. It is not other than Avatar Adi Da Himself—a Boundless, and Boundlessly "Bright", Sphere.

Divine Avataric Self-"Emergence"—On January 11, 1986, Avatar Adi Da passed through a profound Yogic Swoon, which He later described as the Yogic

Establishment of His Divine Avataric Self-"Emergence". His Avatarically-Born bodily human Divine Form was Perfectly Conformed to Himself, the Very Divine Person (or Reality Itself), such that His bodily human Form became (forever thereafter) an utterly Unobstructed Sign and Agent of His Own Divine Being.

Divine Condition—The Prior, Eternal, Love-Blissful State of Unconditional Reality. (See also Divine Person.)

Divine Domain—Not "elsewhere", not an objective "place" (like a subtle "heaven" or mystical "paradise"), not a state of mind. Rather, it is the True Condition of all beings, the condition that is always already the case and that cannot be Realized via any mode of seeking.

Divine Enlightenment—Most Perfect Real-God-Realization, a matter of the actual conversion of the body-mind-complex to the State of Divine Conscious Light Itself, liberated from the self-contraction, thus perfectly free of ego.

Divine Form, Presence, and State—Avatar Adi Da Reveals that He appears simultaneously in three Divine Avataric Forms – physical (His Avatarically-Born bodily human Divine Form), All-Pervading (His Avatarically Self-Transmitted Divine Transcendental Spiritual Presence), and Prior (His Avatarically Self-Revealed Divine State).

Divine image-art—Transcendental Realism, the image-art of egoless Coincidence with Reality Itself, created by Avatar Adi Da Samraj.

Divine Mahasamadhi—The passing, or physical death, of the Divine Realizer. When such a One passes, it is understood to be a physical death only, and such a One eternally continues in spiritual form in the Great ("Maha" = "Great") Samadhi ("Samadhi" = "Realized State or Condition") of His Divine Realization.

Divine Nature—The characteristics associated with the Divine Condition (see also Divine Condition).

Divine Person—Avatar Adi Da Samraj manifested as His "Perfect Self-Nature, Eternal Self-Condition, and Infinite Self-State", continuous with Real (Acausal) God.

Divine Reality—The egoless, non-conditional, uncaused Truth of existence, often referred to by Avatar Adi Da as "Conscious Light".

Divine Re-Awakening—Avatar Adi Da spontaneously Re-Awakened to His own "Bright" Divine Self-Nature, Self-Condition, and Self-State (which He had named "the Bright" in His infancy) on September 10, 1970. Please refer to Chapter 16 in Part One of *The Knee of Listening* for a full account of this event.

Divine Translation—The fourth, or final, stage of Divine Enlightenment: *Most Perfectly Beyond and Prior To all-and-All of Cosmic, or conditional, forms, beings, signs, conditions, relations, and things.* (Avatar Adi Da Samraj, *The Dawn Horse Testament*, 384.)

Divine Work—Avatar Adi Da's Work of Divine Revelation and Awakening with devotees, for all beings, for all time.

ego-"I"—The core, ongoing act of "self-contraction", erroneously committed to separate and separative existence.

egoity—The state of being that results from the activity of self-contraction.

Empowerment—The establishment of Avatar Adi Da's Divine Transcendental Spiritual Presence in a place, object, or event.

faculties of the body-mind—Body, emotion (or feeling), mind (or attention), and breath. These four principal faculties account for the entirety of the human being. Devotional Communion with Avatar Adi Da is fundamentally the moment to moment turning of the four principal faculties to Him.

Gautama Buddha—Also known as Siddhartha Gautama, Shakyamuni Buddha, or simply the Buddha. The founder of the tradition of Buddhism. He is believed to have lived and taught mostly in the eastern part of ancient India sometime between the sixth and fourth centuries BCE.

Great Tradition—Avatar Adi Da's term for humanity's total inheritance of all the spiritual, religious, mystical, shamanic, and transcendental paths of the past.

Guru—The syllable "gu" means "darkness". The syllable "ru" means "he who disperses". *Because of the power to disperse darkness, the guru is thus named.* (*Advayataraka Upanishad.*)

Hearing—The devotee has begun to "hear" Avatar Adi Da when there is most fundamental understanding of the root-act of egoity, or self-contraction, carrying with it the capability to transcend this previously unconscious moment-to-moment activity.

heart-Awakening—The opening in the feeling being of Avatar Adi Da's devotees to the Revelation of Divine Reality.

heart-Communion—With Avatar Adi Da, heart-Communion is moment-to-moment turning of the four principal faculties (body, emotion, mind and breath) to Him.

Kali—One of the most popular goddesses in India. Kali is known for destroying ignorance, and she helps those who strive for knowledge of God. She is often portrayed in a ferocious manner.

karma—"Karma" is Sanskrit for "action". Since action entails consequences (or re-actions), "karma" also means (by extension) "destiny, tendency, the quality of existence and experience that is determined by previous actions".

Krishna and the gopis—Krishna is one of the most widely revered Hindu deities. Gopi is Sanskrit for "cowherd girl". The gopis are famous in Hindu scripture for their unconditional devotion to Krishna.

kriyas—Involuntary movements which can result from reception of spiritual blessing.

kundalini—The energy traditionally viewed to lie dormant at the base of the spine, associated with the muladhara chakra, or lowermost psychic center of the body-mind.

Leela—The Awakened Play of a Realized Adept through which he or she mysteriously Instructs and Liberates others and Blesses the world itself. By extension, a Leela is an instructive and inspiring story of such an Adept's Teaching and Blessing Play. This book is a collection of Leelas.

lingam—An elongated oval stone representing the Hindu deity Shiva, used in temple worship.

Lion's Lap—**Avatar Adi Da's** Forest Hermitage residence at Adi Da Samrajashram.

Listening—Avatar Adi Da's term for the beginning practice of the Reality Way of Adidam.

Listening–Hearing–Seeing–Perfect Practice—The entire course of the Reality-Way of Adidam falls into four primary phases: Listening to Him, Hearing Him, Seeing Him, and the "Perfect Practice" of egolessly Self-Identifying with Him.

"lunch righteousness"—The self-righteous attitude that can manifest from fanaticism about maintaining a "perfect" diet.

mantra—A sound, word, or phrase that is repeated by a spiritual practitioner as a form of meditative practice or worship. Sacred sounds or syllables and Names have been used since antiquity for invoking and worshipping the Divine Person and the guru. The sacred Names of Avatar Adi Da Samraj have mantric force, thus can be used to invoke His Presence (for example: *Da*).

Maya—Traditional Sanskrit term for the incomprehensibly complex (and, ultimately, Illusory) web of beings, things, and events that constitutes conditional reality.

mudras—Gestures of the hands, face, or body that outwardly express a state of ecstasy. Avatar Adi Da Samraj also uses the term "Mudra" to express the Attitude of His Blessing-Work, which is His Constant (or Eternal) Giving of Himself to Be the Means of Divine Liberation for all beings.

Murti—Sanskrit for "form", and, by extension, a representational image of the Divine, or of a guru. In the Way of Adidam, Murtis of Avatar Adi Da are most commonly photographs of Avatar Adi Da's bodily human Divine Form.

Naitauba—The Fijian island of Avatar Adi Da's principal hermitage. Also named Adi Da Samrajashram.

Narayan Maharaj—(1885–1945) An Indian spiritual master who lived in Kedgaon, India. His fundamental teaching was "Treat everyone as God".

Non-conditional Reality—The Divine, or that which is eternal, is always already the case, because It is utterly Free of dependence on any conditions whatsoever.

"object"—Avatar Adi Da consistently places the word "object" (and its variants) in quotation marks in order to indicate that, in Reality Itself, there is no such thing as an "object" separate from the "subject".

Oedipal complex—In modern psychology, the "Oedipus complex" is named after the legendary Greek Oedipus, who was fated to unknowingly kill his father and marry his mother. Avatar Adi Da Teaches that the primary dynamics of emotional-sexual desiring, envy, betrayal, "self"-pleasuring, resentment, and other primal emotions and impulses are indeed (as first systematically suggested by Sigmund Freud) patterned on unconscious reactions formed early in life, in reaction to one's mother and father.

"Perfect Knowledge"—When the devotee is in Communion with Him, Avatar Adi Da Reveals that no "object" or "knowledge" or "subject" or "point of view" is True or Real; rather, Reality Itself is shown as the Prior and egoless Condition that is always already the case. "Perfect Knowledge" is one of the three fundamental dimensions of practice in the Reality-Way of Adidam—together with "radical" devotion and right-life self-discipline.

"Perfect Practice"—The most mature demonstration of esoteric practice in the Reality-Way of Adidam, enacted in the domain of Consciousness Itself, rather than from the perspective of body or mind or body-mind.

"point of view"—Avatar Adi Da places this phrase in quotation marks, communicating that, in Reality, every "point of view" is an illusion since all ordinary viewpoints are founded in the false presumption of the separate existence of "I".

Prasad—Sanskrit term for gifts that have been offered to the Divine and, after having been Blessed, are returned to the devotee as Divine Gifts. By extension, Prasad is anything the devotee receives from his or her guru.

Prayer of Changes—A form of Invocation of and Communion with Avatar Adi Da Samraj which is practiced (by His formally acknowledged devotees) in order to bring about positive changes in the psycho-physical world. The Devotional Prayer of Changes is not a form of pleading with Avatar Adi Da Samraj for results. Rather, the Devotional Prayer of Changes is, principally, a specific form of devotional Communion with Avatar Adi Da and, secondarily, a relinquishment of any negative or problematic states of mind and emotion.

Prior—Not occurring previously in time, but always already being so; thus, for example, the unity of humankind is a prior reality.

Puja—A form of worship that honors and celebrates a spiritual teacher or deity.

radical—Derived from the Latin "radix", meaning "root". Thus, "radical" principally means "irreducible", "fundamental", or "relating to the origin". Thus Avatar Adi Da defines "radical" as "at the root", without any political connotations.

Ramana Maharshi—(1879–1950) An Indian guru considered by many to have been one of the greatest sages of the twentieth century, and acknowledged by Avatar Adi Da to have been a great Realizer.

renunciate—One who has renounced. When Avatar Adi Da Speaks of "renunciation", He is not referring to any form of ego-based renunciation (demonstrated as body-and-life-denying asceticism), but to "true and free renunciation"—in which the movement towards "self"-identification with the body-mind-complex and its "objects" is transcended in Love-Bliss-Communion with Him. He often reiterates that such renunciation is not a search, but is rather coincident or simultaneous with (and inherent in) Realization Itself.

Revelation—Avatar Adi Da's Gift of the fully Revealed Substance of, and Way to Realize, the Divine Reality.

Ruchira—Sanskrit meaning "bright" or "radiant".

Ruchiradama—The title for a female formal renunciate devotee in the Ruchira Sannyasin Order.

Ruchira Sannyasin Order—Most exemplary renunciate "Perfect Practice" devotees, embracing formal and legal renunciation in the circumstance of perpetual retreat.

sacrifice—In Adidam, this is understood to be the devotee's relinquishment of self-contracting activity, or the surrender of egoity.

sadhana—Sanskrit for "spiritual practice".

sahasrar—Energy center (chakra) located at or slightly above the top of the head.

Samadhi—Sanskrit word denoting various exalted spiritual states of Consciousness appearing in esoteric meditation and in Ultimate Realization of the Divine. Avatar Adi Da Teaches that, for His devotees, Samadhi is, even more simply and fundamentally, the Enjoyment of His Divine State (or "Divine Samadhi"),—experienced even from the beginning of the practice of Adidam through ego-transcending heart-Communion with Him.

Samraj—From the Sanskrit "Samraja" meaning universal or supreme ruler, paramount Lord, or paramount sovereign. As part of the name "Adi Da Samraj" or "Avatar Adi Da Samraj", it identifies Him as the Universal Lord of the Spiritual Domain, Sovereign Ruler of the hearts of His devotees.

Samraj Mahal—Sanskrit for the "Palace of the Paramount Lord". The name of a principal building at Adi Da Samrajashram.

Sannyas—The formal relinquishment of all conventional social obligations in order to fully concentrate in intensive spiritual practice. In Adidam, sannyas is embraced by members of the Ruchira Sannyasin Order.

Sapta Na—"Sapta" means "seven" in Sanskrit, standing for the seventh stage Realization, and "Na" refers to the Island of Naitauba. ("Sapta Na Sannyasin Hermitage" and the "Sapta Na Sannyasin Order of Adidam Ruchiradam".)

Sathya Sai Baba—(1926–2011) An Indian guru and philanthropist who stated that he was the reincarnation of Sai Baba of Shirdi. Sai Baba's materializations of vibhuti (ash) and other small objects (such as rings, necklaces, and watches), along with reports of miraculous healings, resurrections, clairvoyance, bilocation, and alleged omnipotence and omniscience, were a source of both fame and controversy.

Satsang—The Hindi word for "true, or right, relationship" or "the company of Truth". In Adidam, this term was used in the earlier years of Avatar Adi Da's Teaching Work to indicate living in ego-surrendering, ego-forgetting, ego-transcending relationship to Avatar Adi Da Samraj.

Searchless Beholding—The practice of searchlessly Beholding Avatar Adi Da is the regarding of His bodily human Divine Form, free of any seeking-effort, and, in due course, the searchless "Locating" and "Knowing" of His Divine Transcendental Spiritual Self-Transmission.

Seeing—The fully technically responsible form of Spiritually Awakened Communion with Avatar Adi Da Samraj. (See Listening-Hearing-Seeing-Perfect Practice).

self—The primal illusion of human existence is that "I" is a "self" that is separate from everything and everyone else (or all that is "not-self"). In His writings, Avatar Adi Da consistently places the word in quotation marks to indicate the illusory nature of "self".

self-contraction—The root-activity that is responsible for the fundamental erroneous presumption of separation, all-pervading in ordinary human life.

Self-Nature, Self-Condition, and Self State—A phrase used by Avatar Adi Da to indicate His own True "Self" (or "Identity"), Which Is the True "Self" (or

"Identity") of Reality Itself, and, thus, the True "Self" (or "Identity") of everything that appears (or what Avatar Adi Da refers to as "all-and-All").

seven stages of life—Avatar Adi Da Samraj has "mapped" the potential developmental course of human life as it unfolds in the context of the gross, subtle, and causal dimensions of existence, describing this course in terms of six stages plus one. The first three stages account for the potential maturation of physical, emotional, and mental aspects of life. He explains that the next three stages account for, and correspond with, all possible orientations to religion and spirituality that have arisen in human history, all of which retain some vestiges of "self". His own Divine Avataric Revelation is the seventh stage of life: Most Perfect Realization of the "Bright", or Reality Itself, Prior to "self" and all experience.

seventh stage Realization— Enlightenment, or the Realization of the "Bright" Reality Revealed through the Incarnation of Avatar Adi Da Samraj, transcending the entire course of human potential. In that Awakening, it is suddenly, tacitly Realized that there is no "difference" between Consciousness Itself and the "objects" of Consciousness. Thus, Avatar Adi Da Reveals that Enlightenment eliminates every trace of dissociation from the body-mind complex and the world. Consciousness Itself, or Being Itself, Is all there is, found to be Love-Bliss-Full. Every "thing" and every "one" is inherently recognized to be only a modification of the One Divine "Brightness", or Divine Conscious Light.

Shakti—A Sanskrit term for the Divinely Manifesting Spiritual Energy, Spiritual Power, or Spirit-Current of the Divine Person.

Shirdi Sai Baba—(d. 1918) An Indian spiritual master. Shirdi Sai Baba was known to use a bag of coins as a metaphor for his devotees, each coin representing an individual devotee. Avatar Adi Da cited this as a precedent for his manner of relating to His devotees as representative of humankind at large.

Shiva—One of the three chief divinities of the later Hindu pantheon, the other two being Brahma and Vishnu.

Siddha—Sanskrit for "a completed, fulfilled, or perfected one", or "one of perfect Accomplishment, or Power". Avatar Adi Da uses "Siddha" to mean a Transmission-Master who is a Realizer of Reality Itself to some significant degree.

Siddhi—Sanskrit for "Spiritual Power" or "Accomplishment". When capitalized in Avatar Adi Da's Teaching, "Siddhi" is the Spiritual, Transcendental, and Divine Awakening-Power that Bhagavan Adi Da spontaneously and effortlessly Transmits to all. Bhagavan Adi Da refers to His Siddhi as "Heart-Power".

Spiritual—One of the two fundamental qualities of Reality Itself, the other quality being "Transcendental".

Sri Aurobindo—(1872–1950) An Indian nationalist, philosopher, yogi, guru, and poet. He joined the Indian movement for independence from British rule, for a while was one of its influential leaders, and then became a spiritual reformer, introducing his vision of human progress and spiritual evolution.

Sri Hridayam Siddhashram—The name Avatar Adi Da originally gave to the ashram on Melrose Avenue in Hollywood. Sanskrit for "Ashram of the Realizer of the Heart".

Submission-Work, or Teaching-Work—The intensive period (1972–1986) of Avatar Adi Da's Submission to devotees' questions, life-level doubts, and sufferings, undertaken in order to Reveal His Divine Reality-Teaching for all beings. His Submission-Work began to be "shed" in 1986 (with the Initiation of His Divine Avataric Self-"Emergence").

Sukra Kendra—Sanskrit for "Bright House", Avatar Adi Da's most sacred temples, in which He established the Force of His Person with a unique intensity.

Sri Ramakrishna—(1836–1886) A famous mystic of 19th-century India, a devotee of the goddess Kali. His followers eventually established the Ramakrishna Order of monks. His chief disciple, Swami Vivekananda, founded the Ramakrishna Mission and the Vedanta Society.

Tapas—Sanskrit for the purifying heat that develops as a result of intense spiritual practice.

"Tcha"—A word Avatar Adi Da used to express His Pleasure with someone's devotion.

The Way of the Heart—An alternative name for the Reality Way of Adidam, used by Avatar Adi Da since the mid-1980s.

The Way of Understanding—The first name used by Avatar Adi Da to refer to the Reality-Way of Adidam. This name was used from the earliest days in 1972.

Teaching-Submission—See Submission-Work.

Transcendental—One of the two fundamental qualities of Reality Itself, the other quality being "Spiritual"

Tumomama—The original name Avatar Adi Da gave to His Hawaiian Sanctuary.

Most Ultimate Divine Self-Realization—Divine Enlightenment, or Most Perfect Real-God-Realization.

Upanishads—A collection of Vedic texts which contain the earliest emergence of some of the central religious concepts of Indian esotericism.

Vibhuti—Ash from a ceremonial fire, used in religious worship in Hinduism, usually placed on the forehead.

Yoni—The Yoni is a round stone with a hole in the center. In Hinduism, the symbol of the goddess Shakti, the feminine generative power and, as a goddess, the consort of Shiva. The lingam united with the yoni represents the inherent nonduality of reality.

FURTHER CONTACT

For more about this book, here are some resources:

Get in touch with Gerald on his website and Facebook:

storiesofthespiritualmaster.com

www.facebook.com/gsheinfeld

www.facebook.com/storiesofthespiritualmaster/

To purchase a 16-track live recording of Gerald telling
some of the stories from this book, go to:

www.cdbaby.com/cd/geraldsheinfeld

◆ ◆ ◆

For further information about Avatar Adi Da Samraj and the
"Radical" (at-the-root) Reality-Way of Adidam Ruchiradam,
here are some recommendations:

For more information on Avatar Adi Da Samraj
and His Teaching go to:

www.adidam.org

and

www.consciousnessitself.org

To purchase books by Avatar Adi Da Samraj go to:

www.dawnhorsepress.com

(Two books recommended for a basic introduction
to Avatar Adi Da's Life and Teaching are
The Avatar of What Is and *The Gift of Truth Itself*.)

To see videos of Avatar Adi Da Samraj go to:
www.youtube.com/AdiDaVideos

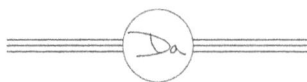